SKIES TO CONQUER

A YEAR INSIDE THE AIR FORCE ACADEMY

Diana Jean Schemo

WILEY

John Wiley & Sons, Inc.

To the Air Force Academy Classes of 2007, 2008, 2009, and 2010,
without whose sweat and struggle, insight and, above all, trust,
this book would not exist

Published by John Wiley & Sons, Inc., Hoboken, New Jersey
Published simultaneously in Canada

Library of Congress Cataloging-in-Publication Data:

Schemo, Diana, date.
    Skies to conquer: a year inside the Air Force Academy/Diana Schemo.
        p.   cm.
    Includes index.
    ISBN 978-0-470-04637-1 (cloth)
        1. United States Air Force Academy.   I. Title.
    UG638.5.P1S34   2009
    358.40071'173—dc22

                                                    2009034192

Printed in the United States of America

10 9 8 7 6 5 4 3 2 1

Contents

Acknowledgments

In tracking a year in the life of the U.S. Air Force Academy, it became clear, almost instantly, that much of what the training cadets go through is aimed at teaching them that nobody succeeds entirely on his or her own. The same is true for this book. In writing it over the course of several years, I have relied on the patience, understanding, insight, and support of many, to whom I owe deep and abiding gratitude. When I first wrote about the academy, Doug Corcoran, who became my agent, sought me out and helped to develop and refine the proposal for a fuller, more penetrating, look inside the academy's walls. As investigative editor at the *New York Times*, Doug Frantz first drew me into writing about the academy, and he continued to offer invaluable counsel well after we'd both moved on. Stephen Power, my editor at John Wiley & Sons, offered patience and encouragement, along with unfailingly sound editorial advice. Rachel Meyers endured "just one last change" countless times, and always with a friendly word. Alison Mitchell and Suzanne Spector, my former editors at the *Times*, were kind in accommodating my absences as I journeyed to Colorado Springs.

At the academy, I owe my thanks, first and foremost, to the cadets who opened their world to me and trusted me with their stories, unwittingly signing on for endless queries that followed them across the globe, which they endured with remarkable grace. They include Miles-Tyson Blocker,

Elizabeth Simpson, Jonathan Elliott, Brad Bernard, Jonathan Benson, Lucas VanTassel and Grace Anderson. A special thanks goes to Jamal Harrison, who volunteered to be my guide more than once, and whose honesty in discussing and prevailing over his own missteps was perhaps the best advertisement for the academy's capacity to transform lives. The cadets' generosity in sharing their experiences and insights was great; any failings in conveying the nuances of their world are mine alone. Dr. Elizabeth Muenger, the academy's command historian, provided important background on the early days of the academy, and source material. Thanks to the Public Affairs Office, particularly to Johnny Whitaker, for supporting my research. Captain Uriah Orland, that office's answer to the indomitable mail carrier, rose before dawn, in rain and sleet and snow to get me where I needed to be.

I save the greatest thanks for last: to my husband, Roger Breeze, who moved worlds to make room and ended my days with heart, dinner, and a fresh perspective; to Odelya Valanci-Kaufmann, Rosali Babayev, and Mariana Brito, whose efforts allowed me to range far; and to Sarah and Jacob, whose little souls were large in understanding.

Introduction

Few cadets at the United States Air Force Academy would describe themselves as romantics. Weeks out of high school, they begin their military careers in an explosion of criticism and punishment that strips their identities raw and hunts down their defenses with the inexorability of a laser-guided bomb. They learn to fight with mud soaked through their clothes and covering their ears, to shower in thirty seconds, to eat like automatons, and to sound off, or shout, an answer to somebody inches from their face. They can do fifty or more push-ups on demand.

And yet, in an era when air travel has been stripped of its glamour, when commercial flights resemble nothing so much as flying crosstown buses, cadets at the Air Force Academy are probably the last young people who are unabashedly in love with flying. The nine thousand high school seniors who apply to the academy each year, of whom only about thirteen hundred are selected for admission, share an overriding trait: the dream of flight.

Three in four hope to become pilots. Some long to fly an F-15 Eagle, a tactical fighter, while others yearn to pilot the F-16, the lightweight fighter jet that slashes across the sky at twice the speed of sound, pulling turns at nine times the force of gravity. Some seek the bulk of heavy transporters like the C-130 and the newer C-17, the flying equivalent of a Hummer; still others, quirky souls that they are, feel drawn to helicopters.

1

Many of them post pictures of their pet aircraft on their walls like pinups or doodle them in the margins of their notebooks.

The cadets spend hours learning the details of each model. Of course, not all cadets will become pilots. More than half will work in the panoply of supporting roles that keep the air force running and planes flying: as engineers, as communications specialists, in logistical support or maintenance, in accounting, in intelligence, or in special operations. The ideal, however, the dream that inspires thousands of cadets in Colorado Springs, is flight. The most ambitious and successful of them aim to fly fighter and bomber jets, each worth tens, or even hundreds, of millions of dollars.

I first came to know air force cadets after women from the academy alleged that they had been raped and punished by their chain of command when they reported the assaults. When I interviewed the women, I noticed that many shared an unusual, seemingly inexplicable, love for what they had set out to do in joining the academy. They were speaking to me, a reporter, because in many ways their hopes had been crushed, but when I asked the women what had first drawn them to attend the Air Force Academy, the bitterness would disappear, eclipsed by the big dreams of their younger selves. They would recall an air show, a larger-than-life uncle who flew planes, or the heady pleasure of not only zooming beyond expectations but also driving them in new, uncharted directions. Eyes shining, they would talk without embarrassment of their love for their country and of making a difference, of perseverance, and of the quality of leadership.

Remembering their ideals undoubtedly deepened their disillusionment, but the cadets themselves were striking: mature, idealistic, and focused— and, at times, maddeningly controlling. They were completely different from college students anywhere else. At an age when many teens are experimenting with breaking the rules, cadets live with an abundance of rules that circumscribe everything: the places they can walk, the food they can eat, even the distance between the shirts and the socks in their drawers. For the most part, they do it all with pride and purpose.

A year later, the Air Force Academy was back in the news, and again the issue at hand involved the blurring of boundaries. This time, the new commandant of cadets, Brigadier General Johnny Weida, who had been appointed to restore morality, was promoting Christianity among cadets and faculty. In one classroom building, the normally stark white walls were covered with flyers for *The Passion of the Christ*. Jewish groups condemned the Mel Gibson film of unrelenting violence and betrayal as anti-Semitic and historically skewed, but evangelicals saw the film as a vehicle for winning converts. "This is an officially sponsored USAFA event," the ads announced. "Please do not take this flyer down." Lest they miss the point, each cadet found a flyer for a cadets-only showing of the movie on his or her seat in the dining hall. Well after the news cycle rolled on, as it always does, I remained curious about the broader world of the cadets that the rest of the country was coming to know only by the academy's blunders. The nature of those mistakes was intriguing: each suggested deep roots, and a gulf between sensibilities in early twenty-first- century civil society and life inside the academy.

Outwardly, the world that unfolds over the academy's eighteen thousand acres is bound by tradition and ritual, almost a religion unto itself. The cadet career is divided by milestones and punctuated by parades: First and Second Beasts, Acceptance Day, Commandant's Challenge, Recognition, Hundred's Night, Ring Dance, Graduation Day, and so on—the same, year after year. Beneath the fixed order and the reverence for tradition, however, change was constant, coming from all directions and playing out on many levels simultaneously.

As I'd expected, the academy was struggling to redefine the relationships among cadets at different grade levels, openly acknowledging that the historically unchecked, God-like power of upper-class cadets over freshmen had opened the way for abuse. Academy leaders were experimenting. They gradually redrew events like Basic Training and Recognition—the final, grueling training exercise for new cadets each spring—toning them down to conform to the active-duty force, at times sparking tension with older cadets. The leadership ordered cadets, faculty, and staff into hours of lectures on sexual assault and religious tolerance and ordered them to refrain from invoking Jesus during prayers at mandatory events.

That was only the start of the changes that were under way. Within each cadet was a personal universe that was being blown apart and reconstructed, piece by piece. Furthermore, beyond the academy, the role of pilots as heroes of air and space was becoming more elusive each day: more and more of the functions traditionally played by military bombers and fighter planes were being taken over by increasingly sophisticated drones, and the country began confronting the limits of air power in winning wars against guerrillas embedded in civilian populations.

Instead of soaring over enemy territory, dodging radar, rescuing comrades, or bombing bad guys, today's cadets are as likely to end up hunched over the military equivalent of a video game somewhere in Nevada after graduation, controlling an unmanned drone thousands of miles away. The cadets are at once more remote and yet closer than ever to war. Whereas pilots once zoomed in over enemy territory, dropped bombs from miles up in the sky, and returned to base, technology now allows them to see their targets before, during, and after an attack. They can see the house or building exist one moment and vanish the next; they can see bodies flying apart, in high definition. Then they still take in a daughter's dance recital.

This book is about metamorphosis—the main business of the Air Force Academy. It follows the cadets of a single unit, the Fighting Bulldawgs of Squadron 13, as they make their way through a year at the academy. The newest cadets include a recruited athlete from Georgia who openly doubts his decision to attend the academy; a young woman who had gone through Junior ROTC (Reserve Officers Training Corp) in high school and figured that the Air Force Academy offered her the best chance of seeing combat; a Californian who had set her sights on outer space; and the son of a rocket scientist who was homeschooled along with his nine siblings. We also track the upper-class cadets training them: a cadet officer who learned to fly with Martin Burnham, a missionary kidnapped by Islamist terrorists in the Philippines and killed in a siege to win his freedom; a flight jock with two vastly different sides to his nature; an African American cadet with top grades, who nevertheless worries that he must prove his worth.

The year that's covered here is the midpoint of 2006 to the midpoint of 2007. The United States is slogging through its third year of a bloody, seemingly intractable war in Iraq, with more than 3,350 service personnel dead by May 2007. The military is blaming the torture and deaths of prisoners at Abu Ghraib on "a few bad apples." The Republicans suffer stunning defeats in midterm elections, losing their majorities in the House and the

Senate. Ted Haggard, the powerful president of the National Association of Evangelicals, loses his post at the popular New Life Church, which is just outside the academy gates, because of a three-year affair with a male prostitute. The seniors were one of the first classes to apply for admission after 9/11; the freshmen barely mentioned the terrorist attacks in their admissions essays.

The cadets' experiences unfold at America's youngest service academy, built where the Great Plains west of the Mississippi River reach the Rocky Mountains. The city near the foothills of Pikes Peak was historically a sleepy spa town of forty-five thousand residents, where patients with tuberculosis and other illnesses came in the spring and the summer. By the end of World War II, Colorado Springs was losing its raison d'être, thanks to medical advances and the rise of the automobile. Fewer tourists came, and those who did left earlier.

The city fathers saw the Pentagon's search for a new academy site in 1953 as the chance to revive their dying city. They fought hard, and sometimes dirty, to beat the competition for the location of the new Air Force Academy. According to a history by Brigadier General George V. Fagan, some six hundred locations were proposed for the new academy. Ultimately, the choice came down to Colorado Springs and Alton, Illinois. Colorado Springs won over a site selection committee in part thanks to some unconventional moves by a local Ford dealer, R. Soland Doenges, who headed the city's chamber of commerce.

Upon hearing that the committee was leaning toward Alton, Doenges grew a beard, put on sunglasses and old clothes, and traveled to Illinois. In Alton, he stoked antagonism toward the new academy among local property owners, urging them to write letters to their congressional representatives and even giving interviews himself to local papers. In contrast, businessmen in Colorado Springs eagerly welcomed the committee members, entertaining them at the city's premier hotel, stretching welcome banners before their eyes, and hanging posters touting the city as the perfect home—despite concerns about the availability of water, flying in high altitude, and possible respiratory problems. Charles Lindbergh flew fellow committee members over the proposed site, declaring it suitable for flight training. Even the newspapers held back letters from readers who did not want the academy.

After the arrival of the academy, Colorado Springs grew rapidly, so that it is now among the fifty most populous cities in the country. It became a bastion of the nation's most powerful evangelical groups, which have influenced the academy experience as surely as the academy has shaped the city. When Focus on the Family opened its doors in 1993, across the interstate highway, the Air Force Academy sent its parachute team, the Wings of Blue, to float down from the sky, handing the symbolic keys to the city to James Dobson, then the group's president. Monday nights, the Air Force Academy invites religious groups to use its classrooms for weekly Bible study.

Cadets come here from all walks of life. In one sense, they are more representative of the country than are the students at any undergraduate campus, because candidates for admission come from every congressional district. At the same time, cadets here do not exactly mirror the country at large. Rather, they represent a cross section of a particular slice of the United States. The average grade point average of incoming cadets is 3.9, and most are in the top fifth of their graduating classes. The majority has perfect vision—near perfect vision is required for flight training—and almost all have won varsity letters.

"We know they're not quitters," says Rollie Stoneman, the former associate director of admissions. Most are members of the National Honor Society and politically conservative—a tendency that becomes accentuated in the closed universe of the military academy. The cadet body is more Christian and more white than the rest of the nation.

A word about ground rules: Citing more stringent security after 9/11, the academy denied my initial request for unfettered access to the institution and to cadets. Instead, its escorts were to keep an eye on my whereabouts, but not to sit in on interviews unless asked—a rule they mostly observed.

The academy accepts about thirteen hundred students for a graduating class of a thousand. For four years, through a series of ever more grueling trials, the academy breaks down these high school kids, rebuilding the survivors into an elite corps to lead the U.S. Air Force in the coming generations. Tuition and fees are paid for by the taxpayers. Students graduate as second lieutenants, commissioned in the air force, where they must serve for five years. Family income, or the lack of it, does not keep anyone out. (Performance does, however. There are a few poor urban districts from which the academy does not get any qualified applicants, Stoneman says.)

The academy's lexicon differs from that of a civilian university. Cadets are not freshmen, sophomores, juniors, and seniors; rather they are designated by their proximity to graduation, like planes on a runway. Seniors are *first-class cadets*, or *firsties*, while juniors are called *two-degrees* and sophomores are *three-degrees*. Freshmen go by a variety of names, from the neutral *four-degree* or *four-dig* to *doolie*, spelled like the building where they begin their journey, Doolittle Hall, but said to be derived from the ancient Greek word for slaves, *doulos*. For narrative flow, I have occasionally used the civilian terms for class year. And *airman* is the official term for both men and women.

During their four years at the academy, the individual cadets shed the person their parents shaped and educated for eighteen, nineteen, or twenty years in order to become, as one graduate put it, the person the cadet wants to be. More precisely, each cadet melds the person he or she envisions with the new person the air force hopes to make of them.

This is the map of their journeys.

Part One

ON THE HILL

1 | Light Travelers

If Casey Jane Barrett holds fast to one scrap of advice as she stands under a warm June sun in the foothills of the Rockies, about to start her life as a cadet at the United States Air Force Academy, it is this: Whatever you do, don't stand out. As a newcomer, the teenager from Ventura, California—with straight brown hair, freckles, and red-framed glasses—is the lowest form of life at the sprawling academy. She will be reminded of this fact thousands of times, in ways subtle and overt, over the next eleven months—if she makes it to May, that is.

Forget rank. Barrett won't even have a name, and she cannot earn the right to be called *cadet* for another six weeks. Instead, she will be a faceless slug—an embryo, really—in a red cap, moving when told to move, speaking when spoken to, holding back tears, and saving them for after lights out. Her entire identity will now boil down to the label *Basic*—as in, "Basic, what are you smiling at? Is something funny, Basic?" delivered with pulverizing sarcasm. This is not the time to show off, to tap-dance to the top of her class over the backs of her fellow cadets. Attracting notice here will be the surest path to misery, swift and enduring.

Not that Barrett is the type to do that, but then again, what type is she: The patient, kind daughter of Terri and Jeff Marcus who helps her mother train seeing-eye dogs for blind people and pitches in at her mother's fourth-grade class? GI Jane, untried warrior, yearning to roar across sky and space in the planet's most sophisticated, most powerful, flying machines? Or is she just another high school grad, smarter and maybe luckier than most, turning down the University of Michigan to try out a more unconventional future whose peaks would play out miles above the earth's surface?

Today, Barrett carries no answers, only a knapsack, holding thirteen pairs of white panties and nine white sports bras, which she drops under a tent with a growing pile of backpacks and duffle bags from the other freshmen. All of their belongings have been reduced to their skivvies, their identities pared down to that one unlovely, generic title: Basic.

The seventeen-year-old joins a line of hundreds of others from around the country and the world who are set to enter the elite academy. The line snakes around a hill and leads slowly into Doolittle Hall, known as Doolie Hall inside the academy, a modern building where 1,334 freshmen say good-bye to their families on the first floor and check in on the second, officially entering academy life.

At a time when universities across the country are feeling whipsawed by the conflicting strains among students—trying to build college spirit, but also tailoring options ever more narrowly for the "have it your way" generation—military service academies like this one head resolutely in the opposite direction. They do not offer squadron assignments by common interest, politics, or religion, for they deride catering to the individual as a sign of weakness. There are no climbing walls, lavish atriums, or fancy fitness centers. There are no food courts worthy of the name and no coffee in the morning, designer or otherwise.

This is a crucible for the training of warriors, a campaign that begins with war on the individual, an internal battle to erase the ego and create a new, group identity. From the moment the freshmen are out of their parents' sight, as the bus that takes them from Doolie Hall rounds the corner, every encounter is aimed at knocking the newcomers off-kilter, breaking down whatever sense of self-importance they left home with to create a new, common identity around the air force.

Other universities do not even start classes for another six weeks, and when their freshmen arrive, they come loaded with stuff: clothes and computers, books and cell phones, televisions and iPods, skis and rollerblades, bicycles and cars. But here the future leaders of the air force—the group that will one day make up half of all its generals—arrive with only the T-shirts on their backs, their shorts, and white, almost interchangeable, underwear. They surrender cell phones, BlackBerrys, and even watches. Topping off the brief list of items they are permitted to bring is a single book, the Bible, between whose pages they tuck photos from the lives they are leaving behind.

Now, as her time with her family dwindles down to minutes, Barrett starts to fret over, of all things, greeting cards: colossal ones in screaming pink and chartreuse and lavender, with polka dots and stripes; cards with ribbons and fat red hearts, bulging with messages of unabashed hero-worship. ("Way to Go," "Casey Jane, We Love You.") The cards come courtesy of her mother's adoring fourth graders, but to hear Captain Uriah Orland, a recent graduate, tell it in the line to Doolie Hall, they will be Barrett's ticket to hell, marking her as precious and just too darling. Each card guarantees not just her, but her squad mates as well, dozens of push-ups as punishment.

"Thanks, Mom," Barrett says, shooting her mother a nervous, not altogether thankful, smile. Inching toward her future on emotional auto-pilot, Barrett cannot be angry with her Mom, who is soaring just then, almost as if she herself were about to enter the academy as its oldest freshman. Terri Marcus makes up an entire cheerleading team unto herself, tireless in her optimism and not about to feed her daughter's anxieties over the cards.

"I'll make cookies," Marcus offers.

Barrett, nervous already, tries to force a smile, but it comes across as more of a wince.

"This is just getting better and better," says Orland, shaking his head and chuckling. His gaze skips from mother to daughter as he enjoys the show. Orland, assigned to public affairs, is supposed to hang back, but cannot resist.

"She's going to have to do a lot of push-ups," he tells Marcus. "Normally, it's five to ten a letter."

"He's laughing," Barrett tells her mother. "He's laughing at you."

"No," says the captain, his eyes finally resting on the new cadet. His thinning blond hair makes him look older than his twenty-odd years, giving the insult extra authority. "I'm laughing at *you*."

Barrett blanches, for the first of many times through her training here, and worries about the days ahead. Could anything broadcast her as a nice girl—here where warriors are bred—more eloquently than this batch of cards and comforts streaming her way from a bevy of nine-year-olds? Would she be marked from day one? Would her classmates hate her for all those push-ups?

She and her mother consider themselves best friends, but at that moment a distance begins to open between them. Marcus seems unconcerned by the cards, even jovial. In just a few moments, the two women would say good-bye, and for the first time in Barrett's young life, she would not have her mother at hand. Barrett does not know it, but her mother defied her doctor's orders to make the trip here, telling him that she would rather die than send her daughter off alone into the world.

"So, you'll just get stronger," says Marcus.

Unlike Casey Jane Barrett, David Urban does not have family or friends along to wish him luck in the minutes before he enters the military. Tall, with blue eyes and straight blond hair that falls evenly around his head and brushes the top of his ears, Urban comes across, as serious and upright. While he is not fat, an extra ten or fifteen pounds softens the rugged cast of his narrow face, the high cheekbones, and the blue eyes, making him seem more boy than man. Urban is one of ten children, all homeschooled by their parents in a suburb outside Dallas.

Whatever trials, humiliations, and achievements the academy has in store for him, Urban has not a clue. At that very moment, he is mostly looking forward to sharing a bedroom with only one or two roommates instead of three younger teenage brothers. He said good-bye to his family back in Texas, and now he drops his backpack onto the pile with the others. However, he is not really alone.

Getting here, for instance, was really a joint effort, involving not just his parents but also the members of his religious community, who cheered him on, helped with his application, and even tutored him in math so that his score on the SATs reached an acceptable range.

Urban does not know what to expect in the coming weeks. Certainly the academy would be more demanding than Mom when it came to assignments, deadlines, and grades. Having taken courses at a local community college, which he sailed through, Urban thinks that he will probably do well enough academically. Mostly, it is the prospect of juggling the academy's intense schedule, which will judge him on academic, military, and physical standards, that unnerves Urban.

He also wonders how his background, having never attended a regular high school, will go down with the other cadets. Will they keep their distance, assuming that since he was homeschooled he must be socially backward? A stranger to dating, sports, and high school proms? The one who laughs a moment too soon or too loud? Will their assumptions set him apart? For how long?

"I have no idea what I'm doing here," Urban confesses, looking around at the other teens, who are throwing their arms around their parents and siblings and posing for their last photos as civilians. Urban certainly wants to fly, but unlike some of the others, he is no Romeo of the skies, smitten by a particular jet whose features he has marveled over and memorized. A major reason he is standing here is undeniably pragmatic: the free tuition. Given his large family, a college education courtesy of Uncle Sam is not something easily turned down in the Urban household.

In fact, taxpayer-financed tuition is a major draw for nearly all the cadets here, especially with the cost of college soaring and with better colleges across the country offering a relative pittance of available aid to the most needy applicants, however worthy they might be.

In the final moments before the newcomers climb the stairs to the second floor, they and their parents get pep talks from some graduates of earlier years.

Under a small tent just outside Doolie Hall, Jim Shaw, a 1967 graduate and the president of the Association of Graduates, asks the teens how many are from the West Coast. Marcus's hand flies up, then wavers. "Do I count?" Barrett's mother asks, glancing at the families and covering her mouth.

Shaw, graying and jocular, lavishes the new students with praise—soon to become a rare commodity—commending them for deciding to attend the academy with the country at war. For the career-minded, he reminds them that the academy graduates only one-fifth of the air force's officers but half of its generals. The alumni include forty astronauts. Half of the graduates will become pilots, and half will devote themselves to the mundane but gargantuan effort of making the air force run by supporting the pilots as air traffic controllers, mechanics, engineers, accountants, doctors, lawyers, military police, and intelligence officers.

Except for the pilots, those who join the air force are, in a sense, joining the branch of the armed forces that offers the least glory. According to the Defense Department, the navy's Seawolf submarine, for example, carries a crew of 140, while an Arleigh Burke class destroyer carries 276. Their entire crews share in the experience of going off to sea and executing a given mission, whether protecting aircraft carriers from aerial fire or waging underwater battle against enemy submarines. The air force's B-2 stealth bomber, in contrast, costs a staggering $2.1 billion, can drop nuclear weapons, and carries only two pilots. All the other air force personnel are in the background, in silent, largely invisible roles of support.

"Say in a thunderous voice, 'I am good,'" Shaw tells the newcomers in his tent. They do, their confidence not quite rising to the level of a meteorological cataclysm. He has them repeat it until it sounds at least mildly convincing.

"Now don't say that again for another year," he says, adding, "You *are* good. That's why you're here. Keep your sense of humor, and don't laugh on the outside, laugh on the inside."

"Once you hit the South stairwell," he says, glancing toward the building behind him, "you belong to the air force and not Mommy and Daddy anymore. That is when you really start your happy day."

Mindful of the jumble of emotions that surrounds the move and the dam-busting force of her own excitement at her daughter's appointment to the academy, Marcus leans in close and talks to Barrett quietly, their bodies forming an intimate tent. Next to her, Barrett's stepfather, Jeff Marcus, a volunteer firefighter and the father of a Navy Seal, dabs his eyes.

"Don't forget you chose this for yourself," Terri Marcus says softly. "We're proud, but this is you. Are you sure this is what you want?"

Barrett does not hesitate. "One hundred percent," she replies. Then she turns around and climbs the South steps to begin her new life.

Up on the mezzanine, the cadets go from table to table, checking in, lining up, and signing forms that officially seal their entrance to the academy. An hour or so later, they walk down the steps at the opposite end of the lobby, stop by an honor wall inscribed with the names of graduates killed in battle, and cross a small footbridge to the shuttle bus that will whisk them off to the dorms and study halls. They are not quite sure, at this stage, whether it's still okay to talk to their families and their friends. They were told not to even acknowledge their parents.

But now the upperclassmen who will train them, called *cadre*, are telling them something else entirely. "Come on. Wave good-bye to your parents, guys," the cadre on Barrett's bus coo. "They drove all this way to see you off. That's not very chivalrous." The initiates are not sure how to take this. Barrett steals a last wave at her mother, her stepfather, and her younger sister, Taylor, before climbing on to the bus. Others, unconvinced or perhaps just unaccompanied, do not turn around.

The cadre also ask whether any of the new arrivals have been writing about coming to the academy on MySpace. There, a handful of incoming cadets began taunting the upperclassmen over the last few weeks, in what would prove to be a disastrously ill-timed poke at the academy hierarchy (more on this later). As the new cadets file on board, cadre study their faces, pictures of the MySpace rebels fresh in their minds. On this run, there are no matches.

The dulcet tones of the cadre vanish the very instant the bus turns the corner, away from the cadets' parents. "Eyes forward!" a voice booms suddenly, a prelude to the world that awaits them over the next few weeks. The cloying dies and its exact opposite is born, hurling the newcomers into the freshman's life of orders and criticism, mind games, and exuberantly possessive pronouns. The change comes so unexpectedly and so completely that it seems choreographed. (It is.)

"Everyone on this bus sit up straight," the voice hollers. It belongs to Cadet Technical Sergeant Steven A. Mount, a twenty-one-year-old from Texas City, Texas—a young Paul Newman who seems to have gotten lost at the gym: blue eyes, chiseled features, and a neck like a hydraulic lift. "Eyes on me."

Hands drop to laps, and the cadets don't really sit up; rather, they try to shrink into themselves. A few cadets, including Barrett, have the nervous smile also seen at an amusement park when the roller coaster picks up speed.

For Mount, the encounter is pure theater, but with a purpose. He is the first filter, aimed at separating the wavering or weak cadets from the start. Better they should leave now than drag down morale three weeks into training. His tools are tension and intimidation.

Mount remembers his own first day two years ago, when he sat on the bus "scared shitless." Nothing had prepared him for that initial onslaught, not even talking to graduates. Part of him wants to take the cadets aside and tell them to hang in there, that basic training will test them but not defeat them. But all of Mount's training in recent weeks pulls him in the opposite direction, urging him toward toughness. This, he concludes, is the greater service: throwing the new kids off balance, stretching the wire so taut that it cracks open their personalities so that new ones can take shape. In any other setting, what is going on here—tearing down an inner world to rebuild a psyche that will obey without question—would be considered abuse. But the changes Basics submit to are all voluntary. This crushing of individual will to forge a new group identity is the nucleus of virtually every army ever raised, underscoring the first essential element of a fighting force: unit cohesion. Watching it unfold is, in a sense, witnessing devastation and creation at once.

"I do want that initial shock of a deer in the headlights, of 'Whoa, I just got hit by a bus,'" Mount says later, then corrects himself. "Not a bus, a wave. If they can get over that shock and start following orders, listening and being receptive, then I've done my job, and we've done our job."

None of that ambivalence is evident in the man who is shouting at the newcomers on the bus, however. "Your life starts all over right here," he yells. "Right now."

For the next six weeks, Mount tells them, there will be only three answers that Basics may give to the cadet officers who are training them: "Yes, sir"; "No, sir"; "No excuses, sir." They will learn to dig combat trenches, scale improvised fortresses, and sleep as if in a straitjacket. Lest they forget, their status is cemented in slang: they are called *doolies* or *SMACKs* (an acronym for "Soldiers Minus Aptitude, Courage, and Knowledge"). When the cadre order them down for push-ups, they "beat" them—shorthand for hard physical training. The initial phase of basic training is called First Beast. Then the cadets move outdoors for boot camp, also called Second Beast.

"It is our responsibility—no, it is our sole purpose—to bring out the warrior spirit," Mount says. "We will push you beyond your limits."

Although the script echoes every basic-training movie that Hollywood has ever shoved their way, the cadets seem shocked. They keep their movements to a minimum, as if uncertain when they will bump up against an invisible electrified border.

"If you're ready for my challenges, why aren't you sounding off now?" Mount hollers.

"Are you proud to be here?" shouts Cadet Technical Sergeant Jordan Hayes, another of the cadet officers training the newcomers.

"Yes, sir!" the cadets roar from the seats.

As the bus pulls into the cadet area, Mount warns any cadets who are uncertain to fizzle out now. "If you decide to choose the path of mediocrity, do not insult me or my country," he intones. "Do not get off the bus." The new kids can still head back to the mothers and fathers at Doolie Hall, and they can maybe even make it home in time for September classes at the local community college. One woman, spooked by the performance, drops out on the spot.

As the bus pulls into the cadet area, the doors swing open at a concrete ramp, where the air force's core values loom in tall block letters: INTEGRITY FIRST, SERVICE BEFORE SELF, EXCELLENCE IN ALL WE DO.

Until the academy came under national scrutiny for the allegations of sexual misconduct in 2003, the first sign that newcomers saw above the famous ramp read BRING ME MEN. Removing the call was one of a number of changes spurred by the scandal, whose shadow continues to shape the cadet experience three years later.

Upper-class cadets converge on the newcomers, not to greet them but to attack like a formation of fighter planes, firing at them with every step.

"*Move! Off the bus!*" the trainers shout.

"*Hurry up, Basics!*"

"*You're wasting my time!*"

"*You can walk faster than that!*"

"*Faster!*"

"*Faster!*"

"*Faster!*"

The atmosphere is tense. The trainers are doing this time and again, all day long, but for each busload of new students, the experience is freshly disorienting. Basics rush to the footprints that are painted on the ground, the same footprints that launched decades of graduates before them on what many later described as the most formative experience of their lives.

At the moment, however, most are not thinking about history. They are planted firmly in the present. First, the cadre bark about standing at attention: shoulders back, eyes forward, hands cupped and aligned with the seams of their trousers. The cadets think they've absorbed this by osmosis, just from watching movies and reading about it, but now they find that it is actually difficult to master all at once.

Before they have a chance to really get it right, the call rises to the trainers. "Cadre, fall out. Make corrections." It leads to another onslaught, loud and close, as if the new ones were bugs under the big foot.

"What are you smiling about? Is it funny?"

"Do not look around! You're at attention!"

"Quit moving!"

"Don't smile! Keep your eyes forward!"

"Get off my footprints!"

To a freshman craning to see how the others were doing: "You have not *earned* the privilege to look around yet!"

That's rich, I think, chuckling, privately relieved at what I take for a glimmer of humor. Then I look around. Nobody else is laughing, not even the upperclassmen. There are no winks or sideways snickers. We have entered a no-irony zone.

Barrett gets it. She looks scared, as if she woke up to find a wrecking ball swinging straight at her bedroom window, giving her no time to head for the door. Her mouth is set in a kind of frantic semi-grin, which could be seen as a way of containing her nerves or of being halfway to laughter.

It is the second prospect that hangs her. In an instant, an upperclassman, Cadet Cadre Mark Saffold, is upon her. "Are you smiling?" he demands, leaning into her space. "Is this funny, Barrett? Are you having a good time?"

"Correction, please, sir." Barrett says. There is a catch in her throat now, and her smile has morphed into a thin, quivering wrinkle, a fault line on the map of her face that threatens to end in sobs.

Barrett never gets to correct herself. Instead, Saffold critiques her posture. "Head up," he shouts. "Shoulders back."

Barrett pulls her shoulders behind her and straightens her spine, but it is not good enough. "Get your shoulders back. Get them down," Saffold tells her, inches from her ear. She tries harder to straighten herself. "More," he says. She lifts her chin, pushing her shoulders as far back as they can go without losing her balance. Saffold steps back, spends a long moment looking at her and then moves on, just as the cadre wind up the session. Barrett wonders if she got it right or if the upperclassman just gave up on her. An overachiever, she is unnerved, not used to the yelling, not used to feeling like the pebble in someone's shoe, irritating just by being there.

All the shouting and the tension aims to throw the new kids off their game, to bring them down a few notches, and rattle their defenses. It also forces them to function under stress, as they may one day have to do in combat.

The newcomers jog up the entrance ramp, under the academy motto. They stop briefly at their dorms and then go on to Fairchild Hall, which is normally reserved for classrooms but today is a giant factory. It sucks in students who look like freshmen on any campus—in jeans, shorts, T-shirts, and sneakers and with hair at all lengths—and begins their transformation.

Two hours later, it spits them out in uniform, this year's crop in identical red-billed caps, the men's hair buzzed close to the head, the women's either cropped or pinned back. The kids are still fumbling and screwing up, but the new look is the first, outward, and perhaps easiest step in their journey toward a new identity. The clothes give them the benefit of the doubt, admitting them to a fraternity before they have gone through initiation. I wonder if common dress makes them feel part of a new organism and so less lonely, or does it create the opposite feeling: diminished, disconnected from the individuals they have always been. For the moment, they are in neither one place nor the other.

Sitting in the back row of what is usually a biology classroom, miles from her friends who opted for the party life at state college, is

Rhonda Meeker,* alone and almost too hungry for the military grind. A graduate of junior ROTC at her Albuquerque high school, Meeker knew that she wanted to go into the military like her uncle, a marine.

The other schools she applied to were the United States Military Academy at West Point and the United States Naval Academy at Annapolis, but the Air Force Academy offered her the greatest likelihood, she believed, of seeing combat. "If I were to go to West Point, I wouldn't have been able to go infantry," she said. "The navy also limits opportunities for women. The only way I would see combat as a woman was through the cockpit."

What kind of plane does Meeker want to fly? She does not hesitate in her answer. "Anything that shoots," she says.

Before Meeker even got here, she cut her blond hair short, hacking off eleven inches in one sitting, and she would opt to lose even more in a few minutes. Now, in Fairchild Hall's biology classroom, she sits near a model of a man, his midsection cut open to show his guts.

A few minutes later, she is in another classroom turned haircutting salon, getting a razor trim so that the back of her hair clears the collar of her uniform. On a whiteboard somebody has drawn Snoopy and written "Welcome, Class of 2010."

"If you want to take a lot off the top, go ahead," Meeker says bravely. She is seventeen. Her eyes are light brown and large, but there is no mirror for her to see whether she is going too far.

Meeker has not yet met David Urban, who will become her friend in the next year, but he is sitting for his haircut in a neighboring room. In less than three minutes, a razor buzzes over his hair, which falls in a blond shower on the floor and leaves him looking like a newborn chick.

"Look at that. How cute they are," says Hannah Love, a cutter at the academy whose own frosted hair, light on the sides and darker on top, seems modeled on a cupcake. By the time she reaches Urban, she is two-thirds through the 30 or so heads she will shear that day, and she is just hitting her stride. Between Love and the other cutters, they mow through 250 heads in an hour. It probably helps that the runway these kids are aiming for has nothing to do with fashion.

---

*Her name and identifying characteristics have been changed to protect her identity.

After losing their hair, the newcomers lose some blood, giving up four vials to screen for HIV, rubella, and sickle-cell anemia and leave a sample for the military's DNA data bank. The academy also screens women for pregnancy. The previous year, new cadets had to give seven vials of blood, but with the sudden change in altitude, the blood loss was too much, and about eighty cadets passed out. This year, cadets down snacks and drinks as they make their way through the blood draws and immunizations, with constant reminders not to let themselves become dehydrated.

The newest cadets, broken up into groups called *flights*, are still working out the hierarchy and the etiquette: whom they must acknowledge and how they should identify themselves. This is not as simple as it sounds. Within days of their arrival, the cadets are expected to memorize the names of all the upperclassmen who cross their path, greeting them wherever they are and whatever they are doing.

It is but a hint of the mountain of factoids that cadets must commit to memory. They also memorize the menu for the following day, the rules if they should be taken prisoner of war, and an entire little book of air force arcania—all 266 pages—known as *Contrails*. It is red, for their class color.

The group greeting is something else entirely. Each flight is named by its first letter: A for Aggressors, B for Barbarians, and so on. Delivered in unison, the greetings show respect and announce who they are. Shouted as the masses of cadets pour out of a building and onto a field, the greetings are also a loud way to find their mates—a steamroll of a call that shoves everything aside. Pulling this group together right here, right now, is the most important thing.

"*Aggressors lead the way!*"

They are a way of keeping pace—a driving, nearly tribal rhythm that pulls in the stragglers and the undecideds in the group, sweeping them toward a common destination.

"*Cobra strikes first!*"

They are a show of spirit and pride, a dipstick check of the collective testosterone level.

"*Screaming Demons!*"

They are a sign that in the new military life the cadets are choosing, it is not the interior monologue, the self-doubt, or the whirlwinds of uncertainty that count. It is all about performance, hollering for your group at the top of your lungs, and standing strong.

"*High-flying Tigers!*"

They are a challenge to the other flights, an accident of assignment turned into temporary identity. For these are brief alliances that will last only through basic training.

At this early stage, the cadets are not sure whom to salute, so they greet everybody, even me.

"Good afternoon, ma'am," the Executioners thunder as I walk past. They are lined up in a corridor opposite a breathtaking view of the Rockies. "*Heads will roll!*"

Just before three o'clock, they march out of Fairchild Hall and head to Mitchell Hall, the cavernous dining room that is reminiscent of a row of airplane hangars. Along one side of the hall is a balcony where the academy brass and their guests dine, surveying the rows of tables normally filled with thousands of cadets. Because of the high ceilings and the hard surfaces, sound collides off Mitchell's walls and bounces back, amplified to a hard, almost metallic edge.

On this, their first day, freshmen in limbo—hair shorn but still wearing their clothes from home—eat on a staggered schedule, and the mad pressure that will make eating feel like a march through hell is a day away, still just a rumor. They down hamburgers on buns, cold turkey sandwiches, potato chips, and juice to Phil Collins pleading over the sound system, "Take, take me home."

"Is everybody getting enough food?" asks an upperclassman. "Don't be afraid to ask for something." The new ones are still unsteady and fearful, and most eat little. Urban takes turkey on a bun with mayonnaise, applesauce, and white grape juice. Jonathan Benson, a wiry freshman in thick black-rimmed glasses, eats a turkey sandwich and some carrots. A big bowl of salad—lettuce, cherry tomatoes, and a blanket of grated cheddar—sits untouched, as if it were just too much to manage the dressing, the cutting, and the chewing. There is no conversation.

After fifteen minutes, the new cadets head to the labyrinthine underground warehouse that snakes beneath Mitchell Hall. The first face they meet belongs to Eddie Richardson, a jovial, heavyset native of North Carolina, disarming in his friendliness. The kids get one book of stamps and one postcard each. "Write home, and tell somebody thanks for sending you to the Air Force Academy," Richardson tells them.

"You know where Mesquite is?" Richardson asks Urban, after learning that he comes from Texas.

"Yes, sir," Urban answers.

An instant later, Urban realizes the risk of getting warm and fuzzy. He fails to greet a cadre, Erica Juchter, a junior with sleepy eyes that seem, at that moment, to belie a prickly temper. "You going to greet me?" Juchter snarls at him.

"Yes, ma'am," he answers, his eyebrows rising. "Screaming Demons!"

Urban has been in the underground warehouse less than two minutes, and he is already feeling all wrong.

Over the next few hours, the newcomers collect the rest of their gear for the coming year, much of which has been prepared beforehand for them. They each get red billed caps, which will eventually be covered with writing, like a cast on a broken leg. They get boots and dress shoes, sneakers, pale blue pajamas with dark blue piping, blue bathrobes with red piping, black and white T-shirts, swimsuits, underwear, and the camouflage uniforms commonly called BDUs, for "battle-dress uniform." Rhonda Meeker smiles with contentment when she receives the patch with her name already sewn on, as if she had finally made it home to find her place at the table waiting for her.

The cadets also collect linens, which technically they do not receive, but rent, from Goodwill Industrial Services. If they turn the linens in clean, however, they are not charged for their use. "Don't use my linen to shine your boots," warns Debbie Firkins, the no-nonsense doyenne of the sheet and pillowcase brigade for Goodwill. "You'll have to pay for it. That stuff doesn't come out in the wash."

That night, Casey Jane Barrett, though exhausted, has trouble falling asleep. In other rooms, the cadets sob under their blankets, but she is too wound up for even that. Staring out the window at the night sky and at the lights from the other dorms, she thinks of all that she has to do the next morning.

"What have I gotten myself into?" she asks herself for the first time.

2 | The Ordeal of a Meal

In the darkness before dawn, corridors housing Demons A Flight are menacingly quiet. In the dorm rooms where the new arrivals spend their first night, in exhausted yet restless sleep, it would be impossible to imagine the stealth operations under way just outside their doors. In silence, upperclassmen are clearing space in the hallway, fiddling with a laptop, adjusting loudspeakers, and taking up positions outside their doors, grins of complicity crossing their faces.

The torrent erupts at precisely 4:30 a.m., just a few hours after the kids have finished unpacking and have gone to bed. Reveille sounds just as the junior and senior training cadets—"two degrees" and "firsties" in academy parlance—start pounding on the dorm doors and hollering into the cadets' rooms, shouting at them to get up, get dressed, get out, and do it now. The banging crashes through the halls like garbage can lids down an alley and continues—unrelenting, overbearing, and inescapable—to shock the Basics, rather than simply wake them, into their new world. Before the cadets even open their eyes, they will feel off balance and out of step and, inevitably, believe that they've screwed up.

"*Hurry up! Open that door!*" hollers Kevin Pastoor, a two-degree from Parker, Colorado. The avalanche begins, with commands beating down on the cadets from all corners.

"*Get this door open right now! Get this door open! Hurry up!*"

"*Get your shoes on! Get your belts on! Get your things together! Hurry up!*"

"*C'mon! Hustle!*"

"*Help each other out. It's called teamwork!*"

"*Hurry up! Brush your teeth! Brush them faster than you've ever brushed them!*"

"*Move, move, move, move!*"

"Hurry up with your belts!"
"All ready in five minutes!"
"You should be dressed and out here!"
"Shouldn't be out here without your roommate!"
"You're late!"

Blaring through the halls is Guns N' Roses, screaming the menacing, dystopic lyrics to "Welcome to the Jungle," which will become a kind of anthem for the most searing days of the cadets' doolie year.

Up and down the hallways, the newcomers, disoriented and harassed, blinking at this unforgiving morning, scurry into the bathrooms. By instinct, they want to keep their heads low, as if ducking crossfire, but then they risk not greeting an upperclassman—another mistake. Their showers should take no more than thirty seconds, partly so that they have enough time to get dressed, but also to give everybody a chance under the water.

Some cadets, tipped off beforehand, had showered the night before, but the others are now trying to make it through the morning routine, shower and all. The challenge urges them toward failure. Before lining up along the corridor walls, the newcomers have to make their beds, fold their pajamas, wash and dress, straighten their rooms, and check on their roommates. The women also have to fix or at least brush their hair. And they must do it all in seven minutes.

Casey Jane Barrett's room sits at the far end of the corridor. She shares it with Megan Biles, a soccer player from Portland, Oregon, and Nicole Elliott, from here in Colorado Springs. The afternoon before, Barrett said good-bye to her red eyeglasses, and she now sports shorter hair and boxy black military-issue glasses, reminiscent of Politburo portraits. The kids nickname the glasses "birth-control goggles," guaranteed to thwart desire at any altitude. Unfortunately, they prove indestructible.

Barrett and Biles look to Elliott to help them through. Elliott—who is small, quiet, and athletic—spent a year at the academy's prep school, so she knows better than anyone else what to expect and how to prepare. She warned her roommates to shower the night before, to prepare their clothes, and even to fix their hair, but even she had not expected the nerve-jangling assault that woke them this morning.

The three women are among the last to reach the lineup, their tardiness made worse by the fact that the women's dorm rooms, clustered way down the hall, oblige them to walk farther than the men to reach their assembled squad mates. Each extra step represents one more opportunity for criticism and delay, and sometimes (but not this morning) the entire squad gets dropped for push-ups until everybody turns out.

The morning madness, in creating such stress, aims to drive home a point. Unless the cadets can learn to rely on one another and not see their struggles as entirely personal tests, they will fail at a place like the academy and, by extension, in the active-duty air force.

The message is a switch from the traditional military pitch. The army recruitment campaign appeals to the loner with a close-up of a soldier in uniform over the caption "An Army of One," and the figure most emblematic of the dreams that drive cadets here is likely a solitary fighter or bomber pilot. However, the concept works in the real military only if you broaden *one* to mean not a single individual but an entire group. An army of one would fall fast, with nobody to watch its back.

Despite the operatic herding, the cadets make it down in time, marching off to Mitchell Hall. By 5:15 a.m., wearing their BDUs and their black lace-up boots, the cadets are in their seats for their first real meal as a unit. Of course, they had eaten the day before, but those were hurried bites taken on a staggered schedule. This morning, all the freshmen are eating together for the first time. It is their first full introduction to the mind-bending torture that awaits them at meal-time for the coming year.

The squadrons sit at single long tables, their places assigned before they march in, and much of the food is already laid out. Adding to the disorientation for the new kids, the room does not smell like breakfast. There is no aroma of coffee and no tea, for these are not served at the academy. The cadets drink water or juice. The kitchen staff brings the warm food—eggs, bacon, and French toast—in stacked rolling trays that move swiftly down the aisles.

At the head of each table sits a cadre, with another upperclassman often at his side. At the opposite end are three cadets charged with passing the food around—called the load master, the hot pilot, and the cold pilot. They must use specific terms and movements and even a particular etiquette, which the kids are about to learn.

The cadets sit at attention on the edges of their seats, their backs straight and their shoulders down. Their heads are up but their eyes are cast low, looking at the academy's white plates with the eagle emblem at the twelve o'clock position. This is the only place they are permitted to look.

"You will know every detail about your eagle," Charles Chapot, the firstie who is training them that morning, tells them. "You will study it constantly. You will know how many stars there are around your eagle, you will know how many feathers there are on your eagle, you will never look away from your eagle."

The instructions come in excruciating detail—too many to remember, too many not to slip up, and certainly too many to relax and just eat on this first day. In fact, if you are relaxing, you are probably in the wrong place. Breakfast starts with an announcer from the podium telling the new kids, "At ease. Group take your seats."

Chapot describes how that happens: "You will wait until your table commandant tells you to take a seat. At that point, you will sit down. You will move to the left of your chair, one step. With your right hand, you will pull your chair out. You'll sit down from the left-hand side. You will sit on the front one-third of your chair at position and attention. You will be one fist's distance away from the table. Your feet will be on the ground at a forty-five-degree angle."

All this is before they even open their mouths. Once they sit down, there are more instructions. They will line up drinks like a fortress protecting their plates, with the most opaque liquid to the right and the water to the left. "Every time you drink, you will return your glass to its position. You will make sure that it is touching the other glass. At no time will there be a gap."

"When you start eating, do not take big bites. What you do is you pick up your fork and you pick up your knife. You will cut a bite-sized piece. This is a bite you can eat instead of chew. Put it in your mouth. You will put your fork and knife back down on your plate. You will not start chewing until you return your silverware to your plate."

At the far end of the table, hands trembling, Rebecca Rasweiler-Richter, the load master, spears a stick of French toast on the tray. Chapot's reproach is there before the food hits her plate. "You don't take for yourself first," he fires. Rasweiler-Richter's face reddens, and her head sinks back into her collar, almost like a turtle. The sun comes up.

David Urban takes a strip of bacon, two sticks of French toast, a scoop of scrambled eggs, some orange juice, and water. He too comes in for criticism after accepting the pitcher of water with his left hand from the cadet sitting to his left.

"Receive across your body," Chapot tells Urban. Urban bites his bottom lip, as if to reprimand himself in a private punishment. He switches the pitcher to his right hand and crosses it parallel to his shoulders before filling his glass. When he drinks, he touches only the bottom third of his glass.

Barrett takes eggs, three sticks of French toast, orange juice, and water. She makes the mistake of drinking some orange juice and catches Chapot's unwelcome attention.

"Do not drink your orange juice until your water is finished," he tells her. Chastened, she takes neither water nor juice. She reaches for a banana and is stopped again, for not asking first.

"Sir, um, may I make a request?" Barrett tries.

"Is that one of your basic responses?" Chapot asks. Barrett looks around at the other cadets, hoping, perhaps, for a line. They are still, moving neither limb nor eye. "And stop saying 'um.'"

"Correction, please, sir," Barrett tries. She is not sure where to go from there. What combination of words that she is permitted, she wonders, will actually end this ordeal? She'd gladly give up the damn banana. "Basic Cadet Barrett reporting as ordered, sir," she ventures.

Chapot's patience runs out. In less than fifteen minutes, he has to have them across the terrazzo at Arnold Hall, in their seats for a 6 a.m. address from the leadership. "We don't have time for this," he rasps. "Take the banana."

A moment later, all the freshmen are churning out of Mitchell Hall, Barrett behind Urban, Meeker bringing up the rear, all sounding off in cadence.

"Demons A Flight over here, please, sir!" they holler, a driving drumbeat. "Demons A Flight over here, please, sir!" they repeat, until they all stand with their groups on the grounds outside Mitchell and even the lost and wayward have found their way home.

The cadets stop at the honor wall. The morning air is thin at this altitude, chill and clear. They hear about the long blue line and the graduates who have died in battle.

At six o'clock, they march over to the theater at Arnold Hall, named for Henry H. "Hap" Arnold, the legendary U.S. Army and Air Force general who championed the creation of an independent air force after World War II and who oversaw the projects that became pillars of the modern air force: the intercontinental bomber, jet fighters, and atomic weapons.

The cadets file into the theater, and Demons A Flight sits midway toward the front of the auditorium. There is a buzz of voices as the upperclassmen try to establish order, telling their charges to sit up at attention. But the cadets are curious. They are here, waiting to hear something, but they don't know what or why. This state of cluelessness—fully intended—is something they have to get used to.

Throughout the arduous trials of basic training on the hill (First Beast) and boot camp (Second Beast), the cadets have no firm idea what is coming; their schedule is known to everyone but them. They receive no program and little warning—beyond disconnected orders—of what lies ahead. Later in the year, they will at least hear rumors, from friends, through e-mails, and from their own nosing around. At this early stage, however, they are cut off from the outside world—no newspaper, television, or computer.

The purpose, of course, is to accustom them to follow orders unquestioningly, to rely on obedience rather than on individual judgment. The academy system is based on their becoming followers first, then leaders.

For instance, today they are wearing two pairs of socks, white under black, but nobody has told them why: so that they can slowly break in their marching boots. After wearing the boots in the morning, the cadets will switch to sneakers in the afternoon. Stripped of their watches, the cadets have only a dim sense of the hour, and they have trouble keeping track of the days. Sitting in the auditorium, Urban has the peculiar feeling of time unfurled like a banner, every color and thread distinct. He guesses that it is already nine o'clock, halfway to lunch, rather than six.

Once the seats are filled, the room goes completely black, and there is only a figure, lit from below, on the stage. An unseen announcer introduces him. It is Lieutenant Colonel James Jeffers, commander of the Basic Cadet Training Group, architect of the cadets' introduction to academy life, which lasts for six weeks. Thanks to the lighting, his features remain impossible to make out during his speech—part pep talk and part warning—and I wonder if this, too, is deliberate. "I want you to succeed," he tells the new arrivals. "How you succeed is up to you."

"We're not training you just to train. We're training you to win," he says. "And how you fight tomorrow depends on how you train today."

The newcomers hear from Steven B. Cecil, a two-degree who is in charge of Arnold Hall. He strides back and forth across the stage, unsmiling, at first giving them some basic rules—"No food or drink in my auditorium"—but what he is really doing is changing the tone, raising the tension, for what lies ahead.

The hall is still dark, but now the stage glows red at the back. Another cadet, Shawn Green, introduces the squadron commanders for basic training and recites "Invictus," the 1875 poem by William Ernest Henley. The Basics will hear the poem, a kind of warrior's anthem, often during Beast and throughout the year. (Timothy McVeigh, the Oklahoma City bomber, quoted the same poem in his final testament, just before his execution.)

Out of the night that covers me,
Black as the Pit from pole to pole,
I thank whatever gods may be
For my unconquerable soul.
In the fell clutch of circumstance
I have not winced nor cried aloud.
Under the bludgeonings of chance
My head is bloody, but unbowed.

Beyond this place of wrath and tears
Looms but the horror of the shade,
And yet the menace of the years
Finds, and shall find me, unafraid.
It matters not how strait the gate,
How charged with punishments the scroll,
I am the master of my fate;
I am the captain of my soul.

Under the stage, the cadre stand on squares. Cadet Lieutenant Colonel Jesse Martin Ziegler, commander of Demons Squad, is waiting to be introduced. He is functioning on three hours of sleep, having stayed up late watching the Basics in his squadron urinate into cups for their drug tests—one of the less glamorous demands of the job.

Ziegler remembers his own first encounter with the cadre two years ago, at an assembly identical to this one. "These guys are like gods or something," he thought at the time. "They symbolize everything that I want to be." The only differences this time around are the faces up on the stage and in the auditorium—and the fact that he is now on the other side, the one the cubs are looking up to, the one who, in just a few moments, will begin barking the orders. He feels goose bumps on his arms.

Brandon Dues, a firstie who is cadet group commander in charge of Basic Cadet Training (BCT) for all 1,334 incoming freshmen, presents Ziegler and the other cadre one by one, as if they are rock stars. Behind him, fog rolls over the stage floor. As each one is named, a red spotlight falls on the place where he will appear. A mechanical lift raises the upperclassmen from under the stage, so they appear suddenly, as if by magic or fate. Each is in uniform, snapping from parade rest to attention upon hearing his name. Row upon row, they are a flock of demigods, mythic and cool, waiting to be unleashed on the unsuspecting doolies.

"This is your leadership," Dues intones grandly. He tells the new cadets to aim high, that the academy will accept nothing less, that it has no use for the garbage that is mediocrity. He speaks in cadence, his voice rising and ebbing as the menacing strains of "Clubbed to Death" from *The Matrix* trilogy fill the hall. He then invokes the five words that freshmen come to dread more than any others: "Cadre, fall out. Make corrections!"

Suddenly the cadre fly off the stage in all directions, like Valkyries, picking off groups of cadets and criticizing everything that is wrong with them, ordering them to hit the floor or jump, and now. The room is clanging with reproach, but not shame, for the faultfinding is universal and inevitable, the very purpose for which the young cadets are here. In the din, it is impossible to make out any single reproach, but around the room, over and over, the result is the same. Within seconds, almost the entire auditorium of cadets is sweating through push-ups, knee bends, jumping jacks, and squats, and then they are exhorted to do more, faster and better.

It stops abruptly. The trainers are called back to the stage while the cadets return to their seats and catch their breath and their wits. The cadre stand completely still, like statues commemorating this moment.

"*Class of 2010, will you disappoint?*" Dues shouts.

"*No, sir!*"

"*I can't hear you!*"

"*No, sir!*"

"We'll see," Dues answers, and pauses. He paces and looks out over the auditorium. When Dues went through this, the training was longer and harder, and some cadets were injured in the frenzy. In the aftermath of the sexual abuse scandals, however, the bouts of training were shortened, and the cadre now hold back. Right after this, the Basics will turn out to swear their allegiance as cadets, under the gaze of parents who have stayed on for a last look at their cadets before heading home. Dues explains, "With parents and generals out there looking at them, we didn't want them looking all ragged and worn out."

"*Cadre, fall out!*" he orders again. "*Make corrections!*"

Again, the cadre bust off the stage like atoms breaking apart. Barrett thanks her luck that she is in the middle of the row and not on the aisle as the auditorium explodes in another paroxysm of trial and punishment. All around her, again, the room erupts in individual slipups detected and redeemed through brief intense workouts imposed upon the entire group. Then, as abruptly as it began, it is over.

By the time the doolies crowd toward the doors, accompanied by Frank Sinatra singing "The Most Wonderful Time of the Year" on the sound system, the new kids are shocked and psyched, looking up to the hard, trim, mysterious cadre who will be training them for the next six weeks. The cadre have been cast as stars in a show worthy of Las Vegas, and the kids are beginning to see them that way.

Now the doolies are pumped, calling out their groups. Pouring from the auditorium, they split up, scamper, and regroup, like cells under a microscope finding their shape. Barrett comes out into the sunlight as if shaken, even bewildered, as the group around her puffs, "No guts, no glory!" It is not what she should be hearing; it is not the call of her own mates in Demons A flight.

Rhonda Meeker tries to maneuver her way past the crowd, her eyes darting everywhere in search of her group. "Oh, shit," she whispers to herself. She, too, is lost.

3 | In the Running

Terri Marcus, her husband, and her youngest daughter are in the bleachers early, all in oversized phosphorescent green T-shirts. Before them stretches the emerald lawn of the empty parade grounds, a glimmering, deepwater reflection of their shirts. It is only a day since they dropped off Marcus's eldest, Casey Jane Barrett, to begin life as a cadet. Now they are waiting for her to parade out in her battle greens for the first time to take the oath as a cadet. Marcus fidgets with the video camera.

It is Marcus's last chance to see her daughter before the family heads back to Ventura. To Marcus, she and Casey Jane are best friends rather than mother and daughter, and it is hard for her now to imagine life without her. Other families will see their kids' bristly hair and uniforms, the boots and bulky glasses of military life for the first time, and this will be the updated picture they take home with them as they think of their children slogging through Beast in the coming weeks.

Long before the cadets stride out in their mottled green uniforms, they must learn how to parade. They spend what seems like hours, but is actually just one hour, learning how to "size up"—arrange themselves in order of height—stand at attention, pivot, salute, and stand at parade rest, with their legs apart and their hands crossed low behind them. "You're not in the army or the navy, where they cross in the middle of the back," says Kevin Pastoor, who trains them that morning.

Pastoor is slender and quiet, not the type to bellow orders. He looks, rather, as though he would be more at home with a video version of basic training than with this clumsy, hesitating mass of flesh and fear he has before him. How will he turn them into a discernible group, able to follow orders and synchronize their moves, with so little time? Beyond that, how can he get them to thinking beyond their own interests, to identify with their flight mates? For this is the flip side of basic training. It is not just about shaping a new identity in the incoming freshmen; it is also a chance for the upperclassmen, who will graduate as officers in the regular air force, to learn about leading airmen and managing people—teaching, guiding, and inspiring the people who work for them.

In the movie classics, the drill sergeant is toughness personified, eternally barking orders eyeball to eyeball with the hapless private, hammering him into shape. Here, however, future officers experiment with different styles of leadership: studying classmates and officers, looking into themselves, and trying on and discarding personas until they find one that fits. For some, the overbearing, hard-driving approach is the first they reach for, either because all those movies stuck or because it was the style they experienced when they were doolies. Others are seeking their voices as leaders: Some rely on understanding and encouragement to teach the basics, some on shame. Still others use their strength and fitness, challenging the newest cadets to keep up with them.

Today Pastoor is teaching the Demons to stand at parade rest and then to whip to attention. It is, in fact, four changes of position: the hands go from behind to the sides, the back goes tall and straight, the legs pull together and open out at 22.5 degrees, and the head tilts higher. Done right, these are all one seamless movement, like a rubber band snapping into place.

"Atten-hut!" Pastoor calls. "Parade hest!"

He walks up and down the rows, stopping at Barrett. He slips his boot between her heels to check her position and says nothing, moving on.

Sizing up, Rhonda Meeker concludes that she is the shortest in her flight group. (Actually, she is probably tied with Samuel Pang for that distinction.) She seems to droop a little at the realization, bending her knees and looking down at the ground.

Thomas "Brad" Bernard, a football recruit from Georgia with a build like a breathing refrigerator, rolls his blue eyes. He and his roommate, Zachary Taylor, have already graduated from the academy's prep school, so this lesson covers familiar ground.

Pastoor moves on, teaching the cadets to salute. The movement flows from the center of the body, he explains, with the upper arm going parallel to the ground. The hand doesn't sweep but strikes into place, at the brow and parallel to the sky. Striding through the rows, he stops and tells Barrett to fix the tilt of her hand, which is hiding her eyes. She bites her lip.

Jamal Harrison, a two-degree from Texas who is also training the cadets, sees the kids lose their concentration, stumbling in response to criticism, and remembers how overwhelmed he felt when so much was new. "Don't react to your mistakes," Harrison says, walking alongside the rows of "four-digs," as the freshmen are called. "Keep your bearing and fix it."

Pastoor begins to show them how to raise their hands for the swearing in, again breaking the process down into a series of distinct steps. "We're working together now," he says, just before they head for the parade grounds. "You're not individuals anymore." It is still an instruction, not yet a description.

In the stands, the Marcus family, with their screaming green shirts, can almost pass for discreet. Surrounding them are other parents who have stayed on in Colorado Springs more than a day after dropping their kids off, just to catch one more glimpse of them and watch their swearing in. There are fewer than two hundred people in the stands, who probably represent no more than 10 percent of the incoming class. Those who did stay, like the Marcuses, are exuberant in their support, with special T-shirts, posters, colored balloons, and video cameras everywhere.

"We ♥ U Jordan," one family's poster says.

"We ♥ U SCHS 20."

"We are so proud, Goober!!"

"Sal, NJ ♥ U."

" ♥ Megan Petey," says a fuchsia poster board.

As the cadets march out, the parents are taken aback. Most hadn't figured that, with all of them in uniform, it would be so difficult to pick out their own kids, even using binoculars.

"You can't tell the boys from the girls. They all look the same," says a woman standing near Marcus.

"That's why we dressed up this way," Marcus tells her, glancing down at their shirts. "At least she can find us."

Marcus is able to pick Barrett out from among her flight mates, in her bulky goggles and battle uniform, her eyes wide under the brim of her red cap. Marcus is out of the bleachers, heading with her camera for the path that runs alongside Stillman Field. The ground is still wet from rain, so she stands in the mud, watching her daughter raise her right hand. Marcus is sparkling with pride as Barrett is sworn in toward a future as an air force officer.

At home, the local paper carried Barrett's picture and a full article on her appointment to the Air Force Academy. The family had spent months preparing for this moment, researching what to expect, talking to other cadet parents around the country. Looking far ahead to Barrett's graduation, they had even paid dues to join the academy's alumni association the day before, as if nothing could alter their daughter's path. "I've got goose bumps," Marcus says, holding out her arm, tanned and tingling.

It is perhaps a sign of enduring sensitivity to the consequences of the withering accusations made three years earlier that the first briefing many doolies attend after swearing allegiance to the academy covers sexual harassment. The episodes of 2003 are not only behind this ninety-minute briefing, they also shape Beast over the next six weeks and linger over the entire first year of training.

First a handful, then a few more, and ultimately sixty former cadets stepped forward in 2003 to say they'd been raped at the Air Force Academy, many by upperclassmen, and that the academy's leaders had responded by punishing the victims instead of their rapists. The academy's commandant of cadets, Brigadier General S. "Taco" Gilbert III, had famously answered a question about a 2001 assault, in which a cadet said she was raped after an evening of drinking and playing strip poker, by faulting her judgment. "For example, if I walk down a dark alley with hundred-dollar bills hanging out of my pockets, it doesn't justify my being attacked or robbed, but I certainly increased the risk by doing what I did," he wrote.

As pressure mounted in Congress, Air Force Secretary James G. Roche swept out the academy's entire leadership—its superintendent, Lieutenant General John R. Dallager, as well as Gilbert and two others—in a single day in March 2003, stripping Dallager of one of his stars on the eve of his retirement. A report by the air force general counsel at the time found no significant evidence of fault, but an independent commission, headed by Florida Congresswoman Tillie Fowler, found plenty, reporting that "the sexual assault problems at the Academy are real and continue to this day." The commission blamed a culture at the academy that had never fully accepted women as cadets and that largely ignored "serious sexual misconduct problems" that dated back at least a decade. That spring, President George W. Bush, still enjoying popular support as the commander in chief who had just sent troops off to war in Iraq, canceled plans to speak at the academy's graduation.

The victims who went public, seven women who left the academy, hired lawyers, but they took no steps to sue. Rather, they insisted, they simply wanted to force the academy to confront the problem, and they became self-appointed watchdogs and advocates for victims. The victims never expected roses from the air force or from the academy's leadership for speaking out, but they might have been surprised by the resentment that their criticisms provoked among cadets and by the protective instincts their charges kindled toward the academy.

The new kids, itching to show they belong, betray no interest in the briefing. As Dr. Harold H. Breakey, the academy's top official who coordinates the response to sexual assault cases, explains how to recognize harassment and what to do about it, the cadets slump in their seats, and some doze off. He talks about his own life, saying that he was molested as a child; according to earlier surveys of incoming cadets, 25 percent of the women and 8 percent of the men in that room had likely suffered sexual abuse or assault before arriving at the academy.

After the rape allegations first surfaced in 2003, the academy initially did away with confidential reporting of sexual assaults, mandating that any victim who spoke up, whether for comfort, justice, or medical attention, would have to follow through with an official complaint naming her assailant. The academy contended that mandatory reporting would force the problem up from underground, but victims' advocates argued that it would do just the opposite: push deeper into silence victims who needed help but were not strong enough to face the ordeal of prosecution or who feared the consequences reporting might have on their careers.

In 2005, the academy reversed that policy, offering victims the choice of either filing a criminal report or seeking help without filing a complaint but taking steps to preserve evidence in case the victim opted to pursue justice in the future. "With the crime of sexual assault, the body is the crime scene," Dr. Breakey tells them.

"What we're talking about is the invasion of your personal space or privacy," he says. "Not basic training. What we're talking about is brushing up against a breast or buttocks in an intentional manner." He adds, "You're new here, you're Basics, but I still expect you to report anything that's outside normal."

Privately, the female cadets think about the reports of assaults. Some dismiss the accusations by blaming the women for partying with the men in the first place, though not all of them did. Others keep a quiet watch. Uppermost in their minds, however, is the need to belong, and many yearn for nothing more than a friendly hand on their shoulder. When Dr. Breakey opens the floor for questions, there are none.

In MySpace postings, a group of incoming cadets had gone even further to repudiate the rape victims, convinced that there was no real problem before they had ever even spent a night at the academy. They bemoaned the removal from campus of a sign whose clarion call, "Bring me men," had come to be seen as emblematic of institutional favoritism, as if it were the beginning of a sentence that ended with "not women."

The offending words had stood tall above the ramp where new students enter the academy, and for critics of the sign, its removal in 2003 signaled a possible willingness by the academy to change, albeit under intense pressure. Inside the academy and among many of its graduates, however, taking down the words reeked of capitulation. Now, in fact, a group of female cadets who were just starting out were hankering for its return, arguing that in context, it was not at all about preferring men over women, but about cadets outshining ordinary people to fulfill their nation's highest destiny. The line is from "The Coming American," an 1894 poem by Samuel Walter Foss, and the cadets were claiming that in context, the line was inspiring.

The poem reads, in part:

> Bring me men to match my mountains,
> Bring me men to match my plains;
> Men to chart a starry empire,
> Men to make celestial claims.
> Bring me men to match my prairies,
> Men to match my inland seas;
> Men to sail beyond my oceans,
> Reaching for the galaxies.
> These are men to build a nation.

In a culture that venerates tradition, the removal of the sign rankled many.

Another result of the scandal that the new kids mocked gleefully on MySpace was the suspension of Recognition, a grueling two-day marathon of training and hazing that culminates in the formal acceptance of the doolies by their fellow cadets. The Classes of 2007 and 2008 were the only two in the history of the academy to have skipped Recognition. Nevertheless, razzing the members of these two classes for not having gone through the ordeal, when the decision was not even in their hands, did not win the MySpace cadets any friends.

Forget the high grade point averages, the vaunted leadership potential, and the wave of faith they rode in on. As they came to realize, ridiculing the very upperclassmen who would have near total control over their lives for their first six weeks at the academy was either the most breathtakingly brave, stupid, or suicidal thing the new kids on the block could have done.

By the end of the briefing, which also covers underage drinking and drug use, psychological counseling, and suicide prevention, the torpor is near total. If these issues could conceivably matter to them, the doolies are shrewd enough not to show it.

That afternoon, the academy takes its first measure of the new crew's fitness, ordering the doolies on a 1.5-mile run by the field house, ending on an uphill ramp to the finish line. Having been here only a day, the kids have not yet acclimated to the thin mountain air. The upperclassmen constantly make them stop to drink water, and they warn them to keep their knees loose so their circulation doesn't slow down.

Nevertheless, heads ache and breathing comes short, and even a 1.5-mile run is pushing the kids hard at this stage. That afternoon, Demons A Flight is slow in turning out of its rooms. The first doolies out stand in the hallway sounding off. "Sir, we're waiting on our classmates, sir," they repeat, like robots needing a kick. Ultimately they hit the floor, doing thirty push-ups on the spot.

David Urban, a furrow from his cap cutting across his forehead like a tribal scar, heads out on the run confidently enough. He has eleven minutes and thirty seconds to loop back to the finish line. For the women, the time they must beat is thirteen minutes and fifteen seconds.

As the doolies pour out to start the race, their flight commandant, a senior named Lance Watson, watches, then turns to his cadre, his mouth wrinkling in distaste. "They're not sounding off too well," he says. They don't seem to be getting it; they still seem a little lost and aimless. He wants to see more cohesion, more crispness and certainty. "They're not falling out. We've got to get them down doing more push-ups."

After ten minutes and forty-six seconds, the first runner crosses the finish line. The cadre cluster on the sidelines about fifty feet before it, shouting encouragement, advice, and occasional insults. "A flight females representing," they call out as the first women cross the finish line, just under eleven and a half minutes.

Jamal Harrison exhorts a pack of female cadets, who are pacing themselves, to "finish strong." Meeker takes this encouragement as if it were a personal turbo-charged message for her alone. She swings out to the side and passes her group, crossing the finish line in twelve minutes and nine seconds.

Urban makes it in twelve minutes, his face red and his lungs starving for oxygen.

Six seconds later, Barrett crosses, seemingly without much effort. Hard behind her, a group of male cadets bursts ahead in the final stretch for a hot-dog finish. Nevertheless, they are too late. "All these guys saved a little too much if they can sprint like that," says Pastoor.

As the stopwatch sweeps past thirteen minutes, a female cadet runs next to a male, urging him on. "Keep going," she tells him, as he struggles toward the finish line, his mouth hanging open in pain. "Let the air go." His limbs seem weighted by sandbags, each yard's advance a film run in slow motion.

At fourteen minutes, another group of runners appears round the corner. "Oh, man, there are some serious stragglers," Harrison says to the others. As the young ones get closer, Harrison and the others urge them on. "You got it," they call.

"Push it, Basic."

"You're right there."

"You're home."

At ten seconds shy of fifteen minutes, the last male cadet staggers toward the finish line. His face is fire-engine red, the veins popped and throbbing, like blue-grey strings lying outside his skin. "Fight through that pain," the cadre call. "You only got fifty [feet] left."

A few seconds later, the last female cadet sways toward them, moving side to side more than forward. She finally stops and drops her head, hands on her kneecaps, steadying them as she throws up. "Not there," the cadre say, gathering around her. "Get on the grass."

"If you're going to throw up, let it go."

After the run, the Demons line up along a hallway in the field house. "Men, a score above eleven thirty, you're on probation. You need to work on it," says Watson, whose fanatical devotion to bodybuilding sets him apart even from the other upperclassmen. The women who have come in after thirteen minutes and fifteen seconds also have to try again. They have two weeks before their next test.

That afternoon, the Demons pile into a meeting room off the terrazzo, the concrete and grass square at the center of the base's main buildings, to meet their squadron commander, Cadet Lieutenant Colonel Jesse Ziegler, last seen rising from the smoke at the Arnold Hall floor show. Here he is far less intimidating. He tells the cadets to take off their jackets if they are warm. The room has floor-to-ceiling screened windows, which are now open, so a cool breeze blows through the rows of freshmen. Some sit in chairs and others sit on the floor, their jackets on their laps.

Ziegler himself takes a seat, opens a loose-leaf binder on his lap, and begins going over the ground rules of basic training. He tells the freshmen about military time—"no colons between the hour and the minute"— and that they are *never* to be alone during basic training.

"Make sure you start helping each other out," he says. Basic Cadet Training, or BCT for short, "is all about teamwork." Ziegler does not add that in the 2003 scandal, one of the most damning accusations came from a former cadet, Jessica Brakey, who said that her cadre called her out of her tent one night during boot camp, talked to her about his childhood, and ended up raping her.

Ziegler warns the doolies to put away their contact lenses because the dry, dusty weather "will screw up your eyes." The military-issue glasses are not beautiful, he admits to knowing chuckles, but they really are better for the rigors ahead.

As the cadets head out for boot camp at Jacks Valley in three weeks or so, pinkeye will inevitably spread through the incoming class. "Wash your hands five times a day or more," he says.

Ziegler comes up with some startling reminders: "Always wear your underwear, wherever you go, under your uniform. Do not 'go commando,' or whatever you call it. Do not turn underwear or socks inside out. Never wear a uniform more than two days." He flips a few pages. "Personal hygiene," he says. "If you're going to pee in a stall, lift the seat. My cadre don't want to sit in that, and neither do I. Having the bathroom nasty is going to make the illness problem worse.

"We have hand sanitizer, Chapstick, training-related material, a limited supply of unused sanitary protection items." He stops and scratches his head. "That's how it's worded in here," he reports. The cadets seem unsure of whether it's okay to laugh, and they sneak looks at one another.

He warns them that because of the stress, they may become constipated. The women may miss their periods. "I've known Basics who haven't had a bowel movement for as long as three weeks, or through the entire BCT."

Then he offers the men some brotherly advice, fruit of his bruising past as a Basic in haste. "I know you've been shaving for a while by the time you get here, but in the stress of BCT, you may get a little stressed out and shave too hard," Ziegler tells them. "Take a moment, take a breath, and relax."

Coming on the heels of the sexual assault charges were complaints that Evangelical Christian officers were proselytizing the students. Ziegler pledges "zero tolerance" for religious discrimination. "All of you are guaranteed the right to worship or not to worship, as is your choice." Opting out of Sunday mass is "not a problem, it doesn't matter." Then he reconsiders his terminology. "See that word I used? That's probably inappropriate," he says. "If you choose not to go, you'll have personal time in your room."

At the end, Ziegler gets only two questions: "How do we change our socks, when we've only gotten one pair?" and "Sir, when will our first worship services be available?"

Later, Ziegler says his normal style is far less easygoing than he appeared, but he did not think that the briefing called for a hard rider. "The idea was just to make sure they make it through. That's why I was relaxed, I let them all sit down, and I sat down, so they would relax and comprehend everything I was saying." The night before, he had also let some things slide, because he knew the kids had to get up early and needed their sleep. Now he worries that they may see him as a soft touch, just "a friendly old guy who comes around," and that is not what he is.

As a cadet officer during the year, he pushed even his fellow upperclassmen to meet the standards, and he was not easy about second chances when they fell short. "I expect the standard and hope for higher. That's made me step up myself," he says. Most cadet officers, for example, will allow the cadre working under them to take a pass and slip off campus in the evening, provided they've done their work.

In his squadron, however, there are nightly dorm inspections, and the cadre have to sign up for a night out. This has earned him a reputation that was not entirely welcome. "I'm trying to learn to be more flexible." The Air Officer Command, the active-duty air force officer who oversees his squadron, has told Ziegler that he needs to be more personable.

"Some people see me as a big jerk or something like that," he says, running his hand over his head. "I'm working on balancing the hard-core guy, or whatever you want to call him, and the nice guy. So I'm kind of swaying in there, figuring out what I like to be."

As much as the Basics may learn from Ziegler, he is also learning. That, he explains, is why the academy does basic training at Colorado Springs rather than at, for instance, Lackland Air Force Base in Texas.

"You can sit in a classroom, learn about leadership, and read about leadership all the time, and that'll give you a lot of important things," he says, "but once you start doing it, you really start figuring things out."

4 | A New Road Map

When Brigadier General Susan Y. Desjardins got the call to head to the U.S. Air Force Academy, where she would take over as commandant of cadets in late 2005, it was not in the form of a request. Rather, it sounded like an order, telling her she *would* be returning to her troubled alma mater.

Two years earlier, the sexual assault scandal had cost jobs up and down the chain of command. The following year, charges of religious coercion sent the leadership packing. An appointment to the academy, at a time when it seemed to be staggering from one scandal to another, was perhaps not something one could be *invited* to take on. If recent history was any indication, it was the Calamity Jane of career moves.

But Desjardins had other reasons for hesitating before what was, after all, a historic step—making her the first woman to serve as commandant of cadets. (It would actually be the second time she would make history at the academy: she was also a member of the Class of 1980, the first to enter after Congress ordered the military service academies to admit women.) She felt almost like a stranger to the academy, having returned only once for a reunion, in September 2000. She was also troubled by her own lack of experience in education or instruction. She had never spent time teaching or running any of the air force's myriad training programs. She was a command pilot with experience flying C-17 cargo planes,

KC-135 and KC-10 aerial refuelers, and an array of other aircraft. Her entire career revolved around the operational side of the air force: making sure that planes and pilots were where they needed to be, well supplied, and doing what they were supposed to be doing.

At Charleston Air Force Base, her last post before coming to the academy, she served as commander of the 437th Airlift Wing. Desjardins had fifty crews in the air at any one time, with a mission to ferry more cargo through "our little aerial port," as she called it, "than any other base on the East Coast." Her command supported the war effort, doing aeromedical evacuations, bringing in supplies, and backing up special operations forces—in short, flying everything "from cardboard to blood" to the battlefields in Mesopotamia.

"Everything we do is heading that way," she had said, turning east, "and now you want me to go west and you want me to do *that*?" Desjardins, a trim woman in her late forties with short dark hair and quick eyes, a trace of pale blue eye shadow her only concession to anything specifically feminine, was sitting at a small round table in her office.

"It's a huge change in perspective," she told her bosses. "That's a huge change in the way I approach everything. I don't know if I can make that shift." Then someone who worked for her made sense of it. "He said, 'Ma'am, you have seen what it takes. You have seen the dedica- tion. You have seen your airmen work twenty-four hours straight to load an airplane, to fuel an airplane, to fix an airplane, to fly an airplane, with much-needed supplies. You have seen them through aerial drops, you've seen them drop paratroopers—you've seen the commitment and the dedication. Now, you just have to be sure you produce it.'"

Desjardins now half smiles at the recollection. "*You* should go be the commandant," she had said to that young man. Now she adds, "But he was exactly right. I just needed to back up that time line, so that the people we produce out of here have all the tools to be an officer of character, to face those kinds of situations, to be able to lead in that kind of situation."

The assignment made sense in another light as well. The absence of training experience for Desjardins was not fatal. Her boss, Lieutenant General John F. Regni, Class of 1973, had the educational background she lacked: he had returned to the academy after serving as commander of the Air University at Maxwell Air Force Base in Alabama. Her expertise lay in getting things moving, and the glare of national attention prompted by the sexual assault allegations in 2003 had all but paralyzed the academy, suspending practices and traditions like Recognition, the two-day ritual that intensified the vulnerability of the freshmen. The academy was still feeling its way through the tumult in 2004, when the next wave of criticism hit over the place of religion in academy life. Could she get the place back on course?

"That operational flavor that I bring is probably good, because I don't get wrapped up in minutiae," Desjardins says. "I kind of know that this is important and this is not." She assumes that her pedigree as an alumna of the first class of women, as well as her recent combat experience, played into the decision to deploy her here. But three-quarters of the way through her first year here, she is still not sure. "I wasn't really ever told why. I was just told, 'Go.'"

What Desjardins found was a student body divided. The Class of 2006, which was the firstie class when she stepped in, was angry. The cadets had been through so many changes in response to the crises that they had grown cynical and bitter, sealing a place in the new commandant's mind as "the mad class," eager to graduate and get away from the academy. Cadets from the Class of 2007 were in their freshman year when the sexual assault scandal broke. They had been left standing in the road, feeling as if the bus had pulled away without them.

"No one knew what to do," Desjardins explains. Senior officers were afraid to continue the training they knew, in which the upperclassmen were free to ride the cadets as hard as they thought necessary, virtually unchecked—a "disparity of power" that left new cadets vulnerable to abuse, according to an early report by the air force general counsel. Yet they did not really know any other way to run training at the academy. The result was the only one possible under the circumstances: a vacuum.

To the Class of 2006, the disruption came across as the leadership caving in to bad publicity, casting suspicion and mistrust on them all for the actions of what air force officials had described as "a few bad apples."

To the Class of 2007, the inaction came across as indifference, Desjardins realized after having discussions with them. "It was like 'Who's watching us? Who cares about us? Who's going to train us?'" the commandant recalls. "'No one's willing to train us.'"

The academy restored Recognition for the Class of 2009 just a few months after Desjardins arrived. In the inevitable rivalry between class years, the Class of 2009, though freshmen, drew bragging rights over the sophomores and juniors, because the freshmen had endured the exercise whereas the two previous classes had escaped it. Against this backdrop, the trash talk on MySpace by incoming Basics, deriding their cadet trainers for having missed Recognition, is not just a bad joke or an excess of class spirit. It illustrates how thoroughly the academy's traditional hierarchy—its natural order, in the minds of the older cadets—had been turned on its head in the wake of the scandals.

Amid the upheaval, returning to her alma mater felt surreal to the commandant. Aside from some minor differences, everything was familiar. This time, however, Desjardins was here not as a student but as someone charged with reinventing the system for training cadets to become officers. Moving on at times resembled not so much a march as a crab crawl: two steps to the side and one back and around for each inch forward.

Among cadets, there was a huge groundswell of support for bringing back Recognition, but nobody was quite sure how to do it. The cadets proposed five different plans for how to run the spring ritual before the academy settled on one. "We had to figure out a way to bring it back so that the cadets weren't broken down but were recognized for their accomplishment," she says.

One of the plans concentrated on building teamwork, another on leadership, and still a third on class unity. Each version brought up questions about the meaning and the purpose of the ritual. Cadets tend to value Recognition—as well as basic training and every other exercise of their career here—in direct proportion to the toughness of its challenges, but there was more to Recognition than tradition alone. "It's for them to understand and realize that you can't get through this without one another. Through stress, that bond develops. We had to put them under stress for that bond to develop," Desjardins explains.

The other argument for restoring a tradition that some cadets described as organized hazing was one that only alumni could make: the rush that you get "when that upperclassman shakes your hand and calls you by your first name for the first time all year."

The commandant smiles. The memory of that moment seems as close to her as the rows of medals over her heart. The firstie who shook her hand in the spring of 1977, Kevin D. Kirk, had given her a hard time all year long. He was someone whose name that she knew even then she would remember the rest of her life.

"That was the first time he shook my hand. He said, 'Well done, Sue. That was just fantastic.' Who was *that*?" she remembers thinking, shoulders rising in surprise. "I didn't like him at all up until then. He had maintained his professional distance, but he had challenged me physically and mentally all year, and I had met his expectations. Now he was celebrating that by calling me by my first name. It was a feeling of pure happiness and just a sense of accomplishment." By the time he turned to walk away, Desjardins felt invincible. That was the experience she wanted to pass on.

The plan she ultimately chose was developed by the cadets, and it incorporated roles for the Classes of 2007 and 2008, who would be new to the experience. The plan fell in line with the academy's shift toward an "officer development system" that concentrates on giving each class a role that corresponds to segments in the active-duty air force rather than focusing almost solely on training doolies.

Beginning in 2004, the academy brought in instructors from Lackland Air Force Base in Texas to train the upper-class cadets in running basic training and boot camp and to oversee the cadet trainers, or cadre, at work. All these steps, Desjardins hoped, would curb any tendency toward the ritual trials of Recognition going overboard.

"We wanted it to be more professional, proficient, and proactive," she says. In practice, the freshmen are still trained to follow orders from the upperclassmen, learning "to follow, then lead," in the commandant's formulation.

The sophomores, who come to their new squadron at the start of the year, are supposed to serve as coaches and mentors for the freshmen. The juniors correspond to noncommissioned officers (NCOs)—the bridge between the rank-and-file and the upper echelon, responsible for carrying out the orders from above. The seniors, who are just months away from graduating as second lieutenants, correspond to commissioned officers, who are supported by the NCOs and the rest of the squadron. Desjardins has ramped up physical training to match the level at Lackland's physical fitness conditioning course, going from seven training sessions to twenty-seven.

In addition, the academy now regiments the cadets' days and nights much more closely—frequently to the exasperation of the cadets themselves. Breakfast is obligatory. "That was not a popular decision," Desjardins says, shaking her head with a rueful smile, "but we figured that if we made a mandatory breakfast—a mandatory show time when you have to have an accountability for all the people in your squadron; know that they're there, up, dressed, and ready for class; and then they have breakfast—then you have to go to bed earlier because you have to get up earlier."

There is a mandated study time from eight to eleven o'clock, and lights must be out by midnight. Anyone who wants to study later has to go underground—stuffing towels under the door and closing the curtains with maniacal secrecy—or get special permission. Four out of five days a week, the cadets must line up in formation before marching into the dining hall for lunch with their squadrons. This gives the cadets from different squadrons the chance to connect on a regular basis.

The changes, Desjardins believes, are starting to pay off, in 30 to 40 percent fewer injuries and illnesses, better grades, and lower attrition. The Class of 2007, which felt abandoned on some level, has said that it feels a special calling to train the Class of 2010. "I guess it's because the opposite of love is not hate; the opposite of love is indifference," Desjardins told the Class of 2007 during one talk. "That's right," the cadets replied. "That's what it is."

In her office, the commandant forms a triangle with her fingers, and for a moment she almost looks as if she is praying. "They're so committed now to their leadership role, because they saw how it should *not* be done," she says. "They'd rather be hated than not cared about at all."

5 | Broken but Still Standing

It is only July 4, just six days after they entered the Air Force Academy, when David Urban and the other doolies flock to the mailroom for the first time, full of expectation and longing for word from home. They had only just dropped their bags, felt the razor scrape their scalps, and begun their new lives as cadets in training at the U.S. Air Force Academy, but in the grueling calculus of First and Second Beast—facing the constant orders, corrections, and punishments of upperclassmen seventeen hours at a go—each day stretches into the emotional equivalent of a week. By July 4, it feels to Urban and his roommate, Austin Westbrook, a tall teen from Wisconsin with glasses, whose hairline and face seemed to already carry the outlines of his middle-age self, as if the summer is half over.

And so they rush down, encouraged by the other doolies who are coming away from their mailboxes clutching stacks of letters as Lady Liberty holds her torch. The doolies have stayed away from the mailroom until now, hoping their mail would build up. But Urban's box is empty. There is nothing from his family and nothing from the girl he's known for seven years, who is now in Jordan, to whom he has been e-mailing and instant messaging as though she is another chamber in his brain.

Don't they care? He walks back to his room, laughing and joking as if none of it mattered. "But inside, I was crushed," he recalls. Logically, he knew he'd only just left home. "But when you're there waiting for the mail, you don't think about how long it takes to get here. I wasn't think-ing, 'It didn't have time to get here,' just 'Nothing's there.' Do they even care that I'm gone? Why don't they send something?" He shakes his head. "There's no rational thought process going through your mind. It just hits your morale. You lose it, all right."

Exhausted, his spirits already worn, the letdown tips Urban into depression. The next Sunday, instead of staying back in his room writing letters, he goes to chapel for the first time. The service is bigger than the one at his church back home, but the mood and the contemporary music are achingly familiar. Back in Texas, Urban would get up and sing with the congregation, enjoying the release, but here he freezes in his seat, paralyzed and near tears as he remembers his home and family and everything he'd left behind for this new life of relentless humiliation.

Other than at briefings, meals, and prayer, the doolies are not allowed to sit down and are not supposed to talk to one another, even in private (a rule they mostly ignore). Urban would go to his room and stand there, tired and yet afraid to sit, wondering, "What am I doing? Do I even want to be here anymore?" At night he would lie on his bed, sleeping fitfully.

Like most of the other cadets, he never completely messes his bed at lights out. Instead, he lies on top of the already made bed, still as a corpse under a blanket that he folds up in the morning. He hates jumping out of bed before dawn, the instant the upperclassmen pound on his door. He yearns for just a few more minutes to sleep, to ease himself into the day. In his sleep, he begins listening for the sounds of the upperclassmen rousing and coming out of their rooms even before they actually come hammering. He listens for the sound, half awake, and then tells himself, "Just a few more minutes." It's his way of taking control, of tricking his body into thinking that he is getting just a few more minutes to himself before starting the day. But does he even want to be spending his days here?

He remembers his childhood in Washington state, where the family lived near an air force base. The boy watched C-130 transport planes from his parents' bedroom window, and once he saw a C-5 Galaxy, built to do heavy airlifts across oceans, with its massive landing gear down—"one of the most awesome sights ever." If he wanted to fly planes like that, he reasoned, the Air Force Academy, which promises graduating cadets the most pilot slots and offers a top-rate college degree at taxpayer expense, was the place to come—if it would have him.

He couldn't boast great educational credentials. Like his nine siblings, he had been homeschooled, with his mother grading his exams. Toward the end, he slacked off. "By the time I was a senior, my Mom pretty much said, 'I'm tired of trying to get you to do your work. I can't do it. Here's your book. Go. Study if you want to.'" For advanced science and math, like calculus and higher algebra, Urban turned to his father, an electrical engineer who works on PAC 3 missiles—heir to the Star Wars program.

His parents began homeschooling out of a religious conviction, a belief, Urban says, "that God had told them that they should homeschool their children." Undoubtedly, he missed out on social development; his first high school prom was this past spring, at the age of twenty, when he escorted a cousin to hers. However, he credits his mother's lessons with instilling in him a deep sense of right and wrong and with helping him resist peer pressure.

"Growing up, there were a lot of temptations to go off and do things I shouldn't," Urban explains, "and if I went to public schools, it would have been a lot easier to give in to those things. So in a way, homeschooling was a good thing because it kept me away from those bad influences until I was mature enough to understand and keep away from that stuff on my own.

"I know," he continues, "looking back on some of the things I'd gone through, that if I'd been going to public school, there's a very good chance I wouldn't have turned out to be the person that I am."

Getting Urban to the academy had become a project of sorts in his church. His family and his fellow parishioners had coached him and cheered him through every step. One member, an accountant, prepped him for the math portion of the SAT. Urban learned later that as a young man, the accountant had hoped to attend the academy himself, so Urban plans to keep him and the rest of the congregation posted on his odyssey here.

Westbrook, Urban's roommate, is ironing his dress shirt by the window. He listens while lining up the creases on his sleeves. Until just two years ago, Westbrook had planned to become an architect. Then he went to an air show. He was captivated, imagined himself slashing through the sky while everyone below gawked at him. "It made me wonder if I wanted to just sit in a cubicle and design things," Westbrook says.

However, neither Urban nor Westbrook had imagined the physical and psychological demands of the course they had chosen, nor did they realize how thoroughly the institution would set about dismantling their every defense. It wasn't so much that each mistake led to beatings—push-ups or flutter kicks or sit-ups—but that they never knew how long or how hard the beating would go on. Westbrook would steel himself for ten push-ups, only to find as he neared ten that they would have to do ten more, then ten more after that, like successive waves of hell. Their muscles trembled with overuse, ordered, well past their limit, to go even harder. Lance Watson, their flight commandant, lifts weights for fun and calls himself Superman, pushing himself well beyond the point of endurance for the Basics. "Just when we thought he couldn't do anymore, he'd go and do more," Urban recalls.

Once Urban made the mistake of leaning against the wall behind him. "Why are you leaning up against the wall?" Charles Chapot, the cadre training them, demanded.

Urban, cleaning his room now in advance of an inspection, recalls how he felt, hollowed out and unable to go on. He brushes specks of lint off the red blankets on the beds. "I was so . . . ," he says, searching for the right words. "People say 'crushed,' like, okay, your heart is broken. But I was physically and mentally broken. I couldn't push it out anymore, and I couldn't think of anything to say."

"Are you broken? Are you weak?" Chapot hollered. Their heights were not that different, but Urban felt as if Chapot were looming over him, grinding him underfoot. In the warrior world, there is nothing worse than to admit defeat, and Urban would say nothing, but Chapot was unrelenting. "Say it," he insisted, inches from Urban's sweating, pulsing face. "You're weak and broken."

"And so I said it," Urban confesses.

"After that, they called me out in the middle of the hallway, and I had to stand at attention while everyone around me was doing exercises. I could see it was really hard; I was standing there with sweat pouring down my face. I was literally like this," Urban demonstrates, pushing his shoulders back. His eyes are grim, and his lower lip is jutting out like a small cliff on the topography of his face. His mouth trembles, and he seems about to lose control again—a vestige of the shame he felt at the time.

"At that point in my life," he recalls, "I became very grateful for sweat, because sweat hides tears. The emotional impact lasted until the next briefing, and people would come up to me and say, 'Hey man, don't worry about it,' and I would look away. I thought I was stronger than this," he concludes, not looking away now. "The marines go through twelve weeks of basic."

Despite the emotional pounding, neither Westbrook nor Urban have dropped out. Grateful for the prized congressional appointment, Westbrook fears that he will disappoint his family if he steps down.

Worse yet, it would mean that his loved ones were wrong to believe in him, that he wasn't even strong enough to survive the rituals of admission, and that he had deprived somebody else (who would not have quit) of the chance to attend the academy.

Urban opens the drawers in the captains' beds, checking that the shirts are folded and stacked precisely, the underwear is arrayed in neat rows, and the socks are lying like sleeping soldiers. He runs a rag over an iron bar behind his desk and peers into hidden corners, finding dust that had somehow eluded his earlier efforts.

To his surprise, this is the part that Urban likes. At home, the bedroom he shared with three younger brothers was the second smallest bedroom of their house, not much larger than his dorm room. Being able to clean his room and have it stay neat—instead of collapsing into piles of dirty clothes within hours—is an utterly new experience, and it's more important to him than he ever would have guessed. Here, his efforts are not frustrated if he looks away for a moment. His books and his shirts and shorts stay folded and don't somehow migrate to the floor. In the smallest and most personal way, Urban is taking control of something, defining his space and the kind of person he will become: a person who sees to himself; a person who knows where to find his things.

He steps back, impressed. "Wait a minute," he tells Westbrook. "This looks really nice." He flexes his arm, spies a bicep, and smiles to himself.

Amid the despair are other discoveries. He finds that he can do more than he ever imagined—mentally, if not yet physically. At his community college, he would ordinarily get a week and a half to memorize the massive amounts of information that he has to memorize overnight here.

Throughout this time, as the upperclassmen take sledgehammers to their personalities and before they have had a chance to build up their new identities, Urban and Westbrook, who are not even sure they would be friends under ordinary circumstances, have found themselves stumbling toward a new understanding of themselves, of the families they left behind, and of the institution that would, in a sense, become their new families.

Without watches, newspapers, or cell phones and cut off from their computers and easy, instant communication, Urban comes to appreciate the letter that somebody sat down to write, found a stamp for, and went out to mail. "Wow, they wrote that much to me," he finds himself thinking. "That's cool. There's that much more love and thought that went into it."

As the first part of basic training winds down, Urban begins adapting to the rhythm and ways of academy life. The sense of humiliation lifts, and he finds a way to view his early fiasco that allows him to push on. At least now he knows that he has already hit bottom, "hard-core," as he says, and has survived.

"In a way, I think it made me stronger," he notes. As he continues, at the academy and perhaps in battle, he will see others crack, and he might feel the strain himself once again. "Some people break, and I'll still be there," he says, "staring up at the cadre like 'What's next?'"

6 | The Meaning of Knowledge

Three weeks into basic training, uber-firstie Lance Watson is gone as commander of Demons A Flight, walked to his room by an officer and put under room arrest. A doolie from another flight has complained to a counselor that Watson singled him out for humiliation, berating him in front of the rest of his flight. Watson finds the charge ridiculous. He knows that his natural inclination is to drive people hard. That's why his fellow commander, who was having trouble getting the cadet to fall in line, had asked Watson to step in. In calling the cadet out, Watson hadn't done anything different from what he did in training his own flight.

While the academy officials investigate, Watson has to sit out the last two days of First Beast, frustrated, while the next set of trainers scrambles to take over early. As the new trainers rush into place, they wonder about the implications of Watson's removal. Are the boundaries of acceptable training shrinking, and if so, how far?

"It meant a lot to me to be flight commander [of basic training]," Watson says later. "I knew I didn't do anything wrong, and everybody knew I didn't do anything wrong." Although Watson is cleared after a few days and the cadet drops out, the ground remains shaky.

Thus, early on a July morning, with the dew settling like crystals on their dummy M-16s, the doolies who had been under Watson's command are out training mostly with one another, with just two upperclassmen, Cadet Captain Jonathan Elliott, the firstie who is the flight commander for Second Beast, and Nick Mercurio, a two-degree, on hand to correct them.

The cadets stand facing one another in pairs, learning rifle drill. To the count of fifteen, the rifle must go from standing alongside the thigh, like an unwavering buddy, crossing over the heart to land on the shoulder, and the same in reverse back down. Each number on the way to fifteen has its own position; it should strike crisp and clean, inevitable as the second hand on a clock. With the exception of Theodore Ornelas, a wiry kid who has already learned it at the academy's prep school, the assembled doolies are nowhere near the goal.

Other than the fact that they are both in Squadron 13, Elliott and Mercurio have little in common. Elliott, the son of missionaries, his father an academy graduate, worries that his doolies lack sufficient respect and commitment for the charge they have taken on. In some measure, this is due to the MySpace fiasco, which at that moment he and other trainers from his class are taking very personally. Whereas Watson trained the new kids through physical exertion, Elliott's leverage is more psychological.

Mercurio is from Rhode Island, describes himself as "devilishly handsome—that's the legal term," and dreams of writing like Ernest Hemingway. He came west to fly, but an unhealthy patch on the periphery of his retina, which laser surgery was powerless to fix, ruled out pilot training. "I stayed for the fraternity of it," he says.

The SMACKs practice on a concrete walkway near their dorm that overlooks the athletic fields. Rhonda Meeker and Rebecca Rasweiler-Richter, two short, serious blondes—Meeker tilt-a-whirl gung-ho and Rasweiler-Richter quietly competent—coach each other through the drill.

Meeker is from Albuquerque; she decided on the military life as an eleven-year-old in Sacramento, after witnessing gang wars, drug addiction, and drive-by shootings.

Rasweiler-Richter hails from the other end of the country—and not just geographically. She grew up in Greenwich, Connecticut, one of the richest towns in the United States, and she has an adoring family that treks to Colorado Springs to cheer her on at every opportunity.

Meeker cannot seem to get the rifle to rest straight on her shoulder. "In order for it not to be tilted, I have to do this," Meeker says, pulling the rifle at what feels like an angle. She looks down the barrel. "It doesn't look straight," she says.

"Because it's not," Rasweiler-Richter tells her.

Mercurio is watching them. Meeker turns to him. "You're just going to have to drop it down and feel where it's going," he says.

Meeker enjoys the feel of the gun, its heft and its hard edges, as she turns and shifts the weapon. "It feels easier to maneuver if it's charged and ready to fire," she says—a description, it occurs to me, that could also apply to her own eagerness starting out. She looks down the barrel of another Basic's rifle. "You got sand in there," she tells Nicole Elliott, her roommate.

"Is that what it is?" Elliott asks, eyebrows rising like apostrophes.

"It's dirty in there," Meeker tells her with authority.

Meanwhile, Cadet Captain Elliott—no relation to Basic Elliott—suspects that the doolies are holding back on the criticism, going all fuzzy. That's not how they'll learn. "You're not doing each other any favors by being nice," he says.

"Your hands should be red and stinging from slapping the rifle." Elliott shakes his head, as if they have absorbed nothing. "Your rifles are not pogo sticks."

The drill goes on for more than an hour. As with everything they are learning and practicing in these crucial first weeks, it is all about embedding the cadence in their psyches and building up muscle memory—an innate and unmistakable feel for where the rifle should be on each count from one to fifteen.

"By the time you do it the last time, it should be perfect," Mercurio says, as he leads them through repetitions.

The exercise is a microcosm, in a sense, of the transformation that the Basics undergo throughout their initiation as the demands of the Air Force elbow out the preoccupations they brought with them to Colorado Springs—from clothes and haircuts that make a mockery of vanity to the sudden immersion in drills, lore, legend, and countless factoids on the air force in general and the academy in particular. These last are documented in *Contrails*, which the cadets are summoned to memorize like a catechism until the knowledge becomes automatic.

In fact, "knowledge" is what the factoids are called, as if here there is no higher body of information worthy of the name. The usage leads to odd-ball sentences, with doolies fretting about studying their knowledge and upperclassmen griping that the doolies just don't know their knowledge.

"As basic cadets, they come in here with zero knowledge," says Major Tony Schenk, a compact, muscular tank of a man from northern Texas, Class of 1984. "They learn all the ranks and names of upper-class cadre, military codes, insignias, Air Force Academy history, and then the new cadre come in three weeks later, and they have to memorize the staff all over again. It's all about indoctrinating them into the military environment."

Thus, on this morning, the day before they tackle Second Beast, the new kids stumble through knowledge that feels like factoid razor wire, cutting and scraping them with every misstep.

"When did Congress appoint the first and only five star general of the air force?" Cadet Captain Elliott asks, looking across the faces.

"*Sir, the answer is May 1949*," some of the Basics answer. Others say, "*May 1942*."

"Forty-two or '49?" Elliott asks.

"*Sir, the answer is May 1949!*" they roar back.

"Who was that?"

"*Sir, the answer is Harry Hap Arnold*."

Elliott's eyes narrow. Where to begin? Aside from being wrong, the doolies forgot all about rank and title. "Good ol' Hap," he says, walking past the Basics. "Good ol' Hap."

"*Correction, please, sir. The answer is General Harry Arnold*."

"Harry? *Harry???*"

"*Correction, please, sir. Sir, the answer is General Harold Hap Arnold*."

"*Harold?*"

"*Correction, please, sir. Sir, the answer is General Harry Hap Arnold*."

"Harry? How many different names is that?" Elliott asks. "Let's go through them all. Harry. Harold. Hap. Henry." His gaze shines like a lighthouse through fog, searching out their sorry states. "Let's just guess."

"*Correction, please, sir. Sir, the answer is General Harold/Harry/Henry Hap Arnold!*" the Basics shout, bumping into one another's answers and still not reaching any consensus.

Finally, as much from fatigue as from a sneaking suspicion that this could go on forever, Elliott gives in. "Henry," he says. "Not Harold or Harry. Henry."

The cadets exchange looks. It was on a video about the academy's history that they had just seen the day before.

Next question. Who was the first superintendent of the Air Force Academy?

"*Sir, the answer is Lieutenant General Hubert R. Harmon.*"

Who was the second superintendent of the Air Force Academy?"

"*Sir, the answer is Major General James G. Briggs.*"

"G. As in *golf*? Is that what you said?"

"*Yes, sir!*"

"Is it *golf* or is it *echo*?"

"Sir, the answer is Major General James E. Briggs!"

Mercurio steps forward to take over.

"Basics, what is your altitude?" he asks. The right answer is as much about attitude as altitude: at first it comes back with hesitation, with only a few of the cadets speaking up.

"*Sir, the answer is 7,258 feet above sea level—far, far above that of West Point or Annapolis.*"

"Some people know it. Correct yourselves and do it again," Mercurio says, leaning back on his heels.

"*Correction, please, Sir! Sir, the answer is 7,258 feet above sea level,*" the Basics say. So far, so good. The second part, however, is a muddle, voices tripping over one another, and what emerges is something like "far, far above the average at West Point and Annapolis."

The average? West Point is in the Hudson River Valley, and Annapolis, well, it is the U.S. *Naval* Academy. "Which way is it?" Mercurio presses.

"*Correction, please, sir! Sir, the answer is 7,258 feet above sea level, far, far . . .*"

"Far, far above that of West Point or Annapolis," he says, patience fraying. "Correct yourselves and do it again."

"*Correction, please, sir! Sir, the answer is 7,258 feet above sea level, far, far above that of West Point or Annapolis!*"

Finally, Mercurio's thin face lets out a smile. "That is absolutely true," he says, and looks at Samuel Pang, whose limbs seem made of rubber and who is small enough to avoid messing his bed at night by sleeping on top of his desk. "Basic Pang, do not sway back and forth," Mercurio orders.

Thus goes the drill, on and on, question after question—about which air bases host special commands, about the rank that corresponds to three chevrons, about which year the honor code was established at the academy—hour after hour, in preparation for "knowledge tests" they will take every week between now and Recognition in March.

The purpose extends beyond learning the landmarks of their new world, says Master Sergeant Julie R. Begley, who is here from Lackland Air Force Base in Texas to help teach and monitor the trainers. With a war underway, officers are called upon to memorize battle plans, orders, numbers, and much else under conditions far more stressful than these. Without this training, they could never perform under pressure, she says. "When they get out there, they're going to be put in positions, and they're not going to be told, 'You've got three days to memorize this.' Whatever you got to do right now, do it."

So deeply does the academy reach into their psyches that it is not uncommon for the cadets to rise in their sleep, imagining themselves in the throes of some training exercise, of getting dressed down, or of getting ready for inspection. The incidents go well beyond talking or walking in their sleep, and the cadets do not usually wake up. It is as if phantoms of the new people being born inside them seep out at night to have their say—looming anxiously or out of step or revved up—and are then sucked back into sleep.

Casey Jane Barrett, according to her roommate, got up one night and started throwing on her clothes as if about to turn out in the hall that very minute. She ran around and exhorted Megan Biles, her roommate, to hurry up and get ready with her. "*We gotta go! Now!*" she shouted. Biles, a tall soccer player whose cheerful demeanor gives no hint of the determination that brought her here, managed to calm Barrett down and get her back into bed. The next morning, Barrett remembered none of it.

Another night it was Biles who bolted up in bed. "*My shoes are shinier,*" she called out. That was all. She lay back down and instantly went back to sleep. "What? Are you okay?" Barrett asked, blinking herself awake. No answer came back.

Meeker awoke one night to find her roommate pivoting on her heels as she practiced turning to face in different directions. She never actually woke up and had no memory of what happened.

For teenagers just a few weeks out of high school, the first phase of BCT, First Beast, is a demolition job on their psyches and their personalities, a slap in the delivery room at the birth of their military lives. The next part, Second Beast—two weeks of field training at a vast training complex known as Jacks Valley—is about building up, not tearing down. At this point the trainers aim to take the pulp that is left and begin creating a new identity, one that reaches outward to the group and the academy.

The doolies, though, will not be the only ones chafing under scrutiny. For the cadre training them, as well, Jacks Valley will become a test.

7 | The Long Jump

In the women's bathroom, snapshots of rubber duckies—the chubby kind for a baby's bath—stare from picture frames by the sink, and a radio blares hip-hop. In the stalls, Audrey Hepburn, the epitome of impeccable, classy femininity, looks down at you. She wears white gloves and tilts her head coquettishly.

"Basics: You may be Basics, but that is no excuse for leaving this restroom absolutely *filthy*!" she says, an unlikely phrase to have ever passed Hepburn's lips. "Be a lady and *clean up after yourself.* Thank you!!"

The bathroom, industrial yet clubby with us-girls asides, is a private joke, a wrinkle in the otherwise taut fabric that binds Demons A Flight as the new faces prepare to head out for Jacks Valley. Who's up in the men's room, I wonder. Cary Grant? Batman?

Cadre criticisms aside, by now the rubber duckies—not the ones for a child's bath, but slang for the dummy rifles that cadets use for training—are starting to harden the hands of the new men and women, and within an hour the doolies are lined up in the cavernous gymnasium, tackling their physical training test in shorts and T-shirts. To pass, they need 251 points out of a possible 500, touching their toes and doing chin-ups, push-ups, sit-ups, long jumps, and a six-hundred-yard run around the indoor track.

Rhonda Meeker, at the outset, pronounces herself "fanfreakin'tastic" and then looks around at the hundreds of other Basics, none of whom is even smiling. "I guess I'm the odd one out," she adds, ducking her head.

At the chin-up bars, Casey Jane Barrett stands on a chair, trying to pull herself up. She cannot budge. "Widen your grip. Use your back," says an upperclassman who is manning the station. She is hoping to do just one chin-up—the absolute minimum for women. If she could do eight, she would get top points for the event, but that does not seem remotely feasible to her. She moves her hands apart on the bar and slowly pulls herself up, a tight, tentative smile creeping across her face as it clears the bar. "Go for two," cheers Rebecca Rasweiler-Richter, who is her partner on the course. Barrett does not let go but just hangs there for a moment.

From the next line, Jonathan Elliott, the cadet captain, is watching her silently. "Let's go, Casey. Keep pushing," Rasweiler-Richter tells her. Barrett's arms are trembling as she pulls herself up and does another. She lets go and lands on the floor.

Then it is Rasweiler-Richter's turn. She pulls herself up effortlessly, and steadily does one, two, then four, then eight—at which point she has already reached her maximum score—and sails on to ten, eleven, and twelve, finally stopping after thirteen. A practiced gymnast, she smiles in quiet satisfaction but says nothing. Her face is not even red.

At the long jump, Barrett's best leap comes in at six feet and two inches; her partner goes six inches farther. Both pass the minimum for women, five feet and nine inches.

A couple of rows over, Austin Westbrook swings his arms back and bends his knees, as if he is about to somersault off a diving board. When Westbrook does his long jump, however, he falls backward, landing at seven feet and four inches. The upperclassman who is manning the station, Zach Sasser, a junior place kicker on the football team, is not pleased. Falling back is supposed to count as a zero, but Westbrook hadn't been warned. "If you have to, fall forward," Sasser tells him.

At each of the stations, the bar for physical strain is set lower for women than for men, just as it is in the active-duty military. For men, the minimum number of chin-ups is seven. In the long jump, the men must clear at least seven feet.

The disparity has occasionally led to some grumbling; the men argue that if the women cannot meet the same standards as their male class-mates, they should never have been admitted to the academy. That feeling persisted long after women were first admitted to the service academies in 1976. It was part of an underlying culture of resentment toward the presence of women that caught the attention of investigators after the sexual assault scandals of 2003, and research since then has linked the likelihood of rape to the prevalence of such hostility.

But none of that is in evidence among the new kids on this day. Rather, they are all more consumed with just passing the exam, without bothering to compare themselves to others beyond their own partners. At the mats, David Urban has just done a dozen or so sit-ups and is raising himself in deep concentration, his eyes closed. His brows meet in a zigzag as Ashley Perez, the cadet trainer in charge, counts him to twenty, then thirty. His arms cross over his chest, his fingers crook over his shoulders.

At the count of forty-eight, Urban starts biting his lips hard. Outside, lightning crags across the sky, and thunder makes the gym feel like the inside of a drum. Up, down, up, down. At sixty, he slows and squints, and by seventy-three, he is shuddering with the effort. "Let's go, Urban, you can do it," Perez tells him—and he does, finishing up at seventy-eight. His roommate, Westbrook, does the maximum, ninety-five, like a human metronome, with seemingly no effort.

During the push-ups they both struggle, and they begin to feel thankful for all the beatings, the training, that got them in decent-enough shape to at least reach the minimum. At fifty push-ups, Urban catches his breath, and his knees buckle under him. He stops. "My neck," he says, rubbing and twisting it. He is, in any event, well past the thirty-five minimum. At the six-hundred-yard run, Urban clocks 1:53, and Westbrook just makes the minimum at 2:08, with no seconds to spare.

As they finish the run, breathless, hands on their knees, and their heads down, the storm manages to cut the electricity, and the gym suddenly has only natural light. The mood grows calmer without the bright lights; the shouting dies down as the rain pounds the roof. I think of the famous tapestries of the Manufacture des Gobelins in Paris, woven only in natural light. I'd always thought that the absence of artificial light simply allowed the weavers to see the colors in their true state. Now, I realize, it probably also helped their concentration.

Barrett, sitting on the floor with one leg bent in the semidarkness, is relieved to have passed the fitness test. Despite Second Beast's reputation for toughness, she looks forward to tomorrow's trek out to Jacks Valley. In a way, it is a chance to start over in the open air, to get away from her missteps on the Hill—the cadets' nickname for the complex of dorms, administration buildings, and study halls—and give it another go. "It'll be like summer camp," she says, smiling happily.

The next morning, before dawn, the lights are on and the bustle begins as the Basics scramble to line up in the hallway for breakfast. Robert Santos, a diminutive firstie from Florida, plays the acid-tongued commander, using sarcasm to beat his charges into shape. After a few minutes, more cadet trainers join Santos, each more dyspeptic than the last, and I begin to suspect that they have all seen the same movie (maybe even just the night before) and that I am watching each one's interpretation of the same role.

"You have one point five minutes, Basics. Ninety seconds," he says, striding down the halls. At the men's room, he throws open the door. "We've got females who are already outside," he hollers at the men. "That's pathetic."

Santos walks past half a dozen or so cadets lined up in the hall. The rest should all be out. Instead, they are still getting their gear together. "I thought we had thirty-one people in this flight," he shouts, and orders them down "on your butts" for slow flutter kicks, six inches above the ground, "right freaking now!" He hits the floor alongside them.

Nick Mercurio strolls in, sees some of the Basics struggling with the kicks, and whines unbearably, "Sir, we should start over. Oh, this is so hard." Then he shouts, "Stop looking broken!"

"Get your legs straight. What is your freakin' problem?" Santos hollers.

"Please sound broken," Mercurio chimes in. "It's freakin' music to my ears." Then a sound like dogs gasping spreads, a kind of inside joke for the Bulldawgs of Squadron 13.

"I love six inches. I love it," Santos says, either blissfully unaware of the double entendre or playing off it, and then he adds, as if there is nothing better in the world, "I am so irate. It's fantastic."

From the opposite end of the hall, Lorenz Madarang, a Filipino American two-degree, shouts so loud that it seems his lungs might blow out the walls. "*Don't talk in my hallway!*" he booms. "*Don't talk!!!*"

Elliott, the cadet captain, enters the ring next, accusing the Basics of having abused the freedom he gave them the day before by failing to get completely ready for today's trek. Spying an inside-out collar here and plackets that are not buttoned there, he scolds the Basics for poor teamwork. They should never have allowed their roommates out before checking them over for such slips.

"We have way too many 'me monsters' in this flight," Elliott tells them. His phrase brings to mind not the selfishness that loses lives in battle, but PacMan. "People are looking after themselves instead of the guys and gals next to them."

Given the altitude and the physical demands, dehydration is always a big worry. "Hydrate, or you die," Santos orders. The Basics suck on the tubes from their CamelBaks, canteens they carry like backpacks, gasping between gulps. "Restrain the sounds of weakness coming out of your mouths," he tells them, then launches into another rant.

"If you don't want to put in the effort, *leave my academy*, because I don't want you. The air force doesn't want you!" he hollers.

All of this unfolds before breakfast, which is huge: scrambled eggs and ham, hash brown patties shaped in identical ovals, bananas, cereal, breakfast bars, peanut butter, milk, juice, and—for the Basics—unceasing corrections.

As they wait for the meal to begin, the Basics recite the air force command structure, more or less in unison, and the Code of Conduct, which describes the rules if anyone is ever taken prisoner of war:

I am an American, fighting in the forces which guard my country and our way of life. I am prepared to give my life in their defense. I will never surrender of my own free will. If in command, I will never surrender the members of my command while they still have the means to resist. If I am captured, I will continue to resist by all means available. I will make every effort to escape and to aid others to escape. I will accept neither parole nor special favors from the enemy. . . . I will never forget that I am an American, fighting for freedom, responsible for my actions, and dedicated to the principles which made my country free. I will trust in my God and in the United States of America.

Finally, Cadet Captain Elliott hollers, "*Eat!*"—not out of anger or enthusiasm, but simply to be heard above the chorus of recitations rising from the tables. There is, however, no mad rush by the Basics, no wolfing down of food before their long march. The Basics eat at attention in small bites, watching the eagles at the tops of their plates.

Major Tony Schenk surveys the vast room, the order at the tables, the voices mixing with the ping of metal utensil against plate. He loves this day, and the two weeks ahead in Jacks Valley, more than any other. "We have to worry about things there that we don't even have to think about here: sun exposure, dust, thunderstorms, lightning," he says, his eyes brightening at the trials ahead.

"Such a tradition!" he says, his spine straightening, his head rising with anticipation.

8 | The Seesaw

As the Basics line up for the five-mile march to Jacks Valley to begin Second Beast, their billed red caps pulled low over their eyes, the sarcasm is like a jazz riff, improvised, with one put-down tipping into the next, ever more creative. Before heading out, Samuel Pang asks to use the bathroom, and for this, the mockery of his superiors is merciless.

"My grandfather and Pang have to go to the bathroom every three minutes," Lorenz Madarang announces in a whine.

"It's pathetic," Miles-Tyson Blocker, a junior from Riverside, California, replies, shaking his head at Pang's back.

"Maybe we need some Detrol," Nick Mercurio throws in, looking over the assembled Basics. Detrol is a medication that is often given to old people who have lost control of their bladders and wet their underpants.

"That would work," Blocker says.

"Does anybody else need to go?" Jonathan Elliott asks.

There are no takers.

From her place in line, Casey Jane Barrett stands unsmiling in her way-ward black glasses. She is not merely unamused, however, she is in misery: she has lost about fifteen pounds in the last three weeks and has endured more hollering in that short time than in the entire seventeen years before.

She thinks of home, a clean and cozy ranch in a leafy enclave in Ventura, California, with a posse of friendly dogs and a picture of her stepbrother, a Navy Seal, on proud display. A swimming pool curls around the backyard like an unfinished thought. She would stay up past midnight watching television and wake up sometime around noon.

Her friends are still enjoying the summer, surfing at the Southern California beaches, before starting college. Barrett could have gone with them. She had won admission to a respectable roster of colleges, and the University of Michigan had even offered a generous scholarship. However, she wants to become an astronaut, and nothing, for her, compared to the thrill of being accepted at the Air Force Academy. Her admission became a family project, with her mother and her stepfather plugging almost instantly into the extended social network of academy parents, and she became something of a local celebrity in her neighborhood. The family made bringing her here into a little vacation, stopping first in Las Vegas to catch a bunch of shows.

In the last month, however, her life has changed entirely.

Barrett had always been very close to Terri, her mother and best friend. When Mom needed help with her class, Barrett had pitched in, and they shared gossip and tips like old school chums. Together they trained seeing-eye dogs for the blind, and her mother's class of fourth graders more or less adopted Barrett as their role model and pen pal.

Now, aside from occasional phone calls, Barrett is on her own, a peon in a place whose imminent mission—to pummel her personality into molding clay—she had not really stopped to consider amid all the excitement of getting in.

The training is coming hard, battering mind and body. In a series of letters home, she seesaws between despair and exhilaration. Her smile, a nervous reaction in times of uncertainty, is getting her into trouble. One broke out before a general—"not a good idea," she writes in one of her letters home—exhibit two in Barrett's gallery of "stupid things I've done." Exhibit one is "called my squadron commander, who is a guy, 'Ma'am.'"

Barrett falls sick one day in the gym and is taken away in an ambu-lance. Her blood pressure is climbing—forty points when she stands.

She has trouble breathing, her throat is raw, and she feels as if two boots are crushing her temples. Doctors diagnose strep throat and a cold virus. Barrett is confined to bed for the following morning; instead of waking at 4:30 a.m., she sleeps until 6:30 a.m. and skips training until noon.

Unluckily for her, though, twenty-two other Basics also report sick at the same time. This makes Barrett look like just one more malingerer.

The next day, Cadet Captain Elliott drops by, questioning whether she is really sick. "He didn't say, 'I don't believe you,' exactly," Barrett recalls afterward. "He said, 'You understand, one quarter of Demons went to sick call today. That's an outrageous number.'"

In basic training, the girl who was never yelled at becomes the target of unrelenting criticism, like everyone else. Her honesty and integrity have never been questioned before, but she now comes under suspicion of faking illness. "I cough, sneeze, and wipe my nose all day right in front of him, too!" she complains in one letter home. "My voice is completely gone (I sound like a guy), and the doctor said it won't come back until after BCT because I won't have a 'break,'" she scrawls.

Even worse for her, she makes the mistake of separately asking two student medical officers the same question: whether she should go to sick call the following day. The next morning, both of them show up in her room, accusing her of maneuvering to get a break from training. She insists that this wasn't her purpose. The first officer she had asked seemed to be distracted when he answered, so she believed that he hadn't really heard her question. She herself was not even sure that she understood his answer, she adds.

Barrett's punishment is two meals at the staff squadron table in Mitchell Hall. The cadets who are sentenced to eat with the squadron staff get hammered with every bite, criticized for any misstep. The mood is wound so tight, the decibel level so high, that it feels almost impossible to simply ingest food, to chew and swallow and ask for what you want. Barrett's solution is to avoid asking for anything, so she eats only the minimum.

"If you say it wrong, you get yelled at, and you have to really sound off, so that the whole Mitchell Hall can hear you," she says later.

Of course, her mistakes gather steam from there, like an engine without brakes. She forgets to stand when a lieutenant colonel leaves the table. One demerit on a discrepancy form, known as a 341. Another time, she doesn't stand up fast enough after the meal to put on her gear. For this she is sentenced to another meal at the squadron table. In all,

Barrett has endured six meals at the staff squadron table by the time the doolies head out to Jacks. "I am very scared," she writes home. "I hate eating and mealtime."

In another letter home, she jokes to her mother, "You can diet all you want, and I can guarantee I will lose more weight than you, so just eat all the Peeps and chocolate you want!"

But her experience is not entirely a long march of humiliation. In her rundown of "stupid things cadre make us do," Barrett tells her family about getting permission to pick up a fallen napkin at the dining hall. "Sir, may I make a high-speed low pass and return to altitude?" she must shout. Lining up, the Basics sometimes have to say not "Demons A Flight over here, please, sir" but "Puffy Cheeks Flight, over here, please, sir!" and fill their cheeks with air, like a platoon of Michelin men. "When we have to go to the bathroom, we have to puff our cheeks out as well," she writes. Each of her notes ends with stick figure drawings. In one, a cadre stands over her while she does push-ups. "One hundred six," she counts. "Four hundred more!" the cadre barks.

And there are small victories. One day, Barrett's whole table is written up for a variety of infractions, but because she answers all the questions correctly, the training cadre allow her to decide the fate of the reports: file them or toss them. Of course, they go into the trash, and Barrett becomes, briefly, the heroine of Demons A Flight.

Around her, other newcomers are seeking counseling and bailing out. From a class of 1,334, 48 have left the academy.

Barrett tells herself to hang on, that the worst is over and she has survived. "It's only until March. Then we get our prop and wings."

At 7:10 a.m., a marching band strikes up "Ruffles and Flourishes," and Barrett and almost thirteen hundred other doolies begin the march to Jacks Valley, rubber duckies in tow. Away from the comforts of dorm rooms, seated dinners, and indoor plumbing, their hats flowing like a crimson ribbon on the downhill road, the cadets march as one to face the roar of Second Beast.

Part Two

SECOND BEAST

9 | Into the Beast

As the Class of 2010 marches into Jacks Valley to begin Second Beast, training rifles against their shoulders for the fifty-minute trek, the band strikes up "Ruffles and Flourishes" once again. The cadets are heading into a field, where they will stand at parade rest, listening as the commandant of cadets, Brigadier General Susan Desjardins, welcomes them and runs down what the academy expects of them. Robert Santos, who leads them on the march, asks how they feel.

The doolies of Demons A Flight, future Bulldawgs, answer Santos in unison: "Outstanding, sir."

Rhonda Meeker answers differently. *"Fanfreakin'tastic, sir!"* she shouts.

"Is that even a word?" asks Santos, raising his shoulders and looking around.

"Sir, the answer is, it is my word," Meeker hollers.

"I think it's my word," Santos muses. Score one. Meeker suppresses a smile, just barely. In fact, Santos had used the word the day before, riffing on the delights of flutter kicks and other exercises he was imposing to exhaustion as a punishment on the kids.

"That was a good answer, Basic Meeker," Santos says, smiling slightly and striding down the columns of red caps. He too is trying out a role, part brat-pack wit, part George Patton, shrink-wrapped for a stage much smaller than the battlefields of Europe.

The valley looks like the site of a military deployment, dotted with temporary buildings, giant mess tents, and concrete pads on which, in just a few hours, the Basics will erect the tents they'll call home for the next two weeks.

Here the freshmen will climb a five-story tower built of logs, nicknamed the Tiltin' Hilton, relying on their classmates to catch them as they flip on their backs from level to level—an exercise aimed at building trust among them. A fall could leave them paralyzed for life. They will shimmy along ropes stretched over a muddy pit, trying not to fall in, and teeter on logs extended between trees like balance beams. They will learn how to fire combat rifles, claw through mud and under barbed wire curled low to the ground. For the first time, they will be able to talk freely with their classmates instead of having their every move choked by the withering criticism of the upperclassmen.

Alongside the physical and psychological challenges that await the doolies is another battle, of which the new students are entirely clueless. This battle involves their training in the aftermath of the sexual assault scandal in 2003, which sent tremors from Colorado Springs all the way to Washington and back. The accusations forced three separate examinations of the academy's treatment of women, and they cost the institution just about all the goodwill it would have otherwise expected as a service academy in a time of war.

The repercussions of that scandal continue to play out, octopus fashion, in many directions at once. On one level, they spark clashes between the cadre and the noncommissioned officers, or NCOs, from Lackland Air Force Base in Texas who supervise them, sometimes too closely, as if they do not trust them. On another level, they reverberate between the cadre and the new students, a handful of whom trash-talked the upperclassmen on MySpace, for missing out on Recognition, which the Academy brass initially suspended in response to the scandal. Finally, they echo among the cadre themselves, who will make a point of using the possessive when speaking about the academy, its buildings, its demands, and its traditions, as a way of underscoring their pride and protectiveness, their loyalty, even when the institution is itself under assault.

Each year, the academy has tried a different formula for addressing the crisis while still getting its business done. At first it banned many of the practices and traditions that concentrated power among the upperclassmen, like Recognition and Commandant's Challenge, the main fall training exercise.

In 2004, it upended the decades-old tradition of cadets essentially training one another to become cadre—a system that invited toughness and hazing for its own sake. The academy started sending its military trainers to Lackland for a seven-week course, a shorter version of the same course that is given to drill instructors who train professional airmen. The idea was to bring the training of new cadets in line with training in the active-duty air force.

In the fall of 2006, Lackland sent two military training instructors as advisers, imposing figures who went around in Smokey the Bear hats to oversee the conduct of each squadron, providing an extra layer of quality control.

The moves have hardly been welcomed. "When I got here in 2004, it was a very hostile environment to the NCOs," recalls Technical Sergeant Brian M. Boisvert, a short, sturdily built military trainer.

The cadre believe that they have the right to train the new kids as toughly as they were trained. "All of a sudden it's 'I'm not allowed to beat SMACKs. I have to train a Basic.' That's very different in the mind-set of the cadre," Boisvert says.

At Jacks Valley, the NCOs are often close by, looking over the shoulders of the junior and senior cadets, going so far sometimes as to criticize them in front of the SMACKs. The upperclassmen have squared off with the advisers from Lackland over a number of issues, with the Lackland trainers arguing for extra protections for the Basics and the cadet trainers contending that the Lackland advisers are getting in the way, weakening their authority and making it too easy on the Basics.

Thus, while Lorenz Madarang and the other cadet trainers ridicule the new kids over bathroom stops and ask whether they have "expelled the weak sauce" from their bodies, the NCOs push the cadre in an entirely different direction, to make the training regimens less like hazing and more professional.

Good cadet trainers should ease up on the corrections this morning, allowing the cadets to eat breakfast unhindered, says Major Tony Schenk, who has come in from Lackland. They should check the new kids' feet to make sure that their boots fit right and that nobody is in pain. "Any case of infected feet," Schenk says, "means a cadre was not doing his job."

Unless there is a crisis on the order of a roadside bomb, I cannot imagine the cadre I've seen doing something as humble as kneeling down to examine a Basic's toes—and, in fact, they don't. Instead, they tell the SMACKs to look over their own feet and to speak up if they find any blisters or infections.

In the larger sense, the two groups—the cadre and the NCOs— represent vastly different perspectives, which are vying for the soul of the academy. In grafting the standards and practices of the active-duty air force onto the academy, air force officials believe that they have found a rational solution, a way to lessen the gap between the all-powerful upperclassmen and the vulnerable SMACKs. The cadre reject the very premise of those efforts.

Lackland puts a military mindset into a person, says Lance Watson, the Demons A Flight commander at First Beast, but the academy is about more than just doing a job, however well. "The academy is like a brother-hood," he says. "It's a weeding-out process, for the most part. You want to get rid of the people who don't want to be there. That's why it's so hard to get through that institution." The cadets who have endured its trials see themselves as guardians of a trust. To them, the academy is about forging lifelong bonds.

Beyond that, the juniors and seniors who train the new cadets believe that these kids, as a class, deserved to be ridden even harder than most. Only seven of them had posted comments on MySpace, ridiculing the firsties and the two-degrees and questioning their fitness to train the Class of 2010. "Basic is a joke," wrote one.

Though the scribblings disappeared from the Web site a few days after training started, they left the upperclassmen doubting themselves, hankering to prove their mettle. These kids had been foolish enough to voice their derision publicly. What if they had written what the entire Class of 2010 was feeling but was too shrewd to say openly? If that was the perception among these knuckleheads, the upperclassmen won-dered, then how were their superiors—the officers who had survived Recognition every year for nearly a half century and who would be commanding these firsties and two-degrees after graduation—looking at them?

Given the dynamics, the Class of 2010—or the handful that had derided the firsties and two-degrees—was starting out in perhaps the worst possible way. To the incoming kids, taunting the upperclassmen for missing Recognition was nothing more than a show of class spirit. To the older cadets, however, the jibes were much more: these Basics were presuming not only membership but also superiority in a club before they had even earned entry. They were insensitive and egotistical, criticizing the upperclassmen for something entirely out of their control. Furthermore, they were foolish for doing this on a public Web site. The posts amounted to a hot poker on the rawest of nerves, and those nerves happened to belong to the upperclassmen who would now control the doolies' every waking moment and even invade their sleep.

During First Beast, the cadre hunted down the MySpace miscreants and tacked their online postings to their dorm doors so that everyone would know who they were and what they'd said. They might as well have been dropped in a tub of manure, with no showers in sight.

As the new cadets start at Jacks Valley, Pat Cassidy, the senior who is commanding Demons Squadron, has the names and locations of each of the MySpace Seven in his sights. One of the leaders, Cassidy notes with a chuckle, is a full hundred points short of passing her physical training test. Another, Allison Brown*, "is already broken. She's not even in her tent." The cadre plan to stress them past their limits, loading them with extra push-ups and checking their beds and belongings for the slightest wrinkle. Nobody is in the mood to cut them any slack. Jacks could just as well have been a quarry filled with nothing but slack; there would still be none to spare for the MySpace doolies.

If these kids—or the rest of the new cadets, for that matter—come in puffed up, full of their own importance, they will not leave Jacks Valley that way. "We want it to be tough for them, so they have something to be proud of when they're done," Cassidy says, half smiling and shuffling a pebble with his boot.

Actually, of the seven freshmen who were involved in the MySpace taunting, none of them are in Demons A Flight, the precursor to Squadron 13. To some of the cadet trainers, however, it doesn't matter. The actions of those few blanket the entire Class of 2010 with a dubious whiff.

---

*Not her real name.

. . .

Around the Basics, sirens blare as choppers seem to bring the sky down, pounding right over their heads. The cadet trainers who are working the assault course swarm over the doolies, shouting criticism and insults, ordering them to do push-ups at the slightest misstep. The doolies, peering out from under their helmets, haul weighted dummy M-16s and wear bulky mouth guards in bright blue, making them seem clumsy and dim-witted. Drilling them in close arms combat, the upperclassmen teach them to jab an enemy with their rifle butts and smash him to the ground. Knees bent, the doolies aim to become the opposite of how they appear: not leaden, but nimble; not inept, but lethal; not unwieldy, but unstoppable.

"You're low, ready to move," a cadre demonstrates, his steps fluid, rolling one into the other. "Come up with your arm swinging."

The doolies practice the motions over and over in the sun; the aim is, in part, to wear the kids down before they even begin the assault course itself. Although the rifle weighs less than ten pounds and is not onerous to pick up and carry for a couple of minutes, a doolie is not just carrying it from one place to another. The doolies must treat their dummy M-16s like an extra appendage, not letting them down for a moment and lifting them to lunge and thrust and swing in close quarters. The helmets weigh another two to three pounds, and under the sun they feel like portable ovens baking the kids' skulls. By the time they head for the eighteen obstacles of the assault course, the Basics are bone-weary.

The course, which is spread over a cleared forest that rises to a modest hill, trains them for a ground war, with the upperclassmen barking orders at them and goosing them through each obstacle. Every few minutes, a siren screams at them, shoving them on to the next obstacle, while the cadre holler through megaphones, *"Hurry up!"* and, *"Get off my course now!"* Although the academy leaders and the Lackland trainers have thrown in a water truck, and the doolies are allowed brief rests, the course is otherwise geared to increase the stress and test the new kids to the max.

The Demons crawl on their bellies through the dirt, holding their rifles aloft, moving through mazes that are marked by sandbags and barbed wire. At the rifle maneuver, they do a high crawl on their elbows and

Faces camouflaged, ready for combat course. Basic cadets left to right: John Cox, Austin Westbrook, Samuel Pang, Theodore Ornelas, Casey Barrett, Rebecca Rasweiler-Richter, Frank Mercurio.

Combat course, in the foxhole.

Casey Jane
Barrett.

On the assault course.

Under the wire: cadets crawling on their backs, keeping rifles aloft, on the assault course.

Relief after hell: Thomas "Brad" Bernard rinses off grime after the assault course. Flight commander for Second Beast, Jonathan Elliott, is to the left of Bernard.

knees, keeping their bellies off the ground, as they creep through tunnels covered in camouflage netting.

Casey Jane Barrett's mouth is parched, and she feels about to fall from thirst. Nevertheless, she emerges from the tunnels like the others, crouching to pass under a leaden club that juts at waist level from a metal stand, wrapped in padding and tape. The bayonet-armed stuffed enemies in green vests hang from metal stands in the field like dead men.

The cadre order the Basics to kneel around one of the pits, holding the M-16s over their heads. Throughout, the upperclassmen toss "grenades," which are really pinecones, at clusters of Basics and shout, "*Incoming!*" This forces them all to the ground, whatever they are doing. When the upperclassmen run out of pinecones, they simply shout the warning and the kids dive down, wherever they are.

In the middle of the course, the Basics get a brief break and line up for a drink at a water truck that is stationed at the edge of the course. This concession, which is part of the larger effort to make Second Beast into more of a professional training program and less of a haze, drives the upperclassmen into a fury. Watching them, Cadet Captain Jonathan Elliott recalls his own experience slogging through the A-course three years before.

"We didn't have water breaks, on the course or off," he says. "And we couldn't put down the rifle for a second." He bristles as he watches the kids under his charge now, standing still while they drink from cups. "A-course is weak sauce. It hasn't been drizzled in, it's been freakin' marinated in the weak sauce."

At an obstacle up the hill, the Basics face trenches filled with half a foot of mud and water. They cannot dive over the pit, although some try. They have no choice but to crawl through the muck, weighing themselves down in wet filth. "Keep your mouths closed and don't breathe in the water," Elliott warns them before handing them over to the A-course cadre.

The mud and the water fill their boots and seep into their pores. They crawl through, but the mud sucks them in, swallowing their every move. Their rifles become caught, digging into the wet earth. Barrett, her face caked with mud, her helmet tilted sideways, and her mouth slack, looks about to collapse when she starts down the hill.

"At least I made it through," she tells herself. Then the cadre order her and the others to turn around and do it all again. Barrett's knees buckle. She feels herself falling—and she would have collapsed, if not for her teammates. Without discussion, a couple of them converge at her side and hold her rifle behind her to serve as a substitute spine, as they half push and half carry her up the hill. A cadet trainer, Terrance H. Fregly Jr., a senior from Tallahassee whose father was killed in an airplane crash just five months ago, is at their heels. *"Run up the hill!"* Fregly hollers at them. *"Run!"* By the end of the day, he says later, he has given even himself a headache.

"It's all about the guy next to you," Elliott tells them. "If you see somebody struggling, help him out and push yourself."

The Basics crawl on their backs through another obstacle, under barbed wire, their rifles over their heads. They recite the U.S. Military Code of Conduct, pledging, "I will try to escape, and to aid others to escape, and will not take special favors from the enemy." Through their mouth guards, the words sound muffled, as if they are burbling up from under water. Suddenly, the sirens blast. *"Basics, get off my course now!"* shouts the cadre in charge.

The cadets jog on to the next obstacle, where they climb a six-foot wall of logs while carrying their rifles. Then they stand in two columns, holding the rifles over their heads, until the cadre order them to drop to the ground. They crawl on their backs through a curtain of barbed wire hanging from a pole over their heads. Meeker uses the rifle to push the barbed wire out of the way. Over and over, they hit the ground for push-ups or stand holding their rifles high over their heads.

"Incoming!" one of the cadre hollers. He tears into the students for their lack of energy in climbing the wall and for encouraging one another. He wishes them "continued success in your cheerleading career here at the academy." A few minutes later, another one of the cadre, Marcus Remington, a two-degree, stands nose to nose with Meeker, berating her for failing to wait for her partner before moving on. "Are you leaving your buddy?" he asks softly, and then shouts, *"Do not do it! Get back in line!"* She and her partner do the course again.

Technically, each student is supposed to make it through the obstacle course on his or her own, but that is only officially. More important to everyone here is the bond that makes an officer risk his or her life to help a wounded buddy. It is, after all, the purpose of what the cadets are doing: trying to build cohesion and a group identity that will allow each of them to count on their mates in battle. Helping one another may bring on scorn, but the right action is not to abandon one's buddy; it's to help out anyway.

"It's the kind of thing they may tell you not to do, but secretly they really want you to do it," Elliott says. "We want them to do the right thing, regardless of the consequences." Right now, the choices involve seeing a classmate through a rough patch on a pretend battlefield—a game, really. In a few years, however, the stakes become other people's lives and millions of dollars of equipment.

The assault course—indeed, every trial at Jacks Valley—is a baby step on the way to making the cadets effective fighters on the battlefield. Despite the breaks that the Basics are enjoying this year, the A-course remains one of the most punishing and rewarding experiences of boot camp. The Basics will not appreciate it today or tomorrow, the older cadets says, but maybe they will years later.

"A lot of this course is physical, but a lot of this course, as painful as it is, is mental," says Elliott. Back when he did the A-course, the tunnels were buried underground. A cadre stood outside that particular obstacle, shoveling more sand right into the tunnel as soon as Elliott and his fellow Basics burrowed their way out. "It was horrible, just this little sliver of light," he recalls. He remembers finally making it to that bit of daylight, exhilarated and relieved to be peering out, only to have another cadre slam a shovel against his helmet and force him back down in the muck.

"The second I came out, *bam*, the cadre hit that shovel right on my head." As Elliott's class went through the course back then, their cadre watched for signs of weakness or distraction. When they saw a sign, they pounced, grabbing for the Basics' rifles, driving home the lesson that in battle you drop your weapon at your peril.

"At the time, you're just thinking, 'My arms are so heavy, I'm being yelled at, I'm getting so tired of this,'" he remembers, "but learning that you can push yourself and you're capable of more than what you think you are is important. You move up, and you get used to the yelling and the stress. And you say, 'Hey, I've dealt with this situation before. I had people yelling at me. I was tired, this and that, and I was sick and I was hungry and all that stuff.' The Basics are able to reach back and pull that out."

At their last obstacle now, the Basics crawl through barbed wire on their bellies, this time weighed down with the water and the mud, punting with their rifles. Ahead of them is a sign in tall block letters that tells them they have made it: ONLY THE STRONG SURVIVED. A siren blares a steady scream, and suddenly the ordeal is over. The Basics run off the course as if escaping it, as if this is the last day of school and only summer lies ahead. Away from the course, each stops under a hose that is gushing cold water—jubilant, exhausted, and ebullient as the filth falls from their faces and streams off their clothes in a muddy river. Barrett guzzles some water while Meeker sings, "I feel pretty, oh so pretty."

As if the kids have returned from a long trip, the upperclassmen give them news of the day, taking advantage of the fact that the Demons have been news-deprived for more than three weeks. Nick Mercurio offers baseball scores—7–3, 9–4, 8–2—without saying who played.

"Also in the news, Mel Gibson, filming his latest movie, got hit by a fake arrow and fell off a wall. I hope no one's a Mel Gibson fan," Mercurio says, the corners of his mouth pulled down, "because he's now deceased." A week later, this becomes true, in a fashion, as Gibson takes a metaphorical fall. The darling of the Christian right is arrested for drunk driving in Malibu, and his anti-Semitic rant against the Jewish deputy who stops him is all over the Internet.

Then Mercurio is on to Dan Brown, author of that season's bestselling beach read, *The Da Vinci Code*. Brown, Mercurio reports, just came out with "another novel in his Goosebumps for Grownups series," but he doesn't say what it is. "And don't forget the Tour de France. Awesome, awesome ending," Mercurio says, wagging his head as if savoring the sight and leaving the kids to wonder how it turned out.

Cassidy lets on that one cadet in another flight threw up twice on the course but did not give up, instead hanging in there to finish all the obstacles. "I like to see that," he tells the Basics, adding, "I'm going to let him lead push-ups tomorrow."

Then the panting starts, from one end to the other, shoulders heaving, building from a low rumble to a full-throated bark. "Who let the dog out?" Miles-Tyson Blocker shouts, in mock annoyance. "Ugh, ugh,

ugh, ugh . . . arf, arf," the doolies sing, building to a raucous crescendo. It sounds like a kennel ten minutes before lunchtime.

The future Bulldawgs of Squadron 13 are happy.

While the Demons grab lunch, Cassidy brings Martha Liang*, of MySpace notoriety, to sit at the head of an otherwise empty table under the mess tent, and I sit on one of the sides. Tall and thin, she at first seems like a casualty of war, just in from the battlefield. Her face is smeared grey and green from the camouflage paint, which has been only half removed, and she limps, grimacing as she sits down. The night before, she tripped over a rock and sprained her right ankle, which is now wrapped in a stretch bandage. She seems to bear no resemblance to the party girl with shimmering black hair who had been mugging it up on her MySpace page.

At first, Liang says she never posted remarks mocking the cadre on her MySpace page. "A friend put it up there as a joke," she says, speaking slowly.

"So this is all a misunderstanding?" I ask, not without skepticism. "Why not speak up, then?" I do not entirely believe her, but seeing how miserable she seems to feel, I want to throw a blanket over her shoulders and bring her some tea.

Liang says she refrained from telling the upperclassmen that she didn't actually post the insults herself because they have little patience for explanations. "You can't have excuses," she says. So even if she didn't post the remarks, the fact that she let them stand under her name and did not take them down would hardly get her off the hook. Then, too, if the cadre did look into it and found that she had in fact posted any of the comments herself, she would be in even worse straits for having lied about it.

The ill-fated prank began, she says, when a handful of kids, elated by their admission to the academy, thought it would be fun to jump the gun on class spirit, bragging about themselves and putting down the class that would be training them. However, the academy was still alien to the new kids, and they could not imagine the sensitivities at which they were poking.

---

*Not her real name.

During First Beast, the retribution was not so bad, Liang says, mostly just constant criticism and punishments for any infraction. She could mentally remove herself, erect a wall between herself and the barbs. She certainly hasn't been the most popular freshman, because the damage has often spilled over, bringing extra punishments to everyone in her flight. At times she even feels toxic, and it is only through her friendship with another of the MySpace Seven, who happens to be in her flight, that she's managed to make it through the course so far. Anyway, here at Jacks the Houdini trick no longer works. "For Second Beast, you really have to get your head in the game," Liang says.

I ask her if she thinks the cadre have it in for her. It wouldn't matter, she answers; she is already four weeks into training. She seems dispirited, her voice flat, almost on the verge of tears. "I would still stay."

Liang's father was an army man. At home, he would criticize her for being lazy, saying she could accomplish great things but wasn't applying herself. Now she dreams of becoming a pilot and hopes to major in aeronautical engineering. The Air Force Academy was her first choice, so much so that she did not even wait for the responses from the other colleges and universities she applied to—Johns Hopkins, the University of Florida, and the Georgia Institute of Technology—before accepting her appointment to the academy. "I wouldn't change this for anything," she says.

"I actually wrote a letter to my parents, and they wrote back how much I've changed, discipline-wise. That's why I came here. I wanted to become a stronger person. I wanted to become a better person," Liang says. She picks her head up and sweeps a stray hair from her face. "When we run in the morning, we push each other, tell each other to keep going."

At sit-ups, she does more than she ever thought she could, pushing herself through the pain and past what she once took for the limit of her endurance. Despite the difficulty and the hostility, she cannot not imagine leaving. "I don't even know how I'd ever be able to face my parents. They told me every day how proud they were that I got into the academy. It would make me feel miserable."

Today, for the first time, she is feeling somewhat better. Her teammates approached her and told her to forget all those extra push-ups and flutter kicks. "They said it didn't mean anything," Liang recalls, smiling sadly at this unexpected grace. "They said, 'Whatever you did before you got here doesn't count. It's what you do now that counts.'"

It occurs to me that maybe that is why she has not spoken up to deny the injuries she carries under her name.

That afternoon, after lunch in the mess tent, the morning's euphoria has scattered and landed underfoot, like confetti after a parade. The Demons gather around an SUV, where they learn how to staff the gates of military installations, inspecting cars and picking up on suspicious signs. Technically, the gates are called entry control points, or ECPs, in military parlance. The exercise is hardly academic. Each day's paper seems to carry news of another car bomb exploding in Iraq, often by suicide bombers who turn up at the gates of military installations.

Matthew Eggert, a junior from Columbus, Ohio, who is majoring in aeronautical engineering, tells the Demons that on this hypothetical day in Iraq, the threat level is very high. Every car is to be searched, but there is more. They are also supposed to watch for anything amiss: a loose wire, a dubious story, a jittery driver. "Obviously, you need to focus on the vehicle, but at the same time you need to be vigilant of any activity happening out here," he says.

First, he tells the Basics, they should isolate the car they are about to search, ordering the driver off to a separate area. That way, if the car does blow up, "we don't have to rebuild everything." Eggert, squinting in the sunlight, gives the Basics a moment to absorb what he is saying. He tells them to check the identification of the driver and his purpose for coming. "Now, if you get something kind of fishy, like maybe 'I'm bringing some hot chocolate in,' that may set off a lightbulb in your head, right? Like 'It's hot out here, we don't need any hot chocolate.'"

Even if nothing looks suspicious, during a high threat level like the one they are simulating, gatekeepers should check everything coming into an installation. Keeping the car door open, as a barrier between the airman and the visitor, Eggert tells them to step a safe distance away, and to have the driver open the trunk and the compartments.

"Sometimes compartments may be rigged," Eggert tells them, adding that they should keep a close watch on the driver for signs of skittishness.

When the airmen step forward to actually check the car, they should be thorough, checking especially for any loose wires above the accelerator and searching the visor, the roof, the doors, and under the driver's seat.

"Anytime there's something you're not comfortable opening yourself, there's no shame in getting the driver back up here to open it. At the same time, use your gut. If something seems suspicious, there's probably something wrong, and you can call for help," Eggert says. Only a few of the Demons—Meeker, Rebecca Rasweiler-Richter, and Theodore Ornelas—are actually paying close attention. Barrett looks somewhere past Eggert's shoulders and yawns. Brad Bernard and Zach Taylor, the football players, look around, as if they have no connection to Eggert's demonstration.

"Sometimes, if it's dangerous, you might have the lowest-ranking person there open it up," Eggert says, then laughs. He looks at the Basics, but none of them is laughing. I wonder if they are apprehensive or just inattentive. In fact, when they graduate, they will do so as second lieutenants; it is unlikely that they will ever be the lowest-ranking person in uniform who is checking cars at a gate. As jokes go, it wasn't a howler, but then again, the bar for would-be comics isn't very high just now.

Eggert tells them that it doesn't really matter where they start in their search of a car, as long as they have a system. He prefers to start by the driver's seat. If the driver has a weapon and gets nervous, he might shove it nearby, possibly right by his feet. "That's why I like to start here," Eggert says, reaching under the seat. He tells them to be sure to inspect the roof, the doors, and the seat cushions.

"You're looking for wires hanging out, evidence that it may have been tampered with. It might even be connected to some sort of device." He moves to the back, opens the trunk, and looks under its floor, telling the Basics that they should also watch out for anything a deliveryman would typically not have. "You're looking for some sort of maybe military intelligence, something that links the driver to the enemy, anything that this guy really shouldn't have on him." Given the language barrier, however, it is not at all clear how an airman might tell the difference between instructions for a homemade bomb and a doughnut recipe.

Preparing for the warrior course, the Demons learn to camouflage their faces and their hands. A junior, Robert Reynaud, teaches them the right way to use makeup to conceal themselves. He tells them to use darker face paint on the high points of their faces, like their cheekbones, which are more likely to catch the light, and to use lighter paint on the rest.

Meeker smears green, in a shade resembling comic-book puke, over the hollows of her cheeks and a darker grey-green over her cheekbones, chin, and forehead. Her teeth shine inordinately white. "A month ago, I was doing this for prom," she says. For a second, I wonder where she went to school, Sadr City? Then I remember: Albuquerque, with eleven inches more hair and cosmetics in less startling shades.

The group marches out to a pine forest, gathering around one of several pits dug into the earth and surrounded by mounds of dirt, called berms, and sandbags. Matthew Molten, a squarely built junior who is in charge of training the Basics on the course, shows them how to fill in a map, so that when night falls, the replacement troops that come in will know the layout.

Another senior, Ezekiel Ignaco, a lightweight on the college boxing team, explains the best layout for foxholes, how to guard the terrain, and how to question strangers and strip them of weapons. The Demons hear about detecting suicide bombers before they get too close. The talk is a kind of on-the-ground primer for fighting a war in which every day is Halloween: the enemies, who seldom wear uniforms, can pose as fruit sellers, car mechanics, deliverymen, or pregnant women, emerging to strike and then melting back into a neighborhood or disappearing with the explosion of a suicide belt. It begins to sink in, for some of the new cadets, that what they are learning connects them to an ongoing battle, which they have chosen to join and in which comrades are already dying.

David Franck, a junior who leads the briefing, explains that the "defensive fighting positions," or DFPs, as the pits are called, aim to secure the perimeter of an area. He asks the Basics to think about how to lay them out. One suggests an arch. "Why is it not an arch?" Franck asks.

"Because if it's an arch, then you're gonna be facing inward and you're gonna end up shooting each other," answers Justin Goodin, a Basic from a small town outside Sioux City, Iowa.

Another Basic suggests a straight line. The upperclassman dismisses that as the "battleship failure. If you get hit in one spot, they're just going to go straight down the line and hit you. They don't even have to change their range." Better to scatter the firing stations like a radio wave. Franck punctuates his talk with the all-purpose rallying cry and response for warriors that at this moment signals that the Basics are keeping up with him: "Huah!"

He tells them to dig the pit roughly to the armpit of the tallest fighter who will be using it, allowing the airman to peer over the edge through a gun sight. "You're going to make it one M-16 wide and two to three M-16s long. Huah?" It strikes my morbid turn of mind that the pit is roughly the size of a grave.

"Huah!" the Demons answer, as if taking a collective breath.

"There's a specialty at the bottom of this puppy. Anybody want to take a guess what it is?"

One Basic suggests digging a trench along the inside rim so that hand grenades will roll to the edges.

"Close," Franck answers. There is no sarcasm or reproach in his voice, only encouragement. The put-downs that dominated upperclassmen's remarks throughout First Beast, and even on the assault course this morning, are nowhere evident now. Perhaps the seriousness of what they have all undertaken, to fight and possibly die with one another, has elbowed posturing aside.

"What you want to do is to have the highest point at the very center of the floor," Franck explains. If they dig channels only along the side walls, any shrapnel should shoot straight up. "So when somebody throws a grenade, you and your buddy are going to start kicking. You're going to get over to the other wall. You're probably going to get a little wounded, but you're still going to be able to fight."

The Demons nod. He has their attention now. Ringing the pit are berms, each eighteen inches tall and eighteen inches wide, made from the dirt they have dug out. The berms are like miniature forts, and by shooting over them, fighters can shoot over and not at their comrades in other foxholes.

The berms are also meant to keep combatants in their respective places. Every foxhole has its Rambo, somebody whose instinct is to "jump over these things and say, 'Hey, there's enemy fire coming in from over there,'" Franck says, shaking his head. "The key is to have an organized defense.

If one person is jumping over there and saying, 'Okay, one bullet here and one bullet there,' the truth is that in the heat of battle, there's probably going to be more random fire. That means there's going to be a friendly shot by a friendly force. Huah?"

"Huah!"

"So you stay between these posts," he adds, catching their eyes, as if to seal the knowledge in their heads. To enter the hole, they must pass their weapon to somebody already below, then jump in and take their weapon back. That way, they won't fire into the hole accidentally and risk killing their buddies, he says. So much for the carrot. If they slip up and "fire" at the wrong time today, the stick is onerous: "We'll find the biggest tree, with as many branches as possible. I think we found one yesterday that's about fifty pounds. You will carry it on your back. Huah?"

"Huah!"

Franck has them role-play responses to strangers who approach the combat posts. He tells them about ordering a stranger to kneel with his hands behind his head, fingers interlocking and ankles crossed. "Anybody know why we want him in this position?" he asks.

"They can't get up and turn as quickly," answers Meeker.

"Huah!" Franck affirms. The stance, awkward and uncomfortable, buys time for the airmen, since getting out of it takes a few seconds.

Meeker volunteers for a demonstration, standing in the pit while one of the cadre starts walking toward her. Her hand stalls for half a second before getting into firing position. Then she drops her gun. Ignaco, the boxer, warns her to keep the M-16 in firing position, trained on the "stranger," at all times. As they redo the approach, Meeker shouts, *"Halt,"* sounding off in the same booming voice that she and the others have used to answer hundreds of questions in the last three weeks. She orders the "stranger" to kneel. "Interlace your fingers and cross your ankles." This time, she keeps her gun on him and is about to go over to seize him.

"Good job, Basic," Ignaco tells her. "Best we've seen in the last two days, and we've only had two days here." The praise is like a song dedicated to Meeker, and she replays it in her head for the rest of the day.

In one scenario, a man who is walking toward the defensive fighting position ignores a call to stop. One day, unless the war ends before their graduation, these cadets may have to decide for themselves: Is it a language problem, or something more? "What do you do, say it again? Stick out your hand and ask him to stop? He keeps walking forward. What do you do? You charge your weapon. He keeps walking. What do you do?" Franck presses.

The Basics mumble possible reactions, with the consensus settling around shooting. Franck tells them to fire over the stranger's head. "Now, at that point, if he still doesn't get the message, you probably know that he's bad. Say he keeps coming toward you after the warning shot." This time, the question is tacit.

"Maybe his whole purpose is to come armed, blow up the DFP, and take you and your buddy out. Your job is to not let that happen. I'll give you an example. Sergeant Harper, great guy. He was in Iraq, and they were doing MOUT operations—military operations in urban terrain—kicking down doors, trying to find insurgents. Kicked down this door, found a bad guy. He runs out the back door, and they chased him down." The insurgent "crawls into another building, and they kicked down that door, and there were two nine-year-old boys with a hand grenade." One of them pulled the grenade's pin. The sergeant and his fire team "had to kill those little boys," Franck said. "It messed Sergeant Harper up, because he has a nine-year-old boy himself. Same height, same build. He had to come back stateside."

It occurs to me that in a few years' time, these Basics will probably not remember what they learn today, given that there will be so much else cramming their heads between now and the day they are drawing gate duty in Iraq, Afghanistan, Kuwait, or one of the many other outposts where the U.S. military flies the flag. Then I realize that the purpose of the exercise is twofold: to introduce them not just to a procedure but also to a perspective. As surely as they are learning about the right way to check for hidden weapons, they are also learning that a nine-year-old can be carrying them, that the bulk under a woman's head-to-toe covering can be a baby in her womb or explosives on her waist.

Franck throws another scenario at the cadets: A woman who is covered in traditional Muslim dress approaches. They order her to stop. She keeps coming. They charge their weapons. She turns and runs away. What should they do?

"Fire?" some voices say softly. "Let her go?" others mumble.

"Let her go," Franck says. "Now, if she runs toward you, that's a different story. It could be her mission is to kill you. She doesn't care if she lives or dies." Franck looks at the faces of the Basics, which don't look shocked, only troubled.

"That's the type of war we're fighting now," Franck tells them. "It's dirty, it's grueling, and it's nothing we've seen before. That's why we're teaching this."

Listening to the briefing, Austin Westbrook feels shaken. He didn't realize that he was on the road to maybe shooting pregnant women and nine-year-olds. How would he react in those situations, he wonders.

David Urban recalls all the moaning he and the other Basics have been doing over training exercises, thirty-second showers, and waking before dawn. He feels ashamed. Compared to the people whom they are now coming to think of as brothers and sisters in arms, Urban and the other Basics have endured nothing nearly as wrenching or even challenging.

Barrett thinks how far removed these scenarios are from what she imagined the job of an aviator to be, flying high above the bloodshed, never directly seeing the splash of brains on pavement. This seems more like the army.

In fact, airmen accompany supply convoys and march with army ground units every day, pitching the same tents, sharing the same battles, and running the same risks of car explosions, sniper fire, and suicide bombers. It is from within these units that they radio air force commanders with information on targets, including ground coordinates for explosives that are dropped not by daring pilots in jet bombers but increasingly by unmanned drones.

Moments later, Meeker and Urban stand in the same foxhole as the entire Demons Squad simulates ground fighting. She is peering around, searching the scrub for enemies on the march. He is drawing a map of their position, radiating concentric circles and marking it with Xs to show other foxholes, trees, and paths. The terrain is mostly scrub, scattered with pinecones and bark, and another flight plays the enemy, which is expected to come from the north and the east. There is little cover and less opportunity for concealment. Barrett crawls on her belly with a clutch of other Demons, all moving on different sides of a trench. Overhead, a whistling sound slices through the air. *"Incoming!"* somebody shouts, and whoever has been standing falls face down in the dirt. Then there is a crash that simulates a mortar explosion.

"Contact left," somebody says. A Basic from another flight creeps along the perimeter and out of sight. Two hundred yards north, a smoke bomb goes off, enveloping that patch of scrub in thick grey smoke. Another whistle sounds, and everybody is silent, waiting too long to react. They would be dead if the mortars had been real.

"What are you supposed to shout?" booms Franck. The answer is too obvious even to say.

Down in the foxhole with Urban, Meeker thinks she sees an adversary. "Is that enemy movement in the north?" she asks. "Check it out."

Franck answers for her. "Enemy will be coming from this direction," he says, pointing east.

She shifts her focus while Urban, who is behind her, is nailed for still working on the map. He scrambles to put it down.

"What's that whistle?" somebody asks. The others answer as they dive for the pinecones. *"Incoming! Incoming!"*

"Fire from the east," Meeker says. She hears the shooting but does not see anything yet. "The firing is getting closer. I have a visual. They're in the bush." She is raising her rubber duckie and aiming when Ignaco steps in. "That is your course commander. He does not have a weapon. Why would you shoot him?" he asks.

Meeker ducks her head and presses her lips together, shrinking down into the foxhole with Urban. She starts humming a familiar, always unwelcome tune. "I'm hearing reveille in my sleep," she reports.

"Just hear it. Don't make it," Urban tells her. "Once we get out of these holes, you can do whatever you want."

She goes back to searching for invaders. "We should do this with paintball. That would be pretty sweet."

Watching the terrain, they see shapes moving a distance away. "One, two, three, four guys," Urban counts, and continues to watch. "There's five."

Suddenly, Meeker fires her M-16. "Yeah. I see 'em, there's like ten of 'em. Oh yeah. Yeah, they're moving out."

"Let's go. Moving forward," shouts the leader of the enemy team as they start advancing.

Gunfire crackles around them as the other Demons catch sight of the enemy flight invading.

"Contact east," Urban says, pointing at a tree. He raises his M-16 to fire, but it jams. "You're dead behind the tree," he shouts. The "enemies," who are freshmen like him, ignore him and creep toward his trench. "Bang, bang, bang, bang! You're all dead. You are all dead!" Urban shouts as his position is overtaken. A cadre, overhearing, laughs to himself. "That's genius right there," he says, to no one in particular.

"I hate being a Basic," Urban complains. "Nobody listens to you."

Nearby, Goodin hauls a wooden log in his arms, cradling it away from his body like an unloved child. He earned the punishment early in the exercise for firing his "weapon" within twenty feet of his target, exempting him from the exercise and rendering him useless to his teammates for the duration. "I should have shouted 'safety kill,'" he says, and looks down at the log, as if wondering whether he could just drop it there.

Just a few days into boot camp, the cadre who are training this year's Bulldawgs are convinced that the kids are slacking off, losing motivation. Tradition would have dictated punishment by push-ups. Instead, Technical Sergeant Boisvert says that the NCO advisers have suggested rifle manual drills. "We're trying to show the cadre that there are other things you can make them do than push-ups, sit-ups, and flutter kicks," Boisvert says.

By now, the Basics of Demons A Flight have accumulated a fine of 265 rifle manual drills, which means raising and lowering their rifles to the count of fifteen 265 times. On this Monday afternoon in late July, it is time to start paying up. For ninety minutes under the hot sun, with a generator in the corner roaring like an airplane on a tarmac, Demons A Flight runs through the rifle drill again and again.

In fifteen counts, the Basics are supposed to raise their rifles, turn them in their hands, slant them over their right shoulders, bring them to the front, and then land them on their left shoulders. They are supposed to be able to do this forward and backward. The Basics start in unison, more or less, but then they stumble over one another as they rush toward the finish. "I want you to know this in your sleep," says Blocker, as he walks through the rows. "Get your tempos together."

They try it again but get no closer. Rather, they seem to be dragging themselves through the exercise now, falling behind on every count. "That was horrible. You weren't even close to being close together," Elliott, their cadet captain, tells them.

After thirty-five repetitions, the cadets break to drink water. "Put up a paw if you feel tired and sleepy," Elliott asks. Nearly all the kids raise their hands. "Maybe you should go to sleep at taps and not stay up and write letters to your mommies and daddies, to your Aunt Tillie, and to your boyfriends. That is why you are exhausted."

Other improvised punishments are more creative. One plays on the lack of knowledge about Second Beast among the new kids to trick them into believing they are being punished when in fact they are not. For example, Boisvert says, some of the advisers suggest telling cadets who might have to march for one and a half hours that one hour of that time is punishment for having slipped up. "The Basics don't know that they would have been marching one and a half hours anyway," he says.

In the front row and off to the side, Brad Bernard moves his rifle through the drill dozens of times—if not with gusto, then at least with a practiced hand, having learned the exercise at prep school. Bernard shoots his buddy Taylor a look that all but screams, "Can you believe this waste of time?" He snorts quietly and looks up at the sky.

As the cadet commandant of basic training, Brandon Dues must mediate the competing visions of cadet training. A high achiever who will graduate with the top military rank of his class, Dues finds himself exhausted by Second Beast, buffeted by two antagonistic philosophies of training: the officers, pushing for oversight, for more rational and humane treatment of the powerless newcomers, and the upperclass cadets, arguing that cadre deserved freer rein to train these Basics, and that altering such long-standing tradition was a mistake. In each encounter, he believes, the chips are stacked against the cadre.

"The political environment has become so sensitive that they just don't trust the cadets," he says. The military training instructors are limiting the physical training that the cadre may impose on the cadets. As reports of pinkeye—a perennial problem during basic training—rise, the Lackland instructors recommend easing up on the training standards.

Also fresh on their minds is the death the previous spring of a major who had broken his neck and died after scaling an obstacle course at Herbert Field in Florida. There was even some doubt, among the academy brass, about whether all the obstacles at Jacks would be approved for basic training, and in fact the approval had come only at the last minute.

Perhaps the most revolting illustration of this capitulation to weakness, in the eyes of many upperclassmen, is the decision to allow cadets water breaks. "It is unsightly and disgusting, in our eyes," Dues says. Most cadre recall their own experiences without such comforts; to them, the pauses in training drop the bar too low and hinder discipline. "We got through it just fine, and they don't need those water stations. It's not going to help you. You only need to consume water if you're exerting yourself more than thirty minutes."

Dues says he is not arguing for abusing the newcomers, but he believes that the academy is tilting too far toward spoiling them. "You can't train an individual to his or her max unless you take care of him, but if we're pampering them too much, they're not going to reach their full potential, either. Giving them a helping hand every step of the way isn't doing them any favors. Life doesn't work that way, and neither does the academy. Basics are going to go through a hard time, and there is a time for sergeants to talk to them, but when it comes time to train, we shouldn't have those interferences. It's not really going to solve a problem."

The coddling, as Dues sees it, demeans all of them. As word of the steps to soften basic training spread, he believes, the cadets at the other military service academies, and even active-duty officers, will come to view academy graduates as their inferiors. Worse, the Basics themselves will never know that they are as tough as their comrades. "They are linked with the negative association of that policy, and also with taking advantage of it."

"In 2003, when we came in, we showed up ready to go," Dues recalls. His class lost out on Recognition and on other trials of the cadet experience—a decision on which his classmates had no vote but for which they reaped the consequences. "We were tied together with being the weak class. We were told even at the academy, 'Oh boy, '07, they're going to be completely worthless because of the training they're not going to receive.' That kind of hurt us. It wasn't true, but you were being unfairly associated with something."

Given all that, the juniors and seniors who are shaping this year's entering class hardly believe that "going soft" is the answer. "If you see an individual who is constantly exerting one hundred ten percent, giving all he can and then some, the cadets don't blame that individual" for training them hard, Dues insists. "They take pride, realize that individual has a good heart, pride, and wants to get the job done.

"We're training America's future, the leaders in the air force. The value of my ring is going to be measured in the quality of training I bring to my subordinates. People want to give back and to ensure that what they're holding on to isn't lost."

One night that summer, Dues goes out with some classmates to talk and watch the stars, shining brilliantly over the mountains. By accident, his Jeep hits a rock, and he finds himself accused of horseplay. "I almost lost my position over that, which would have been kind of silly in the real air force," he says.

"As cadet commander, if I'd been fired for something like that, in my mind it'd be a total shame. I'd failed to do something that was vital to the academy, and I couldn't finish something that I started." The failure would follow him throughout his military career. He certainly never would have graduated first in his class in military ranking, as he ultimately will. "People really don't forget those things."

"We have to understand how our superiors will see things," he says. "You walk a very thin rope. It becomes even thinner the higher up you go."

10 | Of Love and Demons

After ninety minutes of rifle drill, Demons A Flight gets to unwind in the shade of a pine tree, away from the hot and heaving hulk of a generator. Nick Mercurio tells the Basics that one of them, Adam Brunderman, just got their unit's first Dear John letter. Brunderman ducks and shakes his head, embarrassed. Mercurio issues an order: they are each to write a letter to Brunderman's girlfriend that night.

"Don't laugh," Mercurio quips. "Some of you will have the same thing happen to you. Others will wish it happened to them." The laugh goes over big after an afternoon of gripping and flipping a leaden rifle.

Rhonda Meeker turns to Cadet Captain Jonathan Elliott. She stands outside the shade, squinting in the sunlight. An upperclasswoman had singled her out on the assault course, the toughest part of Second Beast. "You know what she called me?" Meeker asks gamely. "Eighty pounds of piss and vinegar." She grins widely, euphoric. You'd think the cadre had called her the queen of England or her American idol. Justin Goodin, another freshman who lost out on the combat course, looks sideways at her.

Officially, the short, slender girl with a parrot's haircut and searchlight eyes has been enrolled at the academy for less than a month; she arrived on the same bus from Doolie Hall and stood on the same painted footprints as everybody else. But in a deeper sense, her journey here began before she even knew the place existed. As an eleven-year-old in Sacramento, she ducked for cover through gang wars on her street, watching families fall apart in mayhem and violence. She saw a friend lose her mother, killed in the crossfire of a gunfight next door.

Meeker knew, with a child's clarity, that if she didn't make her own destiny, life would choose one for her, and it could be fatal. "I had a lot of neighbors who joined gangs," she said earlier that day, between training courses. So precarious was her situation that family friends, an older couple, stepped in to take over her upbringing. She thinks of them now as her parents. "I just thought that I needed to be as independent as possible, and I needed to be as strong as possible, because I saw the world around me as a really cruel and unforgiving place."

It wasn't that she shrank from violence, per se. After all, she chose to attend the Air Force Academy, rather than West Point or Annapolis, because it offered her the best chance of seeing combat. The violence she had fled, though, was all so random. In the chaos and destruction of Meeker's eleven-year-old world, she hungered for something stable and secure, with a less elastic sense of right and wrong. She was seeking more than a job or even a career. She was after a way of life: structure over anarchy, meaning over mindless scheming, and—although it is too early in her time here—a sense of belonging, of family. Her eagerness leaves her painfully out of sync with most of her flight mates, some of whom still aren't sure they even want to be here.

There is no denying her love. She felt it before many of her classmates had even thought of applying to the academy. The summer before, she had come out to Colorado Springs for a seminar and had felt irresistibly drawn. "Really, I can't leave here," she told her parents at the time. "I just had an awesome time." On the plane, she cried all the way back. "Are you happy to be home?" Meeker recalls her parents asking. "I was like 'No.'"

She looks around at the other Demons taking a break with her under a tree. "Anybody got more cookies back there? If you got another Capri Sun that isn't frozen, I'd love it." Catching the drink, she turns back to me. "I'm happy to be here," she says.

All her civilian clothes are now tucked into a couple of boxes that have been put into storage, and she has taken charge of her future without relying on her family for financial support. "That was important to me," Meeker says. Her parents sold their home and moved to a retirement community. There is no girlhood bedroom left untouched, awaiting her return. Life has moved on for everybody in her orbit.

A month before, her friends marveled at the radical change that Meeker was hurtling toward with such certainty. "You're gonna be sitting in a field somewhere, carrying an M-16. Do you really want that?" one friend asked her. "You *gotta* really want that. What about the showers? And the makeup? You gotta wear these seedy clothes. You gotta carry that heavy rifle." As if Meeker hadn't thought about all that. Then Kayla, the friend who knew Meeker better than anybody else on the planet, spoke up. "She wouldn't have it any other way," she said.

"The M-16 is cool," Meeker says now. "I just really like taking it apart, oiling everything down, and cleaning it out. I like the oil on my hands. I don't know why. It's like just 'Wow, I worked today.' You look at your hands and say, 'Wow, I did something useful today.'" She comes across as relishing toughness, delighting in the shock value of attending a formal ball at the air force base back home just hours after firing off rounds on a twelve-gauge shotgun with the boys from her high school's Junior ROTC program.

More than most, Meeker has everything riding on her success here, so she seizes on words of praise as if they are markings in a forest, signs that she is still on the trail and not lost in the world. As she was marching on her very first day at the academy, a female cadre called out to her: "Yeah, [Meeker], that's right! Go, [Meeker] and boys." Meeker smiled that day, as if she had gotten a coded message of encouragement, transmitted from one class to the next. "That was okay," she says now. It made all the day's push-ups and put-downs, the shouting and the goosing, endurable.

She smiles and downplays the stress that leaves her classmates quaking. "It's just fun, not painful. It's like getting to know your mom all over again, her mood swings. It's like living with your mom on menopause.

"This is just like professional hazing," she continues, adding that it is useful for accustoming the cadets to working under stress when they head out to war. I was used to hearing the cadre say this, but not the Basics, who are struggling and sweating their way through each day. In her hunger to become friends with cadre training her, in her explanations, I occasionally get the sense that Meeker cannot bear the powerlessness of her position and so identifies more with the people in charge than with her fellow SMACKs.

On the Hill Meeker remembers not eating until she figured out the precise way to ask for something, and she recalls the misery of watching her comrades get punished for her missteps. "That *sucks*! I feel devastated, absolutely devastated. That crushes you."

Despite the strain, she has no doubts about her choice. "A lot of kids come here, and they're so homesick," she says. "Don't get me wrong. I love my parents. But I'm fine here. I'm happy here. This is home." She loves the marching and the jokes with the upperclassmen after an exhausting training exercise. She loves the Jolly Rancher candy—green apple–flavored—that somebody throws her way at just that moment. She loves the jodies, the rhymes that they all chant as they march. In the afternoon there are often violent rainstorms in the mountains, when lightning crackles like an electric vein from sky to earth, and she loves that, too.

In their bubble, she and the others know only dimly the news of the world in the summer of 2006. "We heard something about Israel invading Lebanon," she says. Before heading out to Jacks, the kids had a day off, which they spent with families who sponsor cadets and informally adopt many of them during their time at the academy. "I tried to collect as much news as I could," Meeker says, "but it doesn't all make sense."

Through the combat training earlier this afternoon, though, it started to make sense as she glimpsed a connection to the news from Iraq. "It really hit home when the cadre started saying, 'Your future brothers and sisters in arms are doing this right now, and you're bitching about doing it. You're in the woods. You're about to join your brothers and sisters in arms, and you'd better be proud.'"

David Urban, who is listening nearby, says he has only a hazy sense of what his comrades in arms are up against and what combat is actually like. "We really don't know that much about it, except for what these guys have been telling us," he says. Some days, Urban adds, he still wonders, "Why are we doing this?"

Yearning so much to make her home in the military, Meeker never imagined that fitting in, making friends and feeling a sense of belonging, might be the hard part. Rather, she expected her real challenge to lie in the academics. Eager to fly in combat and to major in aeronautical engineering, she confided on her first day, "I'd be fine if I didn't need to sleep." Socially, however, she expected no problem. She knew so deeply that she belonged to the military that coming here seemed as inevitable as gravity.

In these early days, however, she has a quirky talent for alienating people, for saying the wrong thing to the wrong person at the wrong time, and this makes her first year through the academy lonelier and more painful than it has to be. Sitting under the tree this afternoon, she confesses her distaste for the women who share her tent at Jacks—and she does so right in front of them. She complains about their high school mentality, deriding their preoccupation with petty issues such as how they look and who said what to whom. She seems not to notice the chill that follows her remarks.

On another training course that day, Meeker recalls, a cadre was following her, urging her on. "He's like 'You're the most spirited cadet I've seen on this course,' and this has totally got me going, and he sends me off. The same guy followed me on all of the courses, shouting, 'Come on, [Meeker]!'"

"Yeah, I'm the [Meeker] being," she says, half to herself. Nodding, she sits on the ground, her elbows resting on her knees, buoyed by the notice she is attracting. "I am the [Meeker] being," she says, more loudly this time.

11 | The Family Line

To the cadets who came before them, these freshmen, even before they stepped off the bus from Doolie Hall, did not impress. Nothing in them seemed aware, let alone proud, of the commitment they were taking on, nor humbled by the sacrifices of their elders—the magnificent long blue line. Maybe not all of the incoming class had gone on MySpace, but there was no way to tell how deep the cynicism and arrogance ran.

Nor is there any way that Cadet Captain Jonathan Elliott, in charge of Demons A Flight during boot camp, is going to let it stand. First, he cannot break down a personality and build up a group identity through a wall encrusted with arrogance. Second, these puppies, even if not all of them had participated, had managed to deeply offend him.

He borrows a term from computer games to tell them to forget about shortcuts for the next two weeks. "There's no easy way out of it," he says. "You can't put in a toad and make it all better. You're gonna have to go through it."

If the U.S. Air Force Academy, as young as it is, has an Old Guard protecting its ideals, Elliott, is it. His father, Gary, graduated from the academy in 1974, served the air force for twenty years, mostly as a fighter pilot, and then flew bush planes for a missionary group in the Philippines. Elliott's brother, Stephen, is attending the academy as well and will transfer into Squadron 13 as a legacy after Jonathan graduates.

Elliott insists that he set his sights on continuing the family line in Colorado Springs back in kindergarten, at an age when most kids are first stringing letters into words. The tie, across the generations, gives Elliott a fierce passion, a kind of first-person ownership of the place, and a disdain for the cadets who lack his love. His passion is not necessarily for the academy as it is today, but for the essence he sees shining at its core.

Elliott's family spent eight years living in the bush in the Philippines, the fruit of his father's work for the New Tribes Mission, a group that proselytizes among indigenous peoples in remote corners of the globe. His father flew in medications and supplies and did medical evacuations. Elliott believes that by helping natives in backwater hamlets with one of their most urgent needs, decent health care, New Tribes gives them the space to veer from tradition, to think about God in new ways. Critics, of course, accuse missionary groups like New Tribes of spiritual imperialism, of insinuating themselves into the lives of natives only to uproot their cultural and religious heritage.

Five years earlier, Elliott was learning how to fly a super cub plane with Martin Burnham, a forty-one-year-old fellow missionary at New Tribes from Rose Hill, Kansas, outside Wichita. Burnham took a break from his work to celebrate his eighteenth wedding anniversary at a beach resort with his wife, Gracia, when rebels from the Islamist terrorist group Abu Sayyaf broke in, kidnapping the couple and several other vacationers and staff from the resort. Six days later, they kidnapped three nurses and an orderly from a hospital.

Abu Sayyaf, whose name means Father of the Sword, originally had visions of creating an independent Islamic state in western Mindanao and the Sulu Archipelago, one piece in a pan-Islamic state that would stretch across Southeast Asia. However, Abu Sayyaf had devolved into a gang of bandits with an ideology, responsible for bombings, assassinations, rape, and extortion.

The terrorists held the Burnhams for more than a year. They beheaded some of the hostages—including Guillermo Sobero, an American contractor from California, and two Filipino employees of the resort—abandoned some hostages, and ransomed others. In a 2003 memoir of their captivity, *In the Presence of My Enemies*, Gracia Burnham wrote that one of the terrorists had told her Abu Sayyaf had collected a ransom to free the Burnhams but still would not release them. The Philippine military hunted the Burnhams' kidnappers repeatedly, each time firing on the guerillas and endangering the hostages. There were seventeen firefights in all, and a year of forced marches and near starvation at the hands of their captors.

During the final siege to rescue the remaining three victims, Martin Burnham and Ediborah Yap, a Filipina nurse, were killed, seemingly by army gunfire, according to Gracia's memoir. Though wounded, Gracia survived, left to raise their children on her own. The following year, Jonathan Elliott stood on the painted footprints, reading the legend above the entrance ramp to the campus: SERVICE BEFORE SELF.

As the assault course cadre run the Basics through hand-to-hand combat maneuvers with their rifles, Elliott remembers that time and says, "I do think about it a lot, about why I'm here: so other children aren't made fatherless by these people." During his captivity, Martin Burnham thanked his kidnappers each evening as they cuffed him to a tree, and he wished them good night. He left behind three children—the eldest, Jeff, is just a little younger than Elliott. "It makes what we do important—protecting our citizens so they can go through their lives," Elliott says.

"I get riled up in discussions with people who say, 'One man's terrorist is another man's freedom fighter.' It strikes a real personal chord with me." He is here, he says, out of a keen desire to "serve my country, especially after seeing the world and seeing what separates us from other countries, so that people are able to live the way they want to live."

These days, Elliott says, the hard edges of basic training have been sanded down, and aggression—even the kind aimed at producing a better fighter—feels outlawed. As a leader, Elliott falls back on sarcasm to push, pummel, and pound the Basics into shape. When they fail to estimate the correct distance from their dorms to Jacks Valley, he throws out numbers willy-nilly, as they seem to be doing, inviting them to be ever more fanciful.

When they stumble trying to figure out the names of the original leaders of the air force, he suggests that the freshmen are such intimate friends with those luminaries that they know them by nicknames. His cadre take their cues from him, deriding the grunts from the Basics who are struggling through dozens of sit-ups as "the sounds of weakness coming from your bodies."

Being a devout Christian, Elliott avoids foul language, so his barbs carry the antiseptic whiff of Sunday school corridors. They lack fire, bouncing off the Basics like BBs. Among the freshmen, the sudden shift from physical punishments to mockery as the club of choice fuels speculation. Perhaps this second group of upperclassmen is not as physically fit as the cadre who trained them during First Beast. Their first leader, Lance Watson, was a machine.

Under Elliott, however, the pressure is mental, and that makes some of the men, in particular, wonder if Elliott—with his boyish face and his slender build—is less physically fit, less able to sustain the punishments himself, than Watson was. Is he weak, they wonder? For the unwritten rule of basic training is that whoever is ordering the beating, or punishment, must endure it alongside the Basics, with energy to spare.

Elliott is no showboat. He does not revel in leading for its own sake or steal a glance at a mirror to admire the slant of his blue beret. First Beast, after all, takes place by the dorm and is more about learning how to march, how to turn out in formation, how to wear the uniform, and how to move and speak at the academy. By Second Beast, it's time to get dirty. The severity of training is not entirely his choice, he notes.

Elliott remembers his own experience in Second Beast as far tougher, with cadre leading his flight on runs before breakfast and between meals. "After the assault course, we went back to our tents, got our rifles, and did a run," Elliott recalls. "Those are the things I thought we'd be able to do when it was my chance. I found that we weren't able to do that. The whys were never passed down to my level. That was just something I had to say, 'Yes, Sir' to."

Upon hearing that some of the Basics have concluded that he resorts to shame because he isn't as fit as Watson, Elliott is quiet for a moment. "I can understand why they feel that way," he says. "Even if I was able to do the stuff that I wanted to, it probably wouldn't be as physically demanding as what Lance could do.

"I try to know when to turn it on and when to turn it off," Elliott continues. As cadre, he sees his job as inspiring the Basics and teaching them how to motivate themselves. When he sees someone who tries, however far afield the effort falls, he steps in, quietly edging them toward where they need to be.

Watching as Justin Goodin goes through one of the group's 265 repetitions of rifle drill, Elliott materializes alongside him, grabbing his rifle to illustrate. "It's one continuous movement," he tells Goodin. "It has to be right from the beginning."

Part Three

JOINING
THE FOLD

12 | Surviving Second Beast

As the Basics line up to begin their post–boot camp march back up to the Hill, the skies once again flash and shudder, and lightning crooks down from sky to earth. Midway through the trek back, the whole operation, from the red-capped freshmen to the senior-year commanders in their blue berets, stops for shelter. Everyone finally piles into buses for the ride back to the dorms—a somehow dissatisfying, yet, to some, fitting, close to training that falls short of the cadre's visions this summer.

If the cadre are thinking that they didn't get to fully grasp the reins as leaders, what with training instructors and officers watching their every move, then some of the Basics, for their part, are also feeling cheated; they complain afterward that the training was not as tough as they had heard it would be. This is not the academy they expected. Just what are they missing out on, they wonder. In the final days before receiving their shoulder boards, the newcomers are suspended in a kind of twilight zone: officially still in basic training but with little actual training going on. Still, they are not fully accepted as cadets.

Nevertheless, at a "warrior luncheon" to honor the Basics for making it through boot camp, David Urban's body cannot make the switch from robot mode. For the first time in nearly six weeks, he may eat without studying the eagle at the top of his lunch plate. He may slide back in his seat and rest against its back, and take bites as big as his mouth can hold. However, he does not; his body stays rigid, unable to relax. He still moves at angles, like a character in a first-generation computer game, perched on the edge of his seat, his back straight as sheetrock. Only by the end of the meal do his limbs loosen and recover the memory of how to relax.

A day before the Acceptance Parade, Urban leans into a chair in his dorm room, marveling at the change in atmosphere. He has a new roommate, Christopher Flynn, a soft-spoken, keep-your-head-down graduate of the prep school. Flynn has straight black hair, dark and serious eyes, and a lean build. He has lost seventeen pounds since arriving at the academy; Urban has gained three, but in muscle. Their hair has grown out, so they no longer look raw, waiting to be formed.

Emerging from their isolation, like bears coming out of hibernation, they are piecing together the world's changes while they were marooned at Jacks. Israel had indeed invaded Lebanon (as had been rumored at Jacks), after Hezbollah had crossed the border and kidnapped several Israeli soldiers, but no, Jack Sparrow did not die in the film *Pirates of the Caribbean*.

Now, when the upperclassmen summon the Basics from their rooms, they knock on their doors and tell them what kind of clothes to put on, speaking like normal people. Gone, for now, are the thunderous morning wake-ups, the constant shouting and punishments, and the feeling of being shoved from behind. The pervasive presumption that the Basics are screwing up whatever they are doing is lifting.

Urban had suffered through Jacks. On the assault course, a cadre decided that he wasn't performing well enough and called him on it. Urban had to do push-ups, then ten minutes of high kicks—running in place and lifting his knees up past hip level. Urban's boots and uniform were heavy, weighted with mud from the pits they had crawled through.

But the doubts about whether he was in the right place, whether he wanted to be at the academy at all, have disappeared. By the time he was being beaten at the assault course, his worries had become more short-term. Could he finish an obstacle when he felt like a busted balloon halfway through? He somehow did, watching his flight mates and often barely catching up with everyone else. His focus was narrow: just make it through. He seems not to have noticed when Flynn reminds him of the mutterings scrawled here and there at Jacks: "IHTFP," code for "I hate this fuckin' place."

"If it was a choice of where would I rather be, here or somewhere else, at this point in time I'd rather be home," Urban says. At home, he had had a good job as a store manager and a scholarship to attend the University of Texas at Austin. He had had freedom and friends. "But for me, it's not about the here and now. It's about what I'm here *for*."

Despite that, Urban rides back from Jacks feeling that Second Beast could have been—indeed, he had expected it to be—tougher than it was. If this was his baptism, the font had been half empty. As Basics, Urban and Flynn know nothing of the behind-the-scenes drama that surrounded their training. They don't realize that the cadre were not calling all the shots, that officers and trainers from Lackland—not upperclassmen—were calibrating the difficulty of the training.

Thus Urban and Flynn conclude that the upperclassmen were not up to the task, that they shrank from having to do push-ups or squats right alongside the Basics. Instead, they used ridicule as a first resort, as if they'd shopped for it at a big box store beforehand and had to get rid of it all at Jacks. The style of leadership—"*Was this leadership?*" the Basics wondered—made the Basics feel small and stupid instead of merely untrained.

"A lot of them would get mad and go off," Urban says. "It's like they're on some sort of power trip. Like they're blowing off at the world."

He and Flynn begin polishing their dress shoes, ahead of tomorrow's parade. They use cotton balls, rubbing hard to coax out a high shine.

Urban has asked Kasey King, a junior, to pin on one of his shoulder boards. "He's the one I most respected slash liked," Urban explains, slicing the air with his hand. "When he got mad, I got the feeling he was a lot more sincere." Then there was Calen Pope, a guitar-playing junior with a well-thumbed Bible, who trained them during their first weeks there. "He would get down with you. He was hard but fair. If he got mad, I knew I did something wrong. I knew it was for something real."

Urban rubs the shoe's rim hard and pauses, mentally going over the twenty or so upperclassmen who had wrung him out here at the academy. He looks up. "If I had more shoulder boards, there are other people I could pick," he says.

Flynn looks over at Urban and laughs. "You don't have to polish the insides," he says.

"I'm going above and beyond, man. 'Excellence in all we do.'"

By now, the tension inside the freshmen has begun to uncoil, and this is a day of preparation but not doing. At mail call, many receive boxes and packages from home, packed with the things their parents suspect they miss most: cookies, chips, sodas, books.

Casey Jane Barrett smiles euphorically, her teeth gleaming and her giant plastic glasses tipping down her nose as she carries away a white box sent priority mail. Rebecca Gleason, an intramural swimmer, gets two boxes, and Brad Bernard, perhaps Squadron 13's most reluctant cadet, carries one upstairs for her. Officially, they may open their packages only once they are no longer lowly Basics—that is, after their formal acceptance as cadets the following day. Urban hauls away a huge box and puts it in a corner under his desk.

At rehearsal for the parade, the silliness overflows. The squadrons are to march out numerically, in neatly defined formations led by their guidons, flag-bearing cadets who stake out each squadron's patch of the grassy field. Instead, some of the guidons stage a mock rebellion, breaking out and scrambling across the field helter-skelter, waving their flags wildly. "Stop. Stop. Stop. We'll have to start all over," somebody says over the loudspeaker, to no avail. "You guys who are doing that crazy stuff with the guidons, cut that shit out, or we'll send you to" the superintendent's office.

Later, Brigadier General Susan Desjardins warns them that any cadets who fall out of the parade, as some seventy-five did at a parade the year before, will be in her office, explaining why. She tells them to drink plenty of water, bend their knees to keep their circulation going, and eat a good breakfast. "It should be a day to show your stuff, and that you have control," she tells them, adding that as freshmen they are to be "loyal followers."

"When you do make a choice, own it," she tells them, "and when you make a mistake, admit it and take your lumps. Explain in detail what you did. Don't be vague. It could be the difference between getting some punishment and being disenrolled."

Desjardins describes the gargantuan effort that is going into the war in Iraq and the dedication of the pilots, the mechanics, the maintenance workers, and the troops on the ground. "Now, I just have to produce it in you. We are a nation at war, and we need you."

"2010. Strength within!" the freshmen roar.

There are no academic classes today, but there is a class on taking classes. Given the demands on student time and the fact that the cadets must prove themselves not in academics alone but also in military and physical expertise, the academy offers students strong support. In a small theater-sized room with upholstered seats, Dr. Thomas Mabry, a retired lieutenant colonel in charge of student academic services, warns that the workload they will soon face is nothing like high school. He asks for a show of hands: "How many of you spent one hour or less a night on homework in high school?" About one-third of the students raise their hands. "Here you should expect to do two hours of homework for each hour in the classroom," he says.

Earlier today, Lieutenant General John Regni, the superintendent, has told them that he aims to keep the cadets on a shorter leash this year. Attendance at breakfast will be mandatory, and so will study time each evening. "In a leap of faith," he says, students will no longer take their exams, the common graded review, all at the same time in order to prevent cheating. "By the way, lest you are tempted to share answers," he adds, "we're going to have different versions of the test, so don't think you can do it." He pauses, perhaps to let the irony sink in. "It's a leap of faith," he repeats, with a half smile.

At the academic briefing, Pat Gottschalk, who runs a class on survival skills like avoiding procrastination and preparing for tests, takes the Basics to the edge of the cliff. "Don't think the strategies that got you here are going to work now," she warns. "You're all smart, but . . ." On a screen, she flashes some report cards: one shows a 0.64 grade point average, another a 1.53. "Understand, they were all like you when they came in," she says, wondering if she is getting through.

Ellick Ruffin, a specialist in reading, offers courses in speed-reading and in improving comprehension and recall—backed by a warning to the cadets that their reading load will soon be more than 120 pages a night.

Durthy A. Washington offers help in writing term papers. "How many of you waited until the night before a paper was due in high school and still got an A?" she asks. About one-fifth of the students raise their hands. "If you want to be disappointed, do that here." Few would suspect that Washington's other job involves helping slackers in just that kind of a pinch: she is the author of several Cliffs Notes, abridging and explaining the works of African American authors, including Ralph Ellison's *The Invisible Man* and Toni Morrison's *Song of Solomon*.

Around the room, some students give in to the seductions of a padded chair and dimmed lights and begin dozing off. When the lights come on, Barrett and Rhonda Meeker bound down the steps to sign up for speed-reading classes. Barrett wants to improve not just her speed but her comprehension as well. Meeker, an A student at her high school, wants the extra insurance.

Urban stretches out and stays put. "I'm not really worried about it," he says later. He has already done five semesters at his local community college, which had snapped him back to discipline after he'd slacked off toward the end of high school at home with his mother in charge. Thanks to his courses at the community college, he counts himself well prepared for the rigors of classes at the academy. "It'll be hard, something I'll look back on as a fond memory," Urban says, "but I don't have too much doubt I'll make it through."

13 | Parting the River

The banner stands almost as tall as Casey Jane Barrett does, fuchsia and stoplight-yellow letters stretching across the uppermost bleachers that flank the academy's parade grounds: CONGRATULATIONS—BEAST IS OVER. WE LOVE YOU, CASEY JANE.

Terri Marcus and Payson, the guide dog that Barrett had trained before coming to the academy, have flown in from Ventura, California, for today's parade. They rose at 3 a.m. and turned up at Stillman Field just after dawn. Marcus is not the only parent to arrive so early—hardly believing, after all the trials and travails, that her daughter has reached Acceptance Day. Today Barrett will take the honor oath, becoming a cadet in full standing at the Air Force Academy.

In Marcus's classroom, the banner she was making seemed enormous, reaching across the entire room as she drew the letters and colored them in. Here, however, over the expanse of the parade grounds, which are broader than a football field, the sign looks puny to her. She worries that Casey Jane will miss it when she marches out.

It has been six weeks since Marcus, her husband, Jeff, and her daughter Taylor dropped Barrett off at the academy. For six weeks her daughter struggled through basic training, crying into the phone when she came down with a stomach virus. For six weeks, Barrett wrote letters home about how she coped with missing her mother, eating lousy food, and running afoul of the upperclassmen who were assigned to train her. For six weeks, Marcus tracked the progress of the Class of 2010 through daily videos on the Association of Graduates Web site—so hooked on it that Marcus felt as if she herself were going through the experience.

In a vote of blind confidence, Barrett's family had joined the graduates' association the day she arrived at the academy. In Marcus's mind, there was no doubt that four years from that day she would be at the stadium watching Casey Jane toss her cap toward a cloudless sky as jets soared overhead, jubilant at her graduation and the stellar future awaiting her.

This morning, of the 1,334 who entered the academy, 1,268 fourth-class cadets stand ready to don the shoulder boards, and Casey Jane, to her mother's effervescent pride, is still standing among them.

Marcus has therefore brought her a small stash of rewards—necessities, really: Barrett's contact lenses; cuticle cream; earplugs; a proper hairbrush; a real bra—nothing frilly with lace, just something more than a reinforced undershirt; and Payson—one of Barrett's four dogs. So attuned to her daughter's needs is Marcus that she even packed a lint roller to pick up the hairs from Barrett's uniform after Payson jumps all over her. Marcus and her daughter earn nothing from training guide dogs; it is just their way of helping out.

At that moment, the dog's and the owner's lives are, strangely enough, on parallel tracks. Like Barrett, Payson has gone through months of training to build endurance, in her case learning to disregard her own itches in order to stand, sit, raise a paw, or freeze her movements on command. After more than a year of obedience training under Marcus and her daughter, Payson will head off to boot camp for six weeks, where she will train intensively for her life's work: protecting blind people from danger. In a sense, the regimen that Barrett has taken on—ultimately to protect her country from danger—is not entirely new to the family.

Watching the field under a full sun, Marcus weighs the tempered blessings of technology and her virtual watch over Barrett. She had followed First Beast, the trek out to Jacks Valley, and the obstacles the cadets faced out there. Then Barrett called home one Sunday and broke down, aching with a stomach virus. Her voice was cracking, and Marcus could tell that she was hurting and barely hanging on. The other parents she'd been in touch with, thanks to the association, had warned her that this might happen, and they had urged her not to surrender to the moments of fear and defeat but to help her daughter triumph over them. Prescription: tough love.

"You don't want to not be there. But it's so sad when you hang up the phone and they've just left you in this stupor, like 'Ohhh, my child,'" Marcus says, hugging herself. Despite all the mother-daughter closeness, Marcus felt helpless in the face of her daughter's suffering. She paced the floor, aching to ring the academy brass to tell them that this was not right, not right at all, and to demand that her daughter be taken to the hospital. But, unsure of herself and afraid of doing the wrong thing, she kept silent. Upon learning that the academy had sent Barrett to the hospital, Marcus felt relieved, glad that she had not stepped in.

"The nicest thing about this is that I never thought once about her safety," Marcus says, adding that she believes that Barrett is undoubtedly safer here than at a civilian university. The sexual assault allegations that dominated the academy just three years ago do not worry Marcus, who is confident that Barrett will never put herself in a position where she could be molested. She would never, for instance, pass out from drinking too much in a dorm room with men, as some—but by no means all—of the rape victims who came forward had done. "No, that's just not something she would do," Marcus says, shaking her head as if chasing off the possibility.

As Barrett marches onto the parade grounds, her left foot marking the beat, she thinks, "Thank God. Thank God. Thank God," private lyrics to the music she is obeying. Never more would she answer to "Basic. Female Basic," as if it were her name, first and last. She thinks of all the ways she's heard it: "Basic, watch where you're going!" "Basic, why aren't you out here?" "Basic, get moving!" She is Female Basic no more.

She sneaks a glance at the bleachers in front of the parade ground, spying her own name like a gift, a ribbon unfurled across the top next to a giant heart. She smiles to herself. Leave it to Mom. She'd told her flight mates: "My mom'll be the one in an obnoxious green shirt, with a dog in a yellow sweater." Even the cadets whose own parents couldn't make it are looking for Barrett's mother—and there she stands.

Barrett hadn't wanted to ask her mother to come for Acceptance Day. Airfare, after all, is not cheap, and they would have only a couple of hours together, at most. But more than she wants to admit even to herself, Barrett is thrilled to see her mother. In fact, there is no one in the world she wants to see more.

Barrett is one drop in the river of blue uniforms that flows onto the field, broken only by the cadets who are carrying the guidons, or squadron flags ahead of each squadron. The sophomores, juniors, and seniors who represent the initiates' future file into place at the back half of the field, opposite the aluminum bleachers half filled with the families of the new cadets.

Marcus peers through her binoculars, marking, with her mental yardstick, where each squadron's freshmen are likely to stand. The freshmen take their places in rows across the front of the field, Barrett and the future Bulldawgs a little over to the left of where Marcus is sitting. From the south, a B-52 bomber, dispatched from Barksdale Air Force Base in Shreveport, Louisiana, streaks across the sky.

General Gregory Martin, Class of 1970, a veteran combat pilot and former commander of the U.S. Air Force in Europe and of the Allied Air Forces for Northern Europe, talks to the students briefly about the charge they are taking on. When he graduated, the United States was locked in the Cold War and fighting in Southeast Asia, where he flew 161 combat missions. "Now this nation is again at war," he says. "It's the global war on terrorism, again a war of ideology. This war will not be short. It will require our very best."

A sudden trumpet blast begins the adjutant's call, the customary signal that a guard, a battalion, or a regiment is about to form. The Basics turn to face the upperclassmen across the field. Raising white-gloved hands to their foreheads, they salute, and the upperclassmen salute back. After each group reports to the commander, the academy superintendent, Lieutenant General John Regni, strides forward as the band fills Stillman Field with the ponderous, triumphal strains of the national anthem.

In a few minutes, the new cadets will take the honor oath, swearing to act with integrity as cadets at the academy. Today, before the parents and the other guests, General Regni says nothing very detailed about the oath and the difficulties that previous cadets have had abiding by it. However, the day before, in a talk with the freshmen alone, he had had plenty to say.

"Five, ten years ago, if you had asked the average person about the Air Force Academy, they probably would have told you that 'Wow. It's a beautiful campus in the mountains of Colorado,'" he tells the new cadets. "Now last year, two years ago, if you had asked that same person on the street what they thought of the Air Force Academy, you'd probably get a different answer. You'd probably get 'Isn't that where they assault women? Isn't that where they don't respect religious differences?'"

Regni had come on board at a turbulent time in the academy's life, after a string of complaints had alleged that top officers and cadets were using their positions to foist Christianity on students. According to a report by Yale University, one chaplain, for example, had urged cadets at a religious service during Second Beast to proselytize the non-believers in their tents, lest they "burn in the fires of hell." (The chaplain denied making the statement.) The year before that, scores of female cadets had called Colorado Senator Wayne Allard to complain that they'd been raped and, perhaps even more wounding, punished by the academy's leadership when they reported the attacks. Although other service academies grapple with similar tensions, only Colorado Springs had found itself crippled by them.

"We went through some serious social issues, and we have earned, as a result, some black eyes," Regni states. "What we're trying to do—and it takes all of us to do this—is to over time rebuild our image so that people will look very favorably upon the United States Air Force Academy. This is the most important thing, the reason I wanted to speak to you."

Around the room, the Basics erupt in dry coughs, as if answering each of the superintendent's points with a barking chorus of congestion. "Mind over matter is a good thing," Regni tells them. He waits for the room to quiet. The coughs that come back with them from boot camp are known here as Jacks Hacks.

On today's battlefields, he tells them, even a corporal, the second lowest military rank, after private, must understand the "strategic implications of the battlefield. Even a corporal who is doing his or her job day in and day out can do something at the very low end of the totem pole that has strategic implications."

Regni shows a PowerPoint slide of a marine corporal draping an American flag over a statue of Saddam Hussein. The image was one of the earliest public relations gaffes of the Iraq War. The marines were trying to re-create their iconic World War II image of raising the flag at the Battle of Iwo Jima, he notes. But the image "played into the fears simmering through the Muslim world, and it was seized by U.S. critics and enemies for strategic advantages," Regni tells them.

"The individual actions that you do, whether you're in uniform or not, are going to speak for our Air Force Academy."

The superintendent flashes a slide with the chemical breakdown of an alcohol molecule. He warns them of the zero tolerance policy on giving alcohol to minors, adding that liquor had figured in many of the rapes that were reported. Even when the cadets go into town, out of uniform, he expects them to behave as if they are still in uniform. "About 98 percent of you get it. About 2 percent don't," he says sharply.

Although he never says so explicitly, the stakes are high for Regni. From Colorado Springs to Washington, the trail is scattered with air force careers that have been derailed or destroyed by the chronic excesses of the academy. The man Regni replaced, Lieutenant General John Rosa, had himself been brought in to run the academy after the sexual assault scandal of 2003 forced out his predecessor. In the 1990s, there were reports of widespread drug use, and in 1993, twenty-four cadets accused cadre of going overboard, by sexually assaulting them, during mandatory training in Survival, Evasion, Resistance and Escape (SERE). (The academy subsequently replaced the SERE program with another covering

Combat Survival Training, which did not address sexual assault.) All of this combined to make the academy possibly the most toxic assignment for a senior officer's career.

Regni looks at the faces—attentive, contemplative, bored—across the darkened room and says that he is aiming for "ten years of no news" on the academy. "One major misstep," he adds, "will put us back in the environment we were in in 2003."

Marcus, adjusting the binoculars she has brought, searches for her daughter and finds her as she marches out; Marcus recognizes her daughter despite the geeky goggles that Barrett is wearing. She watches her back as Barrett and all the other freshmen raise their right hands to take the honor oath:

> We will not lie, steal or cheat, nor tolerate among us anyone who does. Furthermore, I resolve to do my duty and to live honorably, so help me God.

Over the loudspeakers, the wing commander makes it official: "Class of 2010 accepted into the United States Air Force Academy cadet wing." Across the field, the cadets salute one another, white gloves rising like the crest of a wave.

The new cadets may have Recognition in their future, but so far, these kids don't have anything on the Class of 2008, Nick Mercurio says as everyone gets ready for the parade. This Beast had been tame, a lion on Valium, compared to what his class had gone through.

"We had the illusion of authority," Mercurio says to me. One day, an officer berated him for running his Basics to combat training. The officer said they were to run only if they were late. Worst of all, he had criticized Mercurio in front of the Basics.

"Sir, we're running so we won't be late," Mercurio had explained. "If we get there early, we have a few extra minutes." The officer didn't budge.

Where they're from: Basics parade out without shoulder boards.

Where they're going: Upperclassmen parade out to accept Basics into the wing. During the ceremony, upperclassmen change formation to open space for the wing's newest members.

Nick Mercurio pinning shoulder boards on Candy Vickroy.

Lance Watson congratulating Christopher Flynn on Acceptance Day.

Doolies get ordered down for a round of push-ups as family and friends look on.

Casey Jane Barrett with her mom, Terri Marcus, on Acceptance Day.

Thus, fuming and humiliated, Mercurio had had to march the Basics to combat training. Sure, that would toughen them up—but was that the sound of his authority grinding down under their boots?

How are the cadre supposed to do their job, Mercurio rages to himself, if the higher-ups just get in the way? He thinks of one Basic in Demons Squadron, not a future Bulldawg, who is clearly not cut out for the academy in the minds of the cadre. She breaks down, cries daily, and can't do the courses. She has to keep repeating the exercises. Mercurio and the other upperclassmen want to send her packing. Aside from doing the training, they believe that they are there to protect the academy by weeding out the kids who don't belong. "But we have to go through so many hoops," Mercurio says, and the cadre just give up. To the derision of the firsties and the two-degrees who have trained her, the young woman is getting her shoulder boards today along with the rest.

The academy brass sees it differently. The cadre are not quality-control agents, and leadership is not about predicting losers. Major Robert Scott MacKenzie, the air officer in charge of the Fighting Bulldawgs, argues that good cadre will not lose any Basics at all during Second Beast. The best leaders harness the strengths of those under them to serve the greater good. To MacKenzie, a Basic who bolts is a failure, not a triumph, of leadership.

Although MacKenzie's generosity—his belief in second chances and the capacity for redemption—rankles some cadets, it extends to the people directly under him: the upperclassmen, who will also find that when they stumble, his hand is there to help them up, not shove them out.

"If they've made it this far," MacKenzie says, "we want to keep them in."

Officially, the parade is meant to showcase the training, discipline, and precision that basic training has instilled in the hundreds of teenagers who were fresh out of high schools (and homeschools) across the country just a few weeks ago. In their predictability and ritual, the parade's marching, songs, and salutes can feel superficial, even numbing—as they seem to Barrett at this very moment.

But for all that, the parade pulls off something profound: it recognizes the significance of the Basics' efforts and of the journey they are joining. It gives form and dignity to the multitude of physical, intellectual, and psychological changes that have readied these nearly thirteen hundred cadets to take their places in the fabled long blue line.

Now, as the band plays, the Basics form an inverted V. The wedge marches toward the back of the field, where the sophomores, juniors, and seniors in blue—who just days before had been berating the freshmen and pounding them into submission—now open a space for them. Taking their places, the freshmen turn and face the stands where their parents watch and film this new stage in their lives. The four classes of cadets now form a single body.

Then, with a "Congratulations, and welcome to the Class of 2010," the ceremony is over, and the parents scamper across the field to watch as each squadron breaks up. For old times' sake, the upperclassmen order the freshmen down for a round of push-ups, right there on the parade grounds, as their parents watch. Then they are up again, standing at parade rest while juniors and seniors weave through the rows, pinning shoulder boards on the new cadets and offering a white-gloved handshake.

The four-digs, as the freshmen are now called, have chosen the upperclass cadets who will pin on their shoulder boards, and the pairings on the green tacitly reflect their measure of the men and women who have been training them.

Barrett has asked Lance Watson and Grace Anderson to tack on her shoulder boards. Christopher Flynn, David Urban's new roommate, has Watson and Miles-Tyson Blocker do his. Flynn likes Blocker, who would get genuinely upset sometimes on behalf of the Basics, and Watson, who, though tough, sweated right alongside them. "He's a great guy. He really cares about everyone," Flynn says.

Rhonda Meeker has chosen Blocker and Jamal Harrison, who is probably the most approachable of the upperclassmen and thus much in demand that morning.

After all the orders and abuse, of being limited to an infinitesimally small series of acceptable responses, the Basics feel the lowliness of their experience over the past few weeks begin to evaporate. There are still dozens of arcane rules they must follow—walking only along the perimeters of the terrazzo and the hallways, never carrying their backpacks on their shoulders, using only certain stairways and not others, and on and on—but at least they have their names back.

"One thousand three hundred ninety-five days to graduation," muses Harrison.

"So just to be safe," answers Blocker, his best friend, "call it infinity."

While the other doolies are spending the afternoon digging into their packages from home and buying supplies, Barrett enjoys nearly two hours at the hockey field house with her mother. As skaters slash over the ice rink, mother and daughter trade news.

"Oh, did you see this, Mom?" Barrett asks, pulling aside her shirt at the collar to show a raw pink patch by her neck. "My battle wound." On the firing range, the Basic next to Barrett had been firing away, and two shells from his M-16 had landed in Barrett's shirt. One had hit this spot, and the other had seared her back. Barrett had been in the middle of her own practice and had had only thirty seconds to shoot off twenty rounds. Thus, skin sizzling, she had kept on going, scoring twenty-five out of forty hits on a small target.

"What about the guy from Jamaica?" Terri asks. "Did even he make it?"

The cadet from Jamaica, Calvin Hunter, had been through basic training four times now: once with the Jamaica Defense Force, once at Lackland, where he had enlisted, once at the academy's prep school, and now at the academy itself.

"Uh huh," Barrett nods, biting into a hot dog her mother has brought over with giant sodas. "He even got a ride in an F-15 already," she says. Payson noses her way to the food. "No. Hey, that's not for you," Barrett says, pushing the dog's face away. On Barrett's birthday, Terri had sent her a card with Payson's paw print stamped in paint.

This year, the academy has given all the Basics the chance to ride in an air force plane, and most consider it the high point of their training. Barrett went up in a glider, riding in the front seat, with the real pilot in the seat behind, able to override any mistakes she might make. "I flew it," she tells her mother, smiling widely and pushing her glasses into place. "That was pretty cool."

The abrupt changes in altitude hit her in the gut, making her feel nauseated and woozy. She also went up with a handful of other cadets and a member of the academy's skydiving team, Wings of Blue. The Basics were all strapped up, wearing goggles and flight gear. The skydiver opened the door, and a gust of wind blew into the plane. "She sits on the edge, like, leaning there, and we take her legs, flipped her upside down and she went like that."

Marcus remembers having dinner at a restaurant after saying good-bye to Barrett the last time she was here. Marcus had sat next to an entire table of skydivers who had just come from jumping. She herself was on medication for her heart, a little tripped out, so it seemed almost dreamlike to her.

"They were so-o-o-o excited," Marcus recalls. "They're all talking about what fun they had, and they have this little glow in their eyes. I was not interested in talking to anybody but just, you know, just wanted to turn around and say, 'My daughter must feel that way.'"

The treat caused no small measure of resentment among the firsties and the two-degrees, however, because some of them had never flown in any air force plane, not even the gliders used for flight training here.

Barrett's stepfather, Jeff Marcus, fretted that basic training might prove too rough for Barrett. Now that fear is past. She had made it, despite the potholes along the way, surprising her stepfather and possibly herself. Barrett's mother worries more about the academic demands, the "pounding day in, day out." Barrett herself also fears that the course load might be too hard. As a student, she never did well without effort. Typically, she slogged through two or three hours of homework a night in high school. The discipline that she had established from that would serve her well here.

Now she is hoping that the speed-reading course she signed up for the day before will also help with her reading comprehension. In high school, she would read a passage and barely remember afterward what it said. When she took the SAT, her verbal scores paled in comparison to her performance in math, forcing her to retake the test three times. Given the academic load she was now facing, poor reading skills would be the academic equivalent of running up a down escalator: she'd work and work and get nowhere.

Even though Barrett and her mother are catching up like old friends, they do not share everything. That morning, Marcus confided to me that she is keeping secret the seriousness of a heart condition she had recently learned about. When Barrett first entered the academy, her mother had just had an angiogram.

"I told her, "It was awesome, everything went great. I didn't have any blockage,'" Marcus says. "She doesn't know yet that I have a leak between my valves. I don't want to tell her all that. This is not the time."

Marcus had even ignored her doctor's warnings about traveling to Colorado Springs when she brought her daughter here. They were worried about the altitude, but Marcus had been resolute. "I'd rather die. I'd rather go and let what's going to happen happen." She would not let her Casey Jane go without seeing her to the door of her new life.

For her part, Barrett does not confide, to her mother or anyone else, the uneasiness she is beginning to feel about her choice.

14 | Bernard's Knock

Brad Bernard is almost reconnected with the outside world, but not quite. He pokes away at the Gateway laptop he's just been issued, trying every possible combination he can remember to unlock it: 257? No. Tap, tap, tap. 000? Not that, either. Tap, tap, tap. 200? He's still locked out. He puts his hands to his head and looks down at the keyboard, as if trying to shake the code from his brain.

"Man," he says, the accent from his native Georgia stretching out the word. Why are even the simple things so hard here? He pushes himself away from the desk, disappearing into the hall to search for help.

In a crowd that is united by a common passion for things skybound—planes, satellites, and spaceships—Bernard has more earthbound dreams. He does not see himself as a modern-day ace, a cargo pilot, or even a video jock controlling drones from a terminal somewhere closer to home. Tall and hard-bodied, with shoulders so broad they look as if they are meant for decorations, Bernard came here to play football—or so he believes.

As a defensive lineman in high school, Bernard had little help when it came to choosing a college. His best friend, also a defensive lineman, headed off to the Naval Academy prep school at Annapolis. Bernard had zero interest in spending five years on a boat. He did, however, like to ski, and he has a friend in Montana whom he visits every summer for trout fishing.

Bernard had spent last year at the academy's prep school before finding his way to Squadron 13, along with Zach Taylor, another football player at the prep school. Of the prep school's initial class of 212, only 178 made it to graduation, and 165 went on to join the academy. Even the ones who could not keep up the minimum grade point average made it to graduation—an important lesson for Bernard. If he just kept showing up, even if he fell shy here and there, he could make it. Of course, he had to also show that he was trying, but the limits of that could be tested. Five recruited quarterbacks had started out with him at the prep school. Every one of them had quit.

Now that Bernard is here at the academy, he wonders why—not, like every other freshman, from time to time, but every day, from the instant his eyes pop open to the moment he drops off to sleep. With few exceptions, he is frustrated by what he sees as the poor leadership of the upperclassmen, and he doubts, after all, that he will be able to play his best ball here. On game day, he believes, there will be so many demands on the athletes' minds that they will have trouble focusing, despite sidestepping much of the physical and military training required of ordinary cadets.

"That's why you can't get the athletes out here, because they don't want to go through all this," he says. His indecision comes across as indifference, irking the upperclassmen. His fellow freshmen are not sure what to make of him. Some resent his ability to speak his mind, if only just privately to them, and to get away with that attitude. Some marvel at his encounters with the upperclassmen with a dark fascination, as if watching two cars about to crash. When others sit up, he leans back. When they snap to attention, he rolls his aquamarine eyes.

The other day, Bernard saw one of the cadre, perhaps overwhelmed by the training regimen, lean over and throw up on the terrazzo. A few minutes later, he recalled, a Basic did the same, and the same upperclassman "jumped all over him," hollering at him for being weak.

Just the day before, he'd been with a group of other freshmen, leaving the library for the dining hall. On the way there, the upperclassman who was training them had the four-digs wait while the other flights marched in. His was one of the last flights in. After waiting in line for their food, the freshmen had hardly any time to eat. Their escort had fifteen minutes—a relative oasis of time.

"But his people didn't get to eat," Bernard says, his voice rising at the memory. He looks at his hands, opening them as if in apology. "That's the one thing about being an officer: you have to take care of your people. That comes first and foremost. The people, enlisted people, are what make the air force. The officers just sit back and tell them what to do, but they're what's running the air force.

"It is a big deal to us when you realize that your leader is not looking after his people," Bernard continues. As angry and frustrated as he is, though, he will not complain openly about it, at least not yet. "We don't have a say in it," he contends, running a hand through the blond bristles on his head. His cheeks are flushed. "If you do say it here, in this place, it does no good for you. They won't change it. They'll just look out for you more when you're walking, to try to find you making a mistake."

Unlike the cadets who have had generations of family members before them in uniform, Bernard has nobody back home to offer perspective or advice. His parents are divorced, and his mother struggles to pay the bills. His father, he says, has been in and out of jail for drunk driving and for beating up his family. Bernard didn't just leave home for school, he fled it.

"If my parents had money, I wouldn't be here," he says. "No one in my family knows what I'm going through here." It is the truth for many a cadet—not only here but at the other academies as well. However, few say it quite that bluntly.

Nevertheless, he does not leave, and it is not only because of the money. When he went home from prep school for Thanksgiving last year, he couldn't connect with his old high school friends, with their tales of partying and campus life, and the trials of prep school seemed alien to them. "This place kind of grows on you," he says, tilting his head as if mystified himself by the admission.

If Rhonda Meeker had arrived at the academy determined to do more and be better than anyone else, at least outwardly, Bernard is her opposite.

Outwardly, he is perhaps the freshman least eager to succeed, Squadron 13's doubtful warrior.

Yet he is also the one who is most likely to notice any unfairness leveled at his comrades and to be bothered by it. Others, when they see an upperclassman rage at a fellow Basic, are more likely to blame the freshman, to find an error or a flaw in the actions of the underling that must have set off the explosion. Bernard doesn't share the reflexive tendency to accommodate the powerful. It seems almost as if he doesn't care, one way or the other, about rank.

He chose Lance Watson and Blake Turnquist, a two-degree from Minnesota and a forward on the academy's hockey team, to pin on his shoulder boards. Watson was always tanned. He worked out with weights, and with his chin high, he seemed to exude confidence—but that was not why Bernard gave him the only personal tribute it was in his possession to offer. "He took care of his people," Bernard says simply. "He would never have done what that cadre did at the dining hall."

Is Bernard simply a slacker who aims to float above freshman year, a kid scarred by a troubled home who has come to mistrust authority in any form? Or is there germinating, under all that attitude, the seeds of a true leader? For the upperclassmen, and even for Bernard himself, it is too early to know.

Like Meeker, however, he has not escaped notice.

15 | Meeker's Fall

The first time Rhonda Meeker hit the assault course, she felt turbocharged, propelled by that cadre who'd urged her on as "an eighty-pound ball of piss and vinegar." On the training courses, that same upperclasswoman told other cadre to watch out for Meeker, then she smiled at Meeker one day in the lunch line. Meeker wondered if that counted as fraternization, which is officially banned, but she figured that friends are always good—especially since she doesn't really have any. "She's pretty cool," Meeker says.

But by the time that Demons A Flight faced the assault course the second time, four days later, Meeker's spirits were sinking, and the early attention began to boomerang. She had an almost constant headache, and her throat burned, swollen and sore. She could barely speak, let alone sound off with her original gusto. She coughed up gobs of green phlegm. Her chest felt packed in wet cotton: thick, damp, and opaque.

Already petite when she started at the academy, Meeker had begun losing weight, about a pound every other day. She dragged herself through the exercises—the tunnel, the muddy trench, the coils of barbed wire—as though she were barely there. Meeker's sudden downward shift caught the attention of her trainers, some of whom mistrusted her; they'd interpreted her earlier eagerness to please as showboating, as glorifying herself, instead of thinking about others.

Meeker doesn't count many buddies among her fellow Basics in Demons A Flight. Instead, she seems to have a knack for alienating her peers, sometimes openly putting them down, sometimes pronouncing her opinions like edicts. On her second go-through on the A-course that day, each step brought criticism and orders to do the obstacle again—not once, not twice, but three or four times in each instance.

With only Tylenol to fight the pain and the throbbing in her head, Meeker didn't understand where she was going wrong, and nobody would tell her. Whatever she tried, it was not good enough. If somebody would just explain what they wanted from her, she kept thinking, but nobody bothered to do so. Instead, the cadre ordered her to do each obstacle again, over and over. That just enraged her.

Frustrated, she trembled on the edge, fed up and wanting only for the pain to stop, when one of the assault-course cadre ordered her to repeat an obstacle one more time. That was when Meeker crossed a line—the Basic's equivalent of jumping without a parachute. She turned to the cadre who was haranguing her, and shouted, "Why don't you leave me the fuck alone?"

"You don't fuckin' talk to me that way," the cadre roared back. Grenades were exploding all around, and smoke clouds and sirens were blaring to simulate warfare. Instead of punishing Meeker, the cadre did something worse: he ordered all her flight mates down, beating them, instead of her, with push-ups and squats and sit-ups, while he hollered at her. Five times he made them run up the hill with all their gear, weighed down with mud and water, and run down in a squatting position. "From then on, it was a blur," she says.

Meeker might as well have fallen seven thousand feet to the floor of the Grand Canyon and had to get up and walk, crushed bones and all, because this transgression will be picked up and repeated among the upperclassmen as the year unwinds and will hobble her journey through freshman year long after basic training ends. The wounds will heal, but the scarring will be long and painful.

Her flight mates raged at her afterward for her explosion. "Why'd you give up?" they hollered.

"It's bad enough I've got them shouting at me," Meeker fired back, as if indifferent to the suffering she'd brought on her flight mates. "I don't need you shouting at me, too."

At Jacks, she roomed in a tent—her bed apart, in a corner—with about half a dozen women, who thought her an alien creature. Now the anger boils over as she explains how the women ganged up on her. "The boys pulled them off me," she says. "I haven't got any friends here. I'm not going to have friends here. I'll have acquaintances."

"I've never been very submissive to authority. I don't like authority, especially when it's exercised in ways I don't agree with," Meeker says. She'd grown frustrated and had lost her temper when she cursed at the cadre. She can explain, but does not defend, what she did.

"I wanted the pain to stop. I guess everybody did. There's really no excuse for it," she says, polishing her black patent lace-ups with cotton balls before an inspection and the Acceptance Parade. "I was the only one who was having these problems. I don't know what was wrong with me that wasn't wrong with them."

She has not seen any sign of sexual assault or of higher-ups forcing religious dogma on the students—the scandals of recent years that have tainted the academy's reputation—but for the first time, Meeker says, she can understand how such things might have happened. So thrilled by the academy at the start, she has now glimpsed the world beyond the polish and platitudes, and she senses something dark and potentially menacing: if she challenged her superiors, whatever the circumstances, she would lose.

For the first time, she thinks about the scores of women who reported being raped at the academy a few years ago. Despite the official insistence on reporting such crimes, she confides that she would not speak up if she were attacked. Her eyes seem vulnerable and defiant at the same time, and I realize that in the theater of her mind, she has been playing scenes of "what if?" "I hope I can defend myself if I ever have to," she says.

"You've got to stay off the radar," she warns. She senses a tension, especially around the upperclassmen who are vested with the most authority, and the whiff of danger. "They are definitely college kids with too much power."

Her flight mates, especially the women, do not worry about somebody else hurting Meeker, but they see her moods, a certain angry look she would shoot at the cadre when she neared her limit. They see her misery, hear her sob that she cannot leave, that she has no place else to go. More than anything else, they fear that she might hurt herself.

As sure as she has been that she belongs at the academy, others are suddenly equally determined to force her out. One upperclassman and one officer start to track her every move, telling her that she does not belong here, threatening to start the paperwork to remove her. "Give us a reason to not kick you out," they tell her.

"I had people talking to me every other day. That's when I understood and became submissive," Meeker recalls. "I'd say, 'I want to be here. Don't send me home.' I need to be here. It's not like I'm doubting that.

"The cadre are like normal people. They want to laugh. They want order in their lives. They're just like us, but they have rank, and they expect a certain deference because of it. I asked why. That was my problem. Why? They noticed right away that I have this defiant attitude." She shakes her head, vexed that she had missed something so obvious. "I realized too late that they needed me to break."

Watching the MySpace fiasco, Meeker blames both the freshmen, who were naive and arrogant enough to publicly insult their trainers before even getting here, and the cadre, who were determined to humiliate those freshmen. The whole episode, she believes, has taken on more importance than it deserves, and it does not speak well of either side. The cadre seem determined to ride the kids who had posted on MySpace, singling them out, forcing them to do extra push-ups, and generally making their initiation into cadet life as tough as they had accused the upperclassmen of being weak. The cadre speak of correcting an attitude of arrogance, but in unguarded moments they also talk of having broken the MySpace freshmen with a sense of accomplishment.

"See, it's bullshit like that," Meeker declares. "This place isn't what it seems. Like, I know I came here with this illusion that 'Oh, my God, I'm going to the academy. Everybody here is going to be absolutely straight and uptight.' And you know, as anal as I am, it's going to be so military. Nothing's going to go wrong, and I'm not going to have to deal with bullshit."

She rubbed her arms, as if shivering from a sudden gust. "We got high school here, definitely." A few weeks before, she had told Jesse Ziegler, her squadron commander, about a personal issue in confidence. Immediately, he wrote it up in a memo, which landed in her personnel file, read by all the cadre, and the officers overseeing her squadron.

Now the kids are gossiping about it. Meeker feels betrayed but says nothing. "I can't call him out on it," she says. She worries that this disclosure will follow her throughout her air force career, and she wants to get the memo pulled from her file. Ziegler, for his part, was just following the rules.

Watching the cadre, she can figure out which ones are dating each other, which ones are flirting with each other. There's a feel of high school about the place, with kids gossiping and spreading rumors. All of this shrinks their once God-like stature in her eyes. "It's not all bad; kids like to have fun." She looks up and then away. "But there's definitely some disillusionment."

Although she was fuming at Ziegler for betraying her trust by telling senior officers about the hardships of her background, those very hardships had most likely saved her military career. The insubordination, under the circumstances, would ordinarily have gotten Meeker bounced out of boot camp in a hurry, but the senior officers who were deciding her fate knew that she had survived harrowing, chaotic moments in her childhood. Her drive, they realized, is fierce. Furthermore, by her own admission, she has no place to go from here. "That's why they didn't send her home, because they do think of that," Casey Jane Barrett says.

Lately, Meeker has begun replaying in her mind her own training of the kids in her high school's Junior ROTC program. "I had my own little power trips—not like getting them to do push-ups or beating them, but other things. I taught them harshly, and there was no need for that," she says now.

She watches her roommate, Nicole Elliott, quiet and unassuming. You'd never suspect it to look at her, but she scored 500 on her physical fitness test. "You don't toot your own horn," says Meeker, who had finished with 249, just shy of passing. "Do your best and shut up about it," she says, shaking her head. "It'll get around."

Later, going through the lunch line, she looks like a convalescent, shrunk in herself, joyless and measured in step and in word. Several times, she mentions being moved by the civilians who turn out to cheer on the cadets. "They don't know me from anybody, yet they came out, and they're waving, they're happy for us. It's humbling, because you don't know if you have it in you to live up to that. I don't know."

We inch our way through the line. Meeker doesn't take any milk. At the table, she eats only half of her sandwich and doesn't touch her cookies, her apple, or her fruit juice. Wordlessly, she gets up from the table, which brings her a reprimand, swift and sharp, and an order to go back to the table and try it again. The academy spokesman who has to keep me in his sight, Captain Uriah Orland, Class of 2002, and Cadet Captain Jonathan Elliott ask Meeker where she's going. Three weeks ago, she would have sounded off, loud and proud. Now she stares blankly at them, uncomprehending.

"I saw my classmates leaving. Sir, I followed my classmates," she says.

"What are you supposed to do?" Elliott asks.

Brad Bernard towers behind Meeker. He hunches slightly, whispering at the back of her head, "You have to ask to be excused." She turns to look at him, grateful for the kindness, but also aware that Bernard—mindful of his value as an athlete—openly disdains the rules and seems to get away with it.

Meeker then faces Elliott and Orland. "I should have asked to be excused, sir," she says quietly. She then goes back to her chair, asks to be excused, and is given permission to join her classmates who are heading out the door.

"This humility thing is killing me," she says. "I come here and I get somebody like Elliott, who's so sarcastic. No matter what comes out of his mouth, I always hear 'I'm better than you, and I know it.'"

At the Acceptance Parade the next morning, Meeker faces Miles-Tyson Blocker and Jamal Harrison as they pin on her shoulder boards. Harrison and Blocker, the only two African American cadre in Bulldawg Squadron, are serious but not intimidating, shunning the power-trip aspect of boot camp. They soften the rough edges with a laugh, throwing Meeker quiet advice when she needs it. They too poked fun during First and Second Beast, using sarcasm to prod and mock the kids along with the rest, but their advice and instruction were not cruel. They were aimed more at keeping the Basics on track than on dominating their will.

As they pin on her shoulder boards, Meeker does not crack a smile but looks straight and serious, hands behind her at parade rest, her blue dress cap low over her eyes.

"Does it feel good?" Harrison asks.

"Yes, sir," she answers.

"It should."

"You got a good head on your shoulders," Blocker tells her. "Just watch yourself, and you'll be fine."

Meeker is still unsmiling, but something glimmers in her eyes now. "Sir, may I make an extraneous movement?" she asks.

Harrison lifts an eyebrow and quirks his head.

"Sir, may I do a shoulder board dance?" Meeker asks.

Harrison gives permission and steps back.

She raises one shoulder, then the other, her new shoulder boards rising and falling like a seesaw, with her head the fulcrum—an awkward happy dance of inner exultation to music playing in her bones.

Harrison erupts in laughter, shaking his head. "No, you're supposed to look at the shoulder boards when you do that," he protests.

"I love to dance," Meeker says, smiling now.

Blocker looks over the rows of new cadets, with their newly minted shoulder boards, looking dazed at the free hours ahead of them. "You're all Fighting Bulldawgs now," he says. "Those gears haven't turned for a while. You're used to us telling you where to go and when."

Afterward, the cadre who had called Meeker "piss and vinegar" seeks her out. Her name is Casey Bayne, and she is a varsity javelin thrower from El Segundo, California, who started out playing soccer. Tall, blond, and cheerful, she comes over to welcome Meeker into the cadet wing and to shake her hand. "You made it," she says. Meeker nods, pumping her hand back.

"That's what sees me through," Meeker says, as Bayne walks off. She thinks of the encouraging strangers at church on Sunday, who had offered bagels and Starbucks coffee and had handed over their cell phones for the Basics to use to call home. "They're so proud of you," Meeker says, even though they'd never met the Basics before. She smiles, and dimples appear, like unexpected sweetness.

Meeker looks down at her shoulder boards, and the defeat that has been weighing her steps seems to be gone. "My proudest moment is getting these," she says, and looks up to see her classmates' parents and friends hugging them. She is seventeen years old, and her parents and friends are not here. Harrison and Blocker have moved off. She turns to the list of things she must do today: deposit a check; buy a phone card, school supplies, new underwear, and skin lotion; and tack up pictures of friends on her bulletin board. These are all freedoms that she has been denied for six weeks and has now "earned" back. She stops and looks across the academy's campus.

"Okay," she says. "Clean slate."

16 | Back from the Pit

Before Meeker's elation bubbles over into her shoulder board two-step, Harrison says something else to her. As he stands in the sunshine looking at her face, her jaw set and her eyes intent, the two seem to be a study in contrasts: Meeker, still shaken from her basic training ordeal, and Harrison, broad-shouldered and muscular, with angular good looks and a steady eye. What they have in common is not just their uniforms—dress blues, hats low over their foreheads—but the fear of falling off. Speaking quietly, he tells her not to confuse the present with the future, despite the roller coaster that has all but thrown her out of boot camp.

"You're going to have other times, in academics or sports, where you're going to have your mountain covered and you're going to come out on top," Harrison offers. He remembers his own spin at boot camp as a freshman, stoked with doubts and sure he would mess up. There were upperclassmen who had taken him aside when they saw him weakening to say, "You can push through that."

This lesson, that just a few words can build or break a world struggling to form, has stayed with him, making him something like the patron saint of kids who skid late into the formation or who tremble through one more dressing-down—which is just about every new face in Squadron 13 those first six weeks. "I'm just one example you can fall back on. I didn't think I could do this, but look at me now," he tells Meeker.

As a cadre, Harrison himself came screeching into leadership training—the course that prepares the juniors for their role over the Basics—only two weeks before the freshmen had arrived. He could not start with everyone else five weeks earlier, because he was busy trying to salvage his position after a disastrous spring semester. His grandmother in Texas, who had reared him, had died that spring, and his mother, who was already mentally fragile, was falling apart. Harrison could barely see through his worry and grief, let alone concentrate on his course work. In an environment not given to gratuitous praise, where popularity ratings remain irrelevant to a professor's standing, Harrison's grade point average reflected the sudden crisis that consumed him. It practically defied gravity, and certainly probability, sinking to an astonishing 0.8.

Of course, the dreaded notice followed soon afterward. "You have been recommended for disenrollment," it said. For a moment, Harrison felt his insides chill and close in on him. His heart raced. The notice sent him falling through a well of mirrored walls, dropping him into a pit. "It might as well have said, 'You just lost your spot at the academy. You just lost your spot at what you're going to do the rest of your life.'"

Harrison is no flight jock: blood, not jet fuel, runs through his veins, and he is not here to become a pilot. Aside from the academy, he applied only to civilian campuses: the University of Texas at Austin, Texas Tech University, Texas A&M University, and Oklahoma State University. He had attended a Catholic high school, graduating with a mediocre grade point average of 2.8 or 2.9 and an SAT score of about 1060. All the places to which he applied, except for UT-Austin, had accepted him, but when the financial aid offers came in, the family just couldn't do it.

The academy had come through as a great surprise. Given his grades, Harrison had been hoping at best for a slot at the prep school, where he would have a year to get into shape for the military and the educational demands of the academy. Thus he was thrilled. Here money was not an issue; the taxpayers cover tuition, fees, and room and board for every student. In addition, the cadets earn a modest stipend each month at the academy. He could graduate debt-free, with a bit of money in the bank, a great education, and a career lined up.

The warning that he might get kicked out came just weeks before commitment: the formal deadline, just before junior year, for cadets to drop out without having to pay back the government for their education. If Harrison had left then, he could have transferred his credits to a civilian university and would not have had to pay anything for the first two years of his college education. After commitment, any cadet who does not make it to graduation must pay the government back, at a cost that can can reach nearly $164,000. Thus, cadets who do not think they will make it to graduation are better off never coming back after sophomore year.

But that was not where Harrison's heart was going. He wanted to stay. The letter forced him to set aside the pain and trouble that was engulfing him, focus on his own threatened demise, and weigh his choices in an almost coldhearted way. If he gave in to the sorrow and mayhem, where would he be? His grandmother would still be gone; his mother would pull herself together, or not. But if Harrison lost his spot at the academy, he told himself, "I wouldn't have anything to hold onto."

In a sense, the warning made him turn away from the family drama, shove it high on a closet shelf, and slam the door shut, in order to focus on saving his future. Harrison tried to think past the memories, the hopes, and the fears roiling inside him, and he understood that as raw and worried as he was, it really all hardened into a single question: "What can I do if I want to stay?"

Harrison sat down with Major Robert MacKenzie, the helicopter pilot who was his squadron's air officer command, and Master Sergeant Mark Winter, the squadron's military trainer, for what Harrison calls a "come to Jesus meeting."

"Whoa. What's going on here?" Sergeant Winter asked. Harrison explained the turmoil at home but did not dwell on it. Instead, he pledged to put it aside and concentrate on his course work. "I can recover from this," he promised. If they had any doubts about him, this was the moment to boot him out, but they didn't. Instead, he recalls, they mapped out a way to help him, advising him to take a summer seminar and to prepare his best case to convince an academic review committee to give him a second chance.

"Right now, your head's on the chopping block," they told him. "You've got to put yourself in a position for them to have a justification to give you the break you want." They forced him to drop every extracurricular activity, including orchestra, in which he played saxophone and clarinet, and the drum and bugle corps, in which he played bugle, to work solely on boosting his academic performance.

"You're a really good kid," Major MacKenzie told him. "We want you back next semester."

Harrison's gift, although he would never put it this way himself, is an ability to shrink his ego down to human size—a rare skill at an academy where half the class sees itself behind the cockpit of flying fortresses worth hundreds of millions of dollars. When he had to arrive weeks late at the cadre course, he had had the humility to acknowledge his shortcomings before Lance Watson, his boss during First Beast. "I know that it isn't the ideal situation, but I'm here to work, and I can give you what I can," Harrison said.

At the training for cadre, he volunteered for every demonstration, knowing that he would appear clueless to his comrades. For all of them, the three or four days before the first Basics turned up at Doolie Hall was a refresher course. "For me, it was a crash course," Harrison recalls. The training showed him the vast difference between, for instance, marching and teaching marching to somebody who knew nothing about military practices. If he told the kids, "You're out of track," for example, they would not understand his meaning: that they were not marching in neatly formed lines. He had to learn to take the pieces of marching and break them down into everyday words.

As a two-degree, Harrison thinks of himself as poised at dead center. He is no longer a sophomore—just learning, watching, and coaching, but not really in charge of anybody other than himself. Nor is he yet a firstie, familiar with the routine and leading other students. He is taking the reins for the very first time, not just in training the Basics, but also with the sophomores, or three-degrees, all of whom are new to Squadron 13. It is not necessarily hard, but it is alien, "almost uncomfortable," he says.

The shouting, the sarcasm, and the constant put-downs—the trademarks of boot camp for Demons A Flight this year—are not part of Harrison's normal makeup. By nature, he is more circumspect and sensitive, and the memory of his own terror at basic training is too fresh for him to revel in razzing kids who are just trying to make it.

"Am I doing this right?" he recalls asking himself constantly. "I don't really know. Okay, I'll try this and see if it works. Okay, that doesn't work. I won't do that again."

Some of his fellow cadre holler constantly at the Basics. That isn't him, nor is that necessarily bad, in Harrison's eyes. He can see the need for a mix of different personalities and types during Beast, much as the cadets will confront in the active-duty air force after leaving the academy. "It's kind of figuring out who you are and how you can best contribute. Because for some people, the best way they can contribute is to yell, and they're just going to be that guy—tough and overbearing."

At some point, Harrison and Watson see what a hard time some of the kids, especially Meeker, are having. "We just kind of flipped the switch from 'Do this, do this, do this, do this,' you know, making it hard on them, to having a heart and soul," he says in retrospect. "To trying to relate to the person and trying to make them see that, 'Hey, as much as I am yelling and screaming, I am a person, I do care about you, and I'm doing it for you.'"

Meeker, he believes, deserves to make it. He is 99.9 percent sure that she will prevail and will graduate from the academy one day—not because she is intrinsically more talented, stronger, or smarter than anybody else, but because she wants it more. Like the bulldog that is Squadron 13's emblem, Meeker grabs hold of an assignment and never gives up. It was the first thing Harrison noticed about her during basic training, and it impressed him. "If you called her out on something, she would do it and do it and do it until she got it right. She would have an attitude while she was doing it, but she would do it."

Although the upperclassmen and the officers have been dogging her every step, most are not really out to boot her. "Deep down, everybody knows that [Meeker] is capable of making it," Harrison says. "She has everything she needs to do it, but she has an attitude problem. I don't think these people are riding her to get her to fail." He shakes his head once. "Totally different."

Harrison has almost no attitude, so he can see, more clearly than most, perhaps, how Meeker's mental stance is bound to trip her up. He himself still does not feel totally in the clear. If he does not boost his academic standing substantially, he can tumble backward and perhaps lose his shot at graduation. Lieutenant General John Regni might have meant well with the more regimented schedule he has instituted, but it gives Harrison and his fellow upperclassmen less latitude for managing their workload.

"You know what this place is all about?" Harrison asks. "Putting people in a position to say you have to—I don't want to say fail—but you have to give one hundred percent to A, one hundred percent to B, one hundred percent to C.

"Now, what are you going to do?"

17 | Barrett's Roar

The doubts start creeping over Casey Jane Barrett as soon as she slows down, upon her flight's return to the dorms from Jacks Valley. During basic training and boot camp at Jacks, the regimen, the orders, and the reams of air force facts and lore that she had to learn had all overwhelmed her, crowding out any deeper thoughts. From the moment she woke until she fell asleep—usually on the floor, so her bed would be neat in the morning—she focused on avoiding notice by the cadre, and on following the narrow set of rules that covered everything from showering to walking.

As long as the Basics were at Jacks, the regimen and the unrelenting orders aimed at remaking her somehow seemed apart from the flow of her life—a discrete experience, like summer camp, that would end soon. It is only upon their return, with a few days to unwind before their formal acceptance as cadets at the academy, that she begins to wonder whether she belongs here at all.

Barrett realizes, to her surprise, that the cadre are not officers but cadets just like her—college students—who will live down the corridor from her the entire year. "This isn't just summer. It's the same now. It continues on," she thinks. Something clenches inside her gut.

She doesn't share these thoughts with anybody just now. Her mother flies in from home, for just a few hours with her. Her shoulders thrust back as she stands next to Barrett for pictures, Terri Marcus holds on to her daughter as if she were a living, breathing Academy Award. She glows, electric with love and pride. They spend no small share of their few hours together swapping gossip and planning ahead for Casey Jane to visit at Thanksgiving, three and a half months away.

How could she speak up?

Barrett herself doesn't know what to make of her feelings at first. As a teenager, her father had applied to the academy but didn't make it. She, however, had made it. She suspects him of living vicariously through her, enjoying every detail of her journey toward becoming a full-fledged cadet. She has become a local celebrity: her picture appeared in her community newspaper—long straight hair, untroubled face, optimistic smile—with a story about her admission. Another boy in the neighborhood had once gotten as far as enrolling in the academy, but he ended up coming home. She is the one who will make it through.

Three days before her mother stretches the banner across the bleachers in the early morning sun, Barrett begins to feel a wave of horror. She thought she had competed for college and won the sweepstakes: a tuition-free education at one of the country's top institutions of higher education. Now she sees that she has not chosen a college but a way of life—one that she does not particularly like.

"If I still feel this way at Parents' Weekend" a month away, Barrett thinks, hugging her mother in the hockey field house, "I'll talk to her about it."

What would she say?

So many things hit her, but not all at once. Bit by bit, disturbing thoughts—realizations, actually—creep up on her. She had come to the academy to study aerospace engineering, but now she worries about flunking. Her military score is below par, dragged down by endless "knowledge" tests demanding instant recall of arcane facts about planes, the air force, and the academy's history. A future pilot, she had imagined, learns some of this by osmosis: The architecture and technical specifications of planes fascinate her; theoretically, at least, her life could one day hang on such knowledge.

Barrett can't seem to memorize the details, however, and she suspects, at bottom, that she just isn't deeply interested. Now she is considering dropping aerospace engineering for something easier—maybe foreign area studies? "Great," she thinks. "I'm losing that already, because I'm afraid of failing."

She rankles under the unrelenting energy that goes into remaking her. This concerted effort to stamp out her personality feels like brainwashing. She can understand the rationale for the wholesale molding of individuals into a corps, but Barrett likes herself and doesn't really want to change. She does not mind improving herself here and there; she is glad, for example, that she no longer wastes hours each day on television, trotting off to bed at two o'clock in the morning and waking up when most people are sitting down to lunch. What bothers her is that the inner qualities she prizes, such as her spontaneity and warmth, are also going. She had entered the academy a happy, confident, optimistic, and friendly woman, who had been raised on love, not force. Now she feels small, ill-timed, and unsure of herself, as if somebody should be yelling at her all the time.

Barrett looks around at the upperclassmen. She admires their strength, their dedication, and most of all, their cohesion. All of this comes at a price, she thinks. She is trading in pieces of herself, and has already done so in basic training, to become like them. Who would she be in five years? Ten years? Where would she be? Once the shouting lets up, she realizes, to her astonishment, that nothing in her wants to actually become part of their world.

The first person she confides her feelings to is Rebecca Rasweiler-Richter, her roommate. Rasweiler-Richter, a gymnast from Greenwich, Connecticut, comes back to their room and finds Barrett in tears. Rasweiler-Richter's family is as supportive and encouraging as Barrett's, and she cannot imagine wanting to leave. She loves being at the academy and is surpassing every test. "I don't really know what to say," she tells Barrett. "I want you to stay, of course, but you have to do what you want to do."

There. That was not too hard. All Barrett has to do is speak up.

If a cadet screams in the corridors and nobody hears her, will she stay on track?

Barrett does not make it until Parents' Weekend in early September. As soon as her mother arrives home from Acceptance Day, Barrett starts sending her e-mails. She has never failed at anything before. This time, she hasn't exactly failed; she did survive the crucible of basic training. Nevertheless, she fears that her parents will see walking away as a kind of failure.

"I'm having second thoughts," she tells her mother, vague and tentative at first. She describes the growing anxiety, the looming sense that this life, this place, is not for her. She has made it through basic training. She is not wimping out, but this is not the life she wants. She wants to come home.

"Why?" her mother asks, for the first of many times, reminding Barrett of how happy she had been to get in. "Why?" ask both her father and her stepfather. Terri Marcus's family accuses her of saying something when she visited Barrett to make her want to come home. "I said nothing to her," Marcus protests.

Barrett cannot articulate the reasons—not for her mother, not for any of them. She is not entirely sure herself why she feels so certain she does not belong at the academy. Which of the many pieces that are shifting to form her growing conviction are decisive? Even she cannot say.

Her parents once again turn to the support network of other academy parents, just as they had done when Barrett called home sick during basic training. The other parents had warned the Marcuses that this would happen, that freshmen inevitably lose resolve at one moment or another and want to give up. Once again, their advice comes down to "no surrender." Your job as parents, they counsel, is to keep your child in the academy. Do not give in. They will thank you, eventually.

Parents around the country rally to help Terri Marcus keep her daughter from quitting the academy. They call their children, most of them in their last two years at the academy, safely past the Bermuda Triangle that is swallowing up Barrett's resolve. "There's a four-degree who's having trouble," the parents say. "Go and talk to her." They do, again and again. One father sends Marcus two lengthy e-mails. He had helped his daughter through the same sort of crisis two years earlier, and she is still at the academy, on her way to graduating now.

"I want to leave," Barrett writes home, again and again.

"You can do it," her mother writes back. "You can get through this."

Though once so close to her mother, Barrett now rages against her, blaming her for dismissing a decision that is not fleeting but that springs from who Barrett is. Of course getting into the academy had been a great achievement, an honor even, but it is not for her anymore. How can her mother, her closest friend, not understand? How can she try to steamroll Barrett into a future she does not want?

Barrett turns to her stepmother, with whom she has never been close; she writes her an e-mail saying that she has made a mistake in going to the academy.

"Oh, you know, I had a feeling," she tells Barrett, adding, "You know what? I don't care what you do, as long as you're happy."

"I feel like you're the only one who's actually listening to me right now," Barrett writes back.

Her father, though, glimpses that e-mail and grows exasperated. "'I'm listening to you,'" Barrett imitates him saying, her voice whispering and hollering at the same time.

Her mother tracks down the two-degree whom Barrett had shadowed on her initial visit to the academy and asks her to talk her daughter out of quitting. "You need to stay," the upperclasswoman tells Barrett. Suck it up and stop this nonsense, she says, in effect. "Right now."

"I know I'm not happy," Barrett pleads. "I know who I am, and this is not me. This is someone else." She sobs, saying that she does not want to grow into the person the air force wants her to be; it is not the adult she hopes to become. She could put up with all the work, the beating, and the regimentation. It's not that she *can't* handle it. She does not *want* to follow the road this training is taking her down.

By the end of her talk with the two-degree, Barrett has convinced her. "Wow," the upperclasswoman says finally. "You should go home."

Seeing how miserable she is, her eyes red and sometimes tearing up in the hallways, Major Robert MacKenzie talks to her like a friend rather than her military superior, trying to help her find her way forward. He lends her his cell phone, letting her take it to her room and talk privately with her family.

"You know what?" he says. "Ring up the bill. I don't care." He tells everybody in the squadron what she's going through, easing the pressure on her.

Even Cadet Captain Jonathan Elliott comes by. There is no sarcasm in his voice, no wisecracks or put-downs. He has seen how hard she has tried, and he thinks she would make a fine cadet.

"I don't want you to leave," he says. "I'm sorry it didn't work out."

Talking about her feelings to so many people does not make Barrett doubt her choice; rather, it refines her understanding of why she should leave and ultimately bolsters her decision. On her academy-issued laptop, Barrett researches which community colleges would still accept her for the fall semester.

It is somewhat maddening to her that people inside the academy—her cadet trainers, her classmates, and the officers—actually understand her decision to walk away from military life. They credit her with trying it out.

"You can't tell, really, until you're there, and sometimes it really just doesn't work out," Elliott tells her.

Adrian Peppers, a twenty-six-year-old who is the cadet squadron commander for the fall semester, even applauds her resolve. "The fact of the matter is, the Air Force Academy, the military, is not for everybody," he says. "It takes a lot of courage to make that decision."

Her family, however, continues to see her as squandering an opportunity.

After ten days, Barrett begins the paperwork to leave ("out-process," in the military's elegant parlance), seeing all the people on an air force–issued checklist in about two days instead of the usual three. At the obligatory counseling session, the therapist does not try to steer Barrett into staying, and she lends her a phone to call home. She only wants assurance that nothing has happened at the academy to push Barrett out.

Barrett eventually grows so frustrated in her quest for approval from her parents that she gives up trying. Quitting might never be all right with them. Instead of giving in, she tells her family that she is coming home—period. She gives them the date and the flight number. "I will be at Los Angeles airport," she tells them. "If you're not there, I'll take a cab and come home."

Her mother yields first. If there was any way to keep her daughter at the academy, she had tried it. The support and the willingness to help from the community of kindred souls she had tapped into awed and moved her. Marcus loved being part of this coast-to-coast network of parents, but she realizes that this is not about her. Both mother and daughter had gotten caught up in "the chase of getting in," Marcus says later. "I think it must be kind of like getting married: people congratulate you, and you get so caught up in that. You lose sight of what it's all about."

It was about the military way of life, Marcus finally acknowledges, which her daughter could know was wrong for her only through firsthand experience. Marcus does not hide her disappointment. She had thought that her daughter was getting a jump-start on her future: first-rate education, enviable training, guaranteed career.

"I thought they were going to take care of her. I knew it would be very strict, but she'd have something," Marcus says. Days before her daughter is due home, she delivers transcripts and SAT scores to the nearby community college, which offers Barrett a scholarship. Marcus meets her at the airport, accompanied by Barrett's younger sister and her best friend.

But this is not a do-over. The options that existed before she attended the academy are gone. She leaves the academy with something for her efforts: two college credits for her summer of basic training. That means she is now a transfer student. To her dismay, she discovers that the scholarships that four-year colleges had offered her last spring, as an incoming freshman, are no longer available to her as a transfer student. Barrett offers to forgo the credits she earned at the academy, but that would not change her status, she learns. The University of Michigan, which had been ready to give her a generous scholarship just a few months before, is now out of reach. So she enrolls at the community college one town away, and classes will start in just a few days.

Marcus acknowledges that her daughter, usually so accommodating, had to be uncharacteristically adamant to get her way. "For us to allow her out of the academy, she had to really speak up and yell hard," Marcus says after Barrett's return, "because we were just not going to let her come home."

Once she is home, Barrett delights in the small freedoms denied her at the academy: "I can walk on a diagonal," she thinks, and she does. "I can walk on the grass." She washes her hair *and* her body in the shower instead of having to choose between them. It takes her a few weeks to sleep late instead of waking before dawn. She continues going to church on Saturdays and Sundays.

Although she fought so hard to leave, part of her remains in Colorado. In the months after her departure, Barrett stays in touch with her friends in Squadron 13 and lobbies her family to let her attend the University of Colorado at Boulder. Even though she won't go through the academy experience with her former classmates, she wants to be near them.

Marcus, however, tells her that the University of Colorado is out of the question on her schoolteacher's salary. She reminds Barrett that it was her own decision to leave and that choices have consequences. Barrett cannot argue with the economics, but she wonders whether there is an element of retribution in the refusal to send her out of state. "Would you have made a different choice?" Marcus asks her daughter.

"I do see this might not have been her route, but I am still disappointed," Marcus says, months after her daughter's return. "I was really proud to say I had a daughter who was in the Air Force Academy. Who wouldn't be?"

In the weeks and months after she has left, Barrett fights the feeling that she is a failure. For a time, she has trouble convincing her father that she is not.

She does not regret either of her decisions: to attend the academy or to leave when she did. She still has the same goals, to study aeronautical engineering and to eventually work for the space program, but she hopes to find her way in through another, less constricting door.

She thinks back to high school and how everyone—including Barrett herself—thought of her as easygoing and infinitely malleable, a human Gumby without strong opinions of her own. She had discovered the limits of her flexibility in a setting that, paradoxically, sought rigid obedience instead. The commandant of cadets, Brigadier General Susan Desjardins, had described the academy's training philosophy as "follow, then lead." Barrett doesn't want to follow *or* lead. She simply wants to be herself.

"I do have an opinion. That's one thing I learned about myself," Barrett says after her brief odyssey through the Air Force Academy. "I don't want to move through life with everyone telling me where to go, what to think. It changed me."

18 | Wars Distant and Near

At first the class appears like any other in college, aside from the uniforms. Students saunter in, hanging their coats and jackets on carousels that drop from the ceiling in the hallways. They take their seats and make small talk across the room. However, after about ten students show up, there are no more. The door closes. Even core introductory courses, which are taught to hundreds of students at a time in large lecture theaters on most campuses in the country, are taught in classrooms at the academy with no more than a couple of dozen students.

One student rises and stands at attention. "Sir, class reports, ready to learn," he announces at the start of Major John Sherman's philosophy class, an introductory course on ethics. It is a Friday in early September, the beginning of Parents' Weekend, when the parents come to see their kids and may attend classes with them for a day. The major, in uniform and cap, is talking about Aristotle. He is illustrating for his students the character feedback loop: how deliberation leads to choices and actions, which determine character. "The way we get habituated to a response is to do it over a lifetime," he says.

Elizabeth Simpson, a junior in Squadron 13, watches as Major Sherman draws a diagram on the board to break down the concept. As her squadron's representative to the honor board—which is charged with upholding the cadet pledge not to lie, cheat, or steal, or tolerate such acts—these habits are exactly what she is trying to cement into the character of her classmates. "The more temperate you are, the easier it is to be temperate," explains Sherman. The logic applies directly to the honor code, he adds.

As I listen, I think that his philosophy is not esoteric but eminently practical—not only because Sherman has the wonderfully accommodating habit of alerting the cadets to the concepts that will turn up on his exams, but because these men and women are joining the military as it struggles through such fraught issues as the use of torture in wartime, extraordinary rendition, and the indefinite incarceration of terror suspects without trial.

With the rules so malleable and the lines between combatants and civilians so difficult to discern, many of these cadets will be forced to examine their individual consciences on the battlefield. They may find themselves, like the soldiers at Abu Ghraib, following orders in shadowy circumstances, forced to defend actions that arguably violate long-standing international law and that shock the consciences of their friends and families.

However, the conflicts in Iraq and Afghanistan do not come up in classroom discussions at all.

"Aristotle says anger has to be over the right issue, at the right time, and directed at the right person. Make sense?" Sherman asks.

One student asks about the common practice during basic training of ordering an entire unit to do push-ups while the doolie who prompted the punishment must stand and watch.

"Aristotle wouldn't have a problem with that," the teacher says. "You're there as a unit."

What of the practice of destroying the homes of suspected terrorists, rendering their families homeless, or firing on a car holding a terrorist and civilians? What if these civilians include children? The dilemma is not raised, at least not that day.

Simpson, a double major in geography and history, dreams of flying helicopters and says she does not ever want to marry. She picks up her books and heads out to the hall, which is filled by the sounds of her classmates.

In a later class, an advanced seminar on geography research methods, Associate Professor Steven J. Gordon breaks the students into small groups and turns them into amateur sleuths. He holds up a box that is about the size of a cigar box. He has closed it up with rubber bands, and dowels poke out of the sides in a grid pattern. The students must figure out which dowels hold steel washers without opening the box to see.

Next he hands out envelopes of canceled checks. The students study a few checks at a time and build narratives to explain them. In Simpson's group, the initial round of checks includes $1,650 to Forest Lawn Mortuary, $3,200 to St. Joseph's Hospital, and $7,600 to One-Day Body and Paint in the autumn of 1977.

The first scenario reads like the plotline of a film noir. William Whitney, holder of the joint checking account, drinks too much and gets married. His wife puts him in a retirement home and kills him two years later. The story evolves with each new set of checks: the retirement home becomes a private school; William Whitney lives, but his wife and his child die in a car accident. In a later scenario, the wife survives and needs physical therapy.

The exercises, which Professor Gordon took from a Web site hosted by the University of Indiana, introduces students—and their parents, on this day—to the scientific method. "You don't start out with one hypothesis and doggedly stick with it to the end," he explains. "Things change with more data. You don't ever know *the* right answer; it's your best deduction, based on the data you have."

Simpson attends the seminar, which is usually reserved for seniors, thanks to an academic waiver. She is twenty-one years old, from Fort Collins, down the road, with straight blond hair that falls evenly, framing blue eyes and an unlined face sprinkled with freckles. She followed her sister, Rebecca, Class of 2005, into Squadron 13, and is glad she did. The officer assigned to her squadron, Major Robert MacKenzie (Major Mac to his cadets), gives them the space to experiment with leadership, standing by if they seek guidance but not second-guessing them at every turn.

On the terrazzo, lining up for noon formation, Simpson spies an MH-53J Pave Low III helicopter from Kirtland Air Force Base in southeast Albuquerque. The helicopter, which has since been phased out, was the most advanced in the air force arsenal, a heavy lifter often used to drop off and pick up Special Forces and to support them on the ground in enemy territory.

The sight makes Simpson antsy to get out and fly, to start the life she came here for. She watches as the massive grey chopper rises straight up and circles the field, whooshing the grass flat with the force of its wind and whipping her hair from her face. "Oh, my God," she says, her fingertips wiping the dust from her eyes. "That is so sweet."

After lunch, Simpson attends Roger Harrison's class in political philosophy. Harrison, a retired career foreign service officer who holds an endowed chair in political science, was President George H. W. Bush's ambassador to Jordan during the Persian Gulf War and directs the academy's Eisenhower Center for Space and Defense Studies.

"Cadets don't have a lot of time to think," he tells me before they get started. "We try to make this class the exception." Harrison is crisp in bearing and speech. He wears a suit to class and has a white mustache, unusual in a military academy. He is bald on top, and his white hair grows in a tight band from ear to ear. Before each class, he sends out a question that the cadets must answer in an essay. Knowing the myriad demands on their time, he says, "I want it to be my class that they read for."

Harrison's course covers Plato, Socrates, Jean-Jacques Rousseau, John Locke, and Thomas Hobbes, he says at the start, as he takes the cadets through the evolution of Western political philosophy. But he also weaves a heavy dose of Christianity into his survey.

What is moderation in Plato's Republic? he asks. "Paying to each what is owed," a cadet answers. Harrison nods. "Turns out that's exactly what justice is in the soul," he says. He hears a slapping sound from the back and flashes a look at the cadet who gave the answer. "No high-fiving in that corner. The answer," Harrison quips, "was good but not great."

"The soul as the repository of virtue—that's new in Plato," Harrison says. Christianity, he tells them, further refined the belief in the soul as something eternal, though it consigned righteous pagans to damnation. "They're in hell. Why are they in hell? They're in hell because they lived before the possibility of redemption. They lived before Jesus Christ."

Harrison asks a cadet what the Gospel according to Matthew has to say about eternal life. When he fails to answer, the professor's reproach is telling, suggesting an expectation that his students should have an intimate knowledge of Christianity. "You don't know your handbook," Harrison says, before quoting Matthew 16:26 himself: "What shall it profit a man that he gain the whole world, if he loses his soul?"

"If you gain all these worldly benefits, but your soul is out of harmony," he says, "then you are the most unfortunate of men." Harrison introduces Plato's notion of the political state as a larger reflection of the soul, and asks, "Can this be realized? Otherwise, it's just talk. Philosophy." The Greeks found that you "have to combine reason and power."

In preparing its own warriors, the academy seeks a pristine slate, Harrison says. The battle ramp that new cadets climb to enter the academy illustrates the point: The top and bottom of the ramp are not visible to each other; each belongs in its distinct place. A cadet ascends to the academy, disconnected from the world he leaves behind. "People didn't understand the symbolic value" of the design, Harrison says. "We want to wipe clean those souls."

Those souls come to the academy from all sorts of places, he adds. "High school is a terrible experience these days. It's lucky anybody survives it at all. Parents should be arrested," he jokes. "I'm sorry we don't still do that."

Now, he reminds the cadets, they operate on a different plane. "You're not civilians anymore. You take an ethical oath: to protect and defend the Constitution."

A lesson infusing political philosophy with Christian theology would hardly seem out of place at a bible college, but this is the nation's premier academy for training officers to lead the world's most powerful military, whose graduates will fly the most sophisticated and lethal weapons known to man. Still, Harrison's lesson seems to strike neither the cadets nor their parents as unusual in any way.

Speaking later, Harrison acknowledged drawing freely on Christian theology, even assigning readings from the Apostles, but said he was not selling Jesus. Rather, he said, the cadets are largely Christian and many of them are born-again. The texts resonate with them, and help them connect political philosophy to something they know. He described "New Testament revelations" as pivotal, seeding a belief that "God's grace is equal to all. From that germ of an idea to Lincoln's second inaugural address, you can trace a line," he said.

If Harrison was not promoting Christianity, he was certainly recognizing its dominance at the academy and beyond Colorado Springs. At the time, the White House was mixing religion and politics in many spheres. As later reported by *GQ* magazine, the Pentagon's morning briefings to Bush on the progress in the Iraq War featured biblical quotations on their covers.

"The Bush administration was so infused" with Evangelical Christian values, says the Reverend Kristen J. Leslie, an assistant professor at Yale Divinity School who prepared a report that sounded the alarm on the religious climate at the academy. Strong even before President Bush took office in 2001, the Evangelical influence in the military deepened with the support of an administration that actively blurred the lines between church and state. Despite the changing of the guard, that influence remains deep. "It's a problem that the military is not finding a way to name," Leslie says.

Simpson's role on the honor board casts her as a heavy, of sorts, the one who will take a case of cheating or lying before the board, which could put an end to a cadet's career.

"A lot of things here are set up to make you fail," she notes. That may be so, given the demands that students perform to three distinct standards: military, academic, and physical training. Her statement is a common refrain of cadets from the moment they first glimpse the pace of basic training, but the academy also offers more help to students who struggle than almost any other campus would, and that makes the help easy to reach for.

There are resource centers for core classes, and workshops on writing term papers and reading quickly. Professors have office hours every day from 7:30 a.m. to 4:30 p.m., unless they are teaching or at lunch, and cadets who are having trouble keeping up may drop in at any time for extra instruction. The Princeton Review, which ranks colleges, has given the academy its top rating for teacher accessibility.

That is something whose importance David Urban, Rhonda Meeker, and the other freshmen are just beginning to discover.

Less than a month into the school year, Urban realizes that he may have overvalued his five semesters at community college. His success there led him to think that he would sail through math here. Instead, he flunks his first exam in algebra and must take the test again. He is carrying five classes this semester: history, military and strategic studies, calculus, chemistry, and biology.

Preparing to see his parents for the first time since leaving home, Urban imagines their pride. A former neighbor who joined the air force, now stationed in Denver, will also stop by. Urban will wear his uniform to greet them, and he wonders how evident the transformation he is going through will be: the muscles that are taking shape under his clothes, the maturity he is discovering. Once content to blend into the background, he now finds himself standing out more. Just yesterday, he was ordered to his feet with a group of other doolies at his lunch table and told to recite the command chain. He blared the parts of the answer that he knew, hoping his voice would cover for classmates who didn't know the answer.

The change makes him smile now. He came here, in part, because he wasn't entirely comfortable with the person he was, and he wanted to grow in ways that would not have been possible at home. Yesterday he did not know the entire command chain, but at least he stepped up.

Still new, Urban is trying to find his footing, but he hasn't entirely succeeded yet. He and the other doolies are constantly reminded of their lack of status: they may not cross the vast terrazzo that anchors the campus but must restrict themselves to the perimeter and to the white marble strips that mark off the sections of the space. They may not carry their rucksacks on their shoulders or take elevators. They must stand at attention in the presence of upperclassmen, absorb and recite minutiae like the next day's menu, and be called by their last names.

Urban misses his good friends back home, the kind who indulge his quirky comments and who get together when there is nothing special to do. His Texan sense of humor, dripping sarcasm and saying off-the-wall things—random thoughts that pop into his head, really—washes up like dead fish at his feet here. It's not that the cadets don't have a sense of humor, exactly. "It's that the people that I'm around don't appreciate the kind of humor that I have, as much," he says, locking his fingers into a cradle.

Urban landed a spot on intramural Frisbee, but there was one member too many. They went around and polled his teammates, and Urban was voted "most likely to suck at sports," he says. He rubs the back of his neck and shakes his head. Getting kicked off intramural Frisbee—that has to be a low point of some kind. Switching to rugby, though, he has surprised himself. "I'm actually liking it," he says.

The hardest part for Urban so far is the isolation. Aside from a hike to the top of a hill—technically part of the academy—he has not gotten away from the grind at all.

Meeker is feeling her way to the far edge of the academy experience, turning herself into an extreme cadet. She has joined the honor guard, the most demanding of clubs. Like the other freshmen, she is taking five classes: English, chemistry, calculus, engineering, and advanced Spanish. Given the schedule, she is also working hard on her speed reading.

"At this stage, I would die for some baklava," she says. She fantasizes about biting into the rich Middle Eastern pastry, something beyond the realm of Mitchell Hall. "I want good sugar, not Mitch's sugar," she says.

Over the weekend she saw her friends, including her best friend, who is studying education at New Mexico State University. They thought she had changed, gotten taller somehow. Meeker puts it down to "the bus driver hat" she has to wear with her uniform.

Meeker is not entirely surprised that Casey Jane Barrett, with whom she was not especially close at that stage, is now attending a civilian college. "What surprised me was that she waited this long to out-process," she says.

In going for the honor guard, Meeker makes exactly the opposite choice of Barrett: grabbing the military life with an iron grip. The guard is not so much an extracurricular activity as a calling. Its members practice rifle drills, flag retreats, and reveille formations every afternoon, from 4:30 to 7 p.m., then have dinner together. They wear strange black helmets, like relics of World War II, that could double as soup pots.

Given Meeker's fateful explosion at Jacks Valley, when she cursed at a cadre who had pushed her past her limit, the honor guard is a strikingly odd choice, perhaps the closest a cadet can come to boot camp on an endlessly repeating loop. The drills are rigorous, filled with the kind of shouting and beatings that invade her dreams and that most cadets are grateful to leave behind with Acceptance Day.

In another light, however, the choice makes perfect sense. For Meeker, it corresponds most closely to the path she followed in high school in Junior ROTC. If the academy were a uniform, the honor guard would be its lining: a world within a world—with its own language, traditions, and practices—run by "super STRACT military gurus," she says. (The acronym stands for Strategically Ready and Combat Tough.) The first descriptions she hears of the honor guard are probably accurate: "They're a bunch of tools. They're weird." She is charmed. "That sounds familiar," she thinks. "I bet I'll like it."

"They're some pretty hard-core people," she says, grinning. "I've found my niche."

19 | (Almost) All Roads Lead to Jesus

Before coming to the Air Force Academy, Zach Taylor would not have described himself as devout. He seldom felt drawn to worship, and he went along to church mostly tugged by his parents. But on Sunday morning during the backbreaking initiation into cadet life known as Beast, church suddenly becomes a refuge—not so much in the spiritual sense; its appeal is more pragmatic.

"You get to socialize there," Taylor says. Sometimes visitors bring snacks, doughnuts, and coffee for the cadets, and they lend them their cell phones to call home. "It's an hour where the cadre can't get to you."

Taylor's roommate, Brad Bernard, is also quick to seize the opportunity. He has a problem: he's broken his shoulder in football practice, and wants a way out of minutes, the morning regimen in which upperclassmen grill doolies on military knowledge and make them do push-ups, sit-ups, and other exercises. For the doolies, solidarity with their peers in punishment is the paramount purpose of the entire year's training. But when Bernard does attend training in the afternoons, he just stands there, humiliated by his injury, while his fellow four-digs do all the work. His solution: he asks to go to morning worship at the chapel.

In fact, Bernard goes to chapel only sometimes. At other times, he studies in his room or just chills out there. "I know that they called it 'religious time,' but it was also individual time," he says, adding that because he is a college athlete, the National Collegiate Athletic Association's rules should exempt him from much of the training, anyway.

"I'm not going to lie," he admits later. "Sometimes I did use chapel as an excuse. But it wasn't all the time, and it was only first semester," until his shoulder healed.

Bernard's strategy for escaping morning minutes is both shrewd and telling. Ryan Whipple, his element leader, in charge of training Bernard and a handful of other four-degrees, doubts the athlete's sincerity. Whipple, an atheist, takes a more or less accurate measure of Bernard's sudden yearning for Christ, but his suspicions mean nothing: denying a request to attend church is something a cadre like Whipple does at his own peril. Even if Whipple had objected, his decision would have been overturned as it rose through the chain of command. Who wants a reputation in the air force for being hostile to Christianity?

"It was definitely the unspoken rule that if you put on your request that you're going to church, nobody would deny it," Whipple says.

In 2004, stung by reports that Evangelicals, from the commandant of cadets on down, were ignoring the separation of church and state to aggressively promote Christianity among cadets, the Air Force Academy began taking steps to tone down the religious fervor. Brigadier General Johnny Weida, the former commandant of cadets who had famously taught cadets a call-and-response system designed to prompt proselytizing, is gone. (In a sign of the Air Force's ambivalence regarding the issue, Weida was quietly promoted to Major General after leaving.) Major Warren "Chappy" Watties, the Air Force Chaplain of the Year, had also left, after a report by the non-profit group Americans United for Separation of Church and State alleged

This Christmas greeting summoning readers to accept Jesus was signed by more than three hundred officers, faculty, and staff and their spouses. The signatories included the academy's then dean of faculty and the vice dean of faculty, sixteen heads or deputy heads of academic departments, nine professors, the director of athletics, and the football coach. The full-page ad ran for several years in the academy newspaper, which is written and produced by the academy public affairs department. The ads were subsequently discontinued.

that he was urging new cadets to convert their tent mates during Second Beast lest they "burn in the fires of hell." (Watties disputed the quote, but academy officials defended the chaplain's call to proselytize among the Basics as entirely "appropriate.") For a time, the academy ran a fifty-minute religious sensitivity class. It banned the practice of quoting scripture on official e-mails.

The subterranean shifts that produced the unrestrained push for Christianity behind the gates of what is, after all, a taxpayer-financed military base, were decades in the making and extend well beyond the academy. They reflect the growing power of Evangelicals in the officer corps, as well as their domination over the military chaplaincy. With the change has come a new language and style, with chaplains exalting the warrior spirit from the pulpit. Traditionally charged with providing pastoral care to soldiers or airmen on their own religious terms, many chaplains today focus instead on winning souls for Jesus.

Although the primacy of Christianity is not as open or forceful as it was under Weida's watch, it has hardly disappeared. As Professor Roger Harrison's class suggests, an atmosphere persists that presumes the primacy of Christianity, while merely tolerating—or sometimes accommodating—other religious beliefs. On more days than not each week, the academy offers some kind of option aimed at drawing cadets to the cross. On Monday nights the Air Force Academy throws open its doors to religious groups, including hard-core Evangelical groups like the Navigators and the Campus Crusade for Christ, and allows them to use academy classrooms for Bible study. The Campus Crusade says its agenda is to forge cadets into "government-paid missionaries for Christ" by the time they leave the academy as officers. The Navigators are dedicated to creating disciples, whom they call "laborers," who will actively spread the gospel, at the academy and once they are deployed.

Before the attacks of September 11, 2001, when outsiders could visit the academy freely, academy officials allowed the Navigators to trawl the library, proselytizing cadets who were there to study. Evangelical and other religious groups continue to have a special room at the academy, even beyond the Monday night sessions, where cadets can drop in at any time.

As reflected in its name, the Special Program in Religious Education (SPIRE) accommodates an array of Christian groups for Monday night Bible study, alongside a smattering of others. Jewish and Buddhist groups operate under its auspices, as did, for a time, a secular group known as the Freethinkers.

On Thursday, male cadets may attend God Chasers, a cadet-run Bible study group that encourages cadets to infuse every activity with a consciousness of Christ and to religiously mentor cadets of all faiths.

On Friday night, the New Life megachurch runs shuttle vans from the academy to its weekly social known as the Mill, where roughly a thousand young people meet, take in a religious concert, dance, and, if they like, stick around for a sermon.

Lucas VanTassel, a firstie in Squadron 13 who has attended the New Life Church since he was a toddler, once filled in for the church's van driver. He bristles to see cadets with little interest in religion using the Mill to find dates.

On Sunday, cadets can attend the academy's sleek modern chapel—the most popular man-made tourist destination in Colorado Springs—or venture off base to any church they like, staying out for the entire day, their squadron leaders permitting. If they do not attend church, cadets must spend one of their hard-earned passes to go off post. Going to church gives the new cadets freedom they otherwise wouldn't have.

Ordinarily, a cadet who wants to go off base more than a couple of times a year has to fill out paperwork to request permission. One with poor grades would be hard-pressed to earn the privilege of time away. "It isn't a system where you have a few restrictions," Whipple explains. "It's more like you have a few privileges." But a request with a religious tie—say, a church-sponsored ski trip or hike—gets weighed more carefully. "If you're religious, it's like a 'get out of jail free' card," he says.

Whipple says he might judge a cadet's motivation for going on these trips as recreational, rather than strictly religious. "But then you get into the very heavy politically correct culture. Who am I to decide what's important for this person religiously?" A few of Whipple's four-digs are not doing well, but fortunately for Whipple none of them ask to go off base for religious events. He says, as an upperclassman, "It's the kind of thing you live in fear of." Later, he amends that: Fear is not a factor, he says, because he would not challenge the request, regardless of the doolie's standing.

The corollary of the broad license for attending church-sponsored events is a ban on any training or events considered "mission essential" on Sunday morning. That time is set aside for worship, and is never compromised. Cadets of other faiths, however, must choose between religious and military obligations. Jewish cadets and Seventh Day Adventists miss important training events and Saturday morning inspections if they opt to observe the Sabbath and their religious holidays. In fact, there are no Jewish services at the cadet chapel on Saturday morning. Believing Christians can live in harmony—even flourish and grow—in their religion at the academy, but this claim cannot be made by cadets of other faiths.

One recent graduate, who is Jewish, recalls obtaining special permission as a doolie to attend Saturday morning religious services off base. The first time went fine. But the second time she turned out in service dress on Saturday morning, her training commander shot her a look. He was about to start training four-digs, all of whom were in battle dress uniform. "You know why your classmates are all in the hallway?" he demanded.

She understood, at that moment, that keeping her religion would set her apart. "I stopped going to synagogue downtown pretty much the first time that happened," she says. "I could see it wasn't going to be easy."

The academy's main training event that spring culminated on the first night of Passover, when observant Jews would ordinarily attend prayer services and join their families for seders, the ritual meal marking the Jewish exodus from slavery in Egypt. (Academy chaplains did arrange for a seder of sorts on base.)

The Freethinkers crashed hard against the limits of tolerance in 2009 when they sought permission for Christopher Hitchens, author of the 2007 best seller *God Is Not Great: How Religion Poisons Everything*, to address their group on campus. The chief of chaplains warned that he would object to Hitchens speaking on base, arguing that SPIRE aims to promote religious study. SPIRE's rules, the chief of chaplains argued, require groups to highlight their own beliefs without denigrating the beliefs of others. He alleged that Hitchens's stance was disrespectful to religion.

However, the same argument could apply to, say, the Navigators, which are inherently dismissive of faiths other than Christianity,

Following the clash over Hitchens, who ended up meeting cadets at an Old Chicago restaurant, the Freethinkers withdrew from SPIRE. Carlos Bertha, the philosophy professor who sponsored the Freethinkers, reestablished it as a chapter of the Secular Student Alliance, a national organization. But the academy's Extracurricular Activities Board refused to even vote on the new group's bid for recognition. "If your club is based on personal beliefs and opinions, then what keeps us from forming a club for every religion?" George Nelson, an associate athletic director and board co-chair, wrote Bertha in an e-mail. He suggested that the secularists get back under SPIRE's umbrella.

After half a year, academy officials offer to help resolve any practical problems arising from the secularists' unofficial status, while sidestepping the thorny issue of recognition outside the chaplains' authority. Under a new superintendent, they also begin to more actively accommodate non-Christians, scheduling to avoid religious conflicts and creating a rock circle where Wiccans and Pagans can worship. Before the circle is even formally dedicated, however, vandals break it, leaving behind a cross built of railroad ties.

VanTassel, who is rehearsing for the role of an angel in New Life's production of *The Thorn*, its annual Passion Play, says that his thinking about the academy's attitudes and practices changed after hearing the criticism of its religious climate. VanTassel has been going through a shattering firstie year and nearly quit the academy. He came here through hard work and prayer, believing that Christ had opened the way for him to attend the academy to become a pilot and a leader. Instead, he had been dropped from pilot training the summer before his senior year and stuck with a career field, finance, that would maroon him behind a desk.

Like many at the academy, VanTassel considers the accusations of religious bias at the academy overblown. He resents the courses in religious sensitivity. Nevertheless, the criticism parallels questions in his own mind and prompts new ones. He remembers "heathen flight," when non-Christians in basic training were marched back to their quarters while the believers went to chapel.

"Why are we calling these guys heathens?" he asked himself. He recalls General Weida's speeches. The commandant would say, "Air power," signifying belief in Jesus as the son of God. Cadets were supposed to respond, "Rocks, sir." Air power also represented "Heir power," the commandant explained at another briefing, forming the letter *J* with his hand. "Rocks, sir," VanTassel shouted back with other cadets. The call-and-response was meant to raise eyebrows—an opening for the Christian cadets to proselytize. VanTassel once found the double entendre cool, but now he thinks that the commandant's critics were right: he had gone too far.

When VanTassel looks at the futuristic chapel now, he notices that the grandest setting, with seventeen soaring spires and stained-glass windows, is reserved for Protestants, whereas Catholics, Jews, and cadets of other faiths are tucked out of sight on a lower level. Protestants are the majority and therefore need the largest space. But VanTassel wonders what would happen if Catholics were in the majority. Would they be permitted to worship in the main chapel?

"I don't think there's a cognitive push to get people to go to church," he says, "but whoever built the academy had definite ideas. You can see the chapel from anywhere in the academy." VanTassel is a purist when it comes to faith, seeing it as a private matter.

"I've never really liked the idea of going to a group of people who are struggling or hurting like you've got all the answers, when you don't," he says. He avoids God Chasers in part because he believes that it is zealous about doing just that.

"I never got the feeling from going to sermons that it was your responsibility to go out and talk to people in that manner," he says. "You can only know what God has told you to do. That's part of the reason I didn't do Campus Crusade or Navigators. I was very careful with those kinds of groups, because that's more what they're about. It's not like there's only one way to live your life. How they live is between the person and God. For me to come along and say, 'You're doing something wrong. You're in sin' doesn't feel right."

At the same time, VanTassel and other born-again cadets argue that the critics of the academy who insist on divorcing faith from academy life—by barring professors from discussing their personal beliefs, for instance—are demanding too much.

"If an individual feels threatened by somebody else's religious expressions, okay, you feel threatened. If you're not a Christian, you're a minority. If you don't have enough courage to stand up for your religion and say I'm not going to let that bother me, I have to seriously question that individual," VanTassel states.

But by that logic, a non-Christian cannot be left alone in peace. If a Muslim cadet, for instance, is strong in his beliefs, it should not bother him to hear Christians profess their faith, the reasoning goes. If he is weak, well, whose fault is that?

In a group interview at the academy, the chaplains say that they make every effort to accommodate the religious needs of all the cadets, ensuring, for example, that Muslim students can have breakfast before dawn during Ramadan. Part of their work, however, involves tempering the expectations of religious minorities.

"We have to teach minorities about the environment they're coming into," says Captain Hamza Al-Mubarak, the Muslim chaplain. He cites a Jewish cadet who was offended by crosses appearing at Christmastime.

"Christians are celebrating the birth of Jesus, so this is an outward expression of an inward belief," says Captain Ruth Segres, an American Baptist chaplain. The Jewish cadet, she adds, "needs to be sensitive to it."

Throughout the year that I am tracking Squadron 13, I ask many times to speak to Jewish cadets, curious for another perspective on the academy's religious climate. As winter turns to spring and the school year nears its end, I learn why the request is never answered: of the more than a hundred cadets in Squadron 13, none is Jewish. Ultimately, I search farther afield.

Curtis Weinstein, a graduate of the Class of 2007, entered the academy as a somewhat observant Jew. He spent Second Beast fending off a flight mate acting on the chaplain's sermons, who told Weinstein that he would "roast in hell." Weinstein said other cadets cursed him out as a "fucking Jew" and a "Christ-killer" countless times.

Weinstein, whose father, Mikey (Class of 1977), and older brother, Casey (Class of 2004), are both graduates of the academy, eventually turned to his father for help. Mikey, author of the 2006 book *With God on Our Side: One Man's War Against an Evangelical Coup in America's Military*, had received swastikas and hate notes as a doolie, and wrote of twice being beaten senseless over his Jewishness at the academy. In response to his son's reports, he founded the Military Religious Freedom Foundation, which forced an end to the problems of religious coercion by the academy leadership.

After his father went public, the attacks on Curtis Weinstein mostly ceased. Some classmates, like VanTassel, actually sought him out to apologize for the nickname they'd given him freshman year: "Super Jew." Weinstein brushed it off and told VanTassel that he didn't mind the nickname. This reaction offended his classmate, for some reason.

"He doesn't mind when he's singled out *that* way," VanTassel says.

I am at a loss. Isn't there a difference between being called Super Jew and Fucking Jew? I ask VanTassel.

Weinstein confirms the nickname and says that at the time he didn't mind. It is only in looking back that he realizes his classmates were relating to him primarily in terms of his religion, and it seems to have worn him down. By the time he graduates, he professes no religious feeling at all, identifying himself only as "culturally Jewish."

Asked why he has given up practicing his religion, Weinstein is quiet for a moment. "I don't feel like I want to be part of anything that says, 'If you don't believe in Me then terrible things are going to happen to you.'" he answers. Talk of God and faith doesn't "bring up good memories anymore."

But I wasn't asking about Christianity, I remind him.

"Every religious argument that I got into was always because it was Christianity versus my religion," Weinstein explains. "I began to equate religion with being a Christian."

VanTassel recalls looking around his dining table at Mitchell Hall the previous year and coming to a stunning realization. He was sitting with five friends from Squadron 13, all upperclassmen. "We were all white, Christian, Republican, home schooled, and we all owned guns. We just so understood each other," VanTassel says. "We just thought, what are the odds of that—all six of us here, in the same squadron? What are the odds of that anywhere else?"

One of those six was VanTassel's roommate, Matthew Stillman. By the time Stillman entered the Air Force Academy, those closest to him saw in him a warrior for Christ. He had spent three years at 24/7 Leadership Academy in Colorado Springs, which was run by New Life Church. 24/7 combines intensive Bible study with extreme physical training that is more rigorous than anything Stillman would face at the Air Force Academy. The drills he underwent there came directly from the Navy Seal training regimen and included an Iron Man triathlon, which involves biking 112 miles, running 26 miles, and swimming 2.4 miles.

Stillman climbed Pikes Peak and completed the triathlon. He was deprived of sleep, fasted, and hiked for hours on end. Each day's training included hours of Bible study. The course ended with his being kidnapped from the home of a sponsor family. He lived outdoors for five nights in early October, undergoing punishment and interrogations. On the last day, he was led from a prison to a pit and was told that it was his own grave. He felt the barrel of a gun against his skull. "Deny Jesus," his would-be executioner ordered. He would count to three.

"You don't actually know you're not going to die," Stillman says. Hearing the count, he thought to himself, "Oh, my God, I could actually die at this point. As far as I'm concerned, I've already died."

"Congratulations," he heard instead. "You have just completed 24/7 missionary training."

"Once you did that, your whole mind-set changed," Stillman recalls. "If you are really committed, you take it to that higher level." The mock execution did not terrify him, he says. "To a Christian, death has no fear. God loves us and wants to bring us home."

Stillman says he entered 24/7 because at the time he wanted to lead a church or a ministry. The mock execution, coupled with scriptural studies, was aimed at preparing him for the dangers and hardships he might face as a missionary.

The leadership academy seemed a kind of funhouse mirror turned on the Air Force Academy, where the primarily military mission was melding with Evangelical Christian fervor and faculty and cadets opened even the most routine meetings with prayers to Jesus, until outsiders blew the whistle on such practices. At 24/7, it was the reverse: the essentially Evangelical message had fused with extreme military-style training.

The similarities are no accident, Stillman noted. 24/7 was started by Christopher Beard, a New Life member whose brother attended the Air Force Academy. Beard saw that cadets often became more religious as the academy pushed them to the limits of their endurance. He structured 24/7 to recreate the raw intensity of boot camp, using it to heighten religious experience and to build a new, tougher and more militant, generation of Christian leaders.

In this blending of the sacred and the lethal, in the imagined persecution that would bring initiates to give up their lives, and in the trauma of being "executed" before one's own grave, the training did not seem entirely new. It seemed rather, a twist on something familiar: a Christian fundamentalist answer to al-Qaida. Stillman acknowledges the similarities to extremism but says there is "a crucial difference." 24/7 does not train initiates on weapons or in the making of suicide belts. "We're going through it because we're the peaceful ones," Stillman says. "We're not holding guns to anyone's head saying, 'Accept Jesus.' We're having guns held to our heads."

There is also an important theological difference. Stillman believes that he will go to heaven simply for accepting Christ, that his redemption—at bottom—is unrelated to his behavior. The suicide bombers, he says, believe ultimately in the power of their actions. "The devil twists the word of God to make those people believe that they have to earn their way into heaven. They believe in the redemptive power of their actions."

I was intrigued by this theology forged at the academy and at the vanguard of the powerful Evangelical movement. Before his life unraveled, New Life's founder, Ted Haggard, spoke weekly to President George W. Bush. Did Stillman really believe that faith always mattered more than actions?

"A Nazi who murdered thousands of people but accepts Christ a moment before his death: Could he reach heaven?" I ask. "Yes," Stillman says. "What about his Jewish victims?" I ask.

"I believe they would go to hell," Stillman says, "unless they accepted Jesus Christ." A Mormon, who believes that he must do good works on earth to merit redemption, would similarly writhe in hell for eternity, adds Stillman.

"The Bible is very clear on it," he says. "It's so easy to go to heaven. Why would you try any other way?"

(24/7 has since split off from the Colorado Springs megachurch, and its training programs, now in Arkansas, Alabama, and Mexico City, vary with location.)

Stillman stayed at 24/7 for three years, training others who came after him. His sense of purpose changed through the experience, to the point where he could no longer even imagine attending a civilian university. "I knew I was ruined," he said, and laughed. "I felt called to the Air Force Academy."

When he went there, his trainers, his religious community, and even his family expected Stillman to treat the academy as a mission, an opportunity to aggressively spread his faith. At the time, General Weida was in charge, so all doors were open. But Stillman says he is not at the academy to win converts.

"I wouldn't hide it, but at the same time, I'm not in the air force to Christianize the air force. I'm in the air force because God called me to be in the air force, not necessarily to be a missionary in the air force. I know that there are officers in the air force who do that," he says. "But once I get into the air force I have to have a very combat-focused calling, not a very missionary-focused calling."

At the academy, Stillman is among the first cadets to attend God Chasers. He comes to it after a junior catches sight of his book bag, with the 24/7 logo, at freshman orientation. Once classes start, the upperclassman e-mails him about the group. "It was a breath of fresh air for me at the academy," Stillman recalls. "It was part of who I was."

I ask Stillman how, as a combat officer, he would respond to airmen handing out Bibles in Afghanistan or Iraq—incidents that have, in the course of the war, prompted accusations that the United States forces were disrespecting Muslim beliefs. Stillman had just begun 24/7 when terrorists rammed planes into the World Trade Center and the Pentagon. Now, he ventures that the American presence there is "not about bringing Christianity to Afghanistan. It's about bringing choice. I believe in giving people choice."

He would encourage his airmen, if given the opportunity, to share their faith and their Bibles, but he is aware of how sensitive the issue is to Muslims and knows he risks violating the military's ban on proselytizing foreigners. "When I say it's about choice, that's what I really believe. I would rather have to clean up a mess than to be contradictory to the very things we're fighting for. Why would I be fighting for something I wouldn't give my airmen the opportunity to exercise?"

Stillman says he would never take action against airmen giving out Bibles. "To me, those people are just living out their beliefs the best they can."

20 | No Excuses

The yellow school bus trundles down the road in the early afternoon, the Bulldawgs of Squadron 13 uncertain what lies ahead. All of them, from firsties to doolies, are headed for Jacks Valley, the scene of the humiliations they had endured as initiates—for some, not that long ago—or invoked as upperclassmen. It is the weekend before Thanksgiving, the cold is settling in as sunlight shrinks to a smaller corner of their days, and they are all in battle fatigues.

They are in the midst of Commandant's Challenge, the main training exercise of the fall. It will test their operational readiness in a competition that includes all squadrons and all cadets.

If basic training aims to hammer the identity out of entering cadets, pushing them to the edge of their endurance, Commandant's Challenge is a trial for every class. The doolies take exams that test their command of military facts, but the upperclassmen—who before subjected the doolies to the obstacles—will now be running fitness courses alongside them, navigating their way on land, building encampments, and commanding medical care for their buddies in the field. Cadet scores are totaled together to determine the standing of the entire squadron.

"What's an IED?" Megan Biles, soccer player and doolie, asks from the front row of the bus.

"Those blue and red boxes," Peter Sohm, another four-dig across the aisle, tells her. "If you see one, jump on it." Unsmiling, he looks out the window at the Rockies, which have a grey pall over them on this overcast afternoon. "Last time I got off a bus, nothing good happened," he says.

The cadets have been practicing for the challenge for weeks now. Unlike in previous years, however, this year's students do not know what awaits them; they only have word of the general areas in which they are likely to be tested. The idea this year is to more closely approximate the unpredictability of war: the booby traps, the unexpected assault, the screwups. Two years ago, the Bulldawgs were a sorry lot, coming in last of thirty-six squadrons. Last year, they came in fourth. Major Robert MacKenzie (Major Mac) would be working it right alongside them in a show of solidarity.

In exams that morning, the Bulldawgs set up their strongest people to answer questions in different areas. One section of today's exam is based on the *Airman's Manual* and asks about deployment, chemical and biological warfare, and first aid. For the second section, the five cadets who are most familiar with aircraft cluster over a counter in the common room, identifying planes by their silhouettes. Sohm is writing furiously as the cadets surrounding him shout out the names of the aircraft and the clock runs down.

"You guys have seven minutes," someone says.

The next section of the test features two rows of badges. Kasey King, a two-degree, picks up a pen, and he and Sohm write simultaneously on the paper. The badges turn out to be tougher than the planes.

"Just write something down. It doesn't matter," says Syed Saad Javaid, an international student from Pakistan, peering between them. "Just write something down you haven't written yet."

"Time's up!"

Now the cadets in their buses are near the north gate, where a famous B-52 bomber from the Vietnam War known as Diamond Lil stands vigil, its single red star commemorating the enemy plane shot down over Hanoi in 1972. The buses join a convoy heading to Jacks, which is outfitted like a war zone. There are mock bombs along the way, as well as roadside ambushes. Word filters back that up ahead, another convoy has come under attack. The buses are running late, and Major Mac is not sure whether their tardiness will be held against the squadron, lowering its score.

COMMANDANT'S CHALLENGE

From Squadron 13: Jamal Harrison, Adam Dunk, Calen Pope, Miles-Tyson Blocker.

Four-digs of Squadron 13 doing sit-ups, to total their class year.

David Closner, a three-degree, holds open a map. "Are those street signs?" he asks, pointing in the distance. He looks down at the map. "Where's the *X*? Like in the mall, saying, 'You are here.'"

Syed, a black curl spilling over his forehead, turns and grins. "We are here," he deadpans.

At Jacks, helicopters throttle overhead and smoke fills the air. Gunfire crackles in the distance. The Bulldawgs pile out of the buses, breaking up into groups. Their first assignment is to build an encampment, pitching thirty-one tents, and then hike to the destinations marked on their maps. One flight, or group, navigates its way to combat arms training, where the cadets fire off M-16s.

The group I follow, A Flight, reaches an encampment where cadets must don protective gear in case of a biological or chemical attack. They have less than three minutes to pull on jumpsuits and tie up the sleeves. They pull out gas masks that cover their entire heads with aprons that fall over the shoulders. Syed has trouble getting the mask on in time, and King turns to help him, but Syed still comes in late.

From there, they must trek to an event described only as "self-aid buddy care," meant to prepare cadets for treating comrades who are wounded in action. The trek is supposed to take less than an hour, and the navigation itself is part of the challenge. An hour and a half into it, the Bulldawgs are on the side of a hill. It is far too quiet; the only sound is their debate over which way to go.

In the stillness, they see two deer standing among the pine trees. The animals stop and look at the group of cadets, whose voices instinctively fall to a whisper. As they look around, the cadets notice familiar rocks and the bend of a tree that they have seen before. In the distance, they hear a train whistle. They keep climbing to the hilltop, where they glimpse a helicopter hovering over the valley on the other side. They realize that they were supposed to go around, not over, the hill. Essentially, they are pretty close to where they started. They head north, toward the battlefield.

As the light dwindles and the temperature drops, the Bulldawgs finally make it to the valley. They hear screaming as they approach a field, where a "wounded" airman lies helpless. Gunfire explodes nearby like a string of firecrackers, and explosions fill the field with rolling clouds of grey smoke. The airman's leg is "bleeding" in this scenario and he cannot walk. One group of cadets does the first aid, gathering the injured cadet on a stretcher, while a second group fans out to secure the perimeter against enemy fighters.

"Don't forget to say, 'bang, bang,' or they're not dead," calls Nick Mercurio.

"Blam, blam, blibbedy blam," quips Reed Wildman, a three-degree. "My gun's British."

At the self-aid buddy-care tent, the officers in charge are not impressed with the performance of the Bulldawgs. "Hey, you guys are two hours late," they scold. No excuses will help, so neither the late buses nor the circles around the hill are mentioned.

It is already dark, and the buses are starting to line up to take the cadets back up the hill to their dorms. They have to cut the exercises short, but they end up shivering as they wait for enough buses to shuttle them all. Matthew Takanen, a firstie who is flight commander for the group, runs a hand over his eyebrow and lets out his breath in a soft whistle. "What a frustrating day," he says to himself.

Adrian Peppers, the Bulldawg squadron commander, is usually psyched for home football games. They are a welcome break from routine, and they pack loads of spirit. On those Saturday afternoons, parachutists fall over the stadium to kick off the game, and the team mascot, a falcon, the symbol of air power, circles the stadium at half-time, catching a lure in midflight for the finale. Peppers's girlfriend is a cheerleader, seemingly indefatigable and relentlessly upbeat, no matter how hopeless the score or how low the thermometer dips.

Although it is senior night at the stadium, tonight's game, pitting the Falcons against the University of Utah Utes, is one that many cadets are having trouble getting excited about. Because the game falls in the middle of Commandant's Challenge, Peppers and the other cadets of Squadron 13 are thinking more about the work waiting for them back at the dorms, which face inspections on Monday, than about the slender chance that the Falcons will make it to a bowl game.

The team has not played a bowl game since 2002—before the current seniors began as freshmen at the academy. The team enters tonight's match with more losses than wins, five games to four. Even given the trend toward bowl-game inflation—there are twenty-nine bowls that ranked colleges can play in, from the Eagle Bank Bowl to the Bell Helicopter Armed Forces Bowl—the air force would have to clock at least two, probably three, more wins to have a real shot.

Without a victory over Utah, the likelihood of the academy's team reaching a bowl game dwindles to remote, and the season will go down as a case study in mediocrity. A win would mean a fresh start. A local sports columnist, Milo Bryant, has called tonight's game decisive for the team: "the beginning of a last chance or the beginning of the end."

The Falcons are not the only ones toying with glory under the bright lights on this frigid night. Banshee, the team's new falcon, will debut with a show at half-time. A hybrid gyr and saker falcon, Banshee stands nearly two feet tall, her white feathers tipped with silver, and she wears a small leather hood and a ring on her ankle. Her handler tonight, George Waterfield-Copeland, a three-degree and a marine's son who went to high school in Okinawa, wears a massive brown leather glove that reaches halfway to his elbow.

The game does not begin well for the Falcons. Building on a streak of wins, Utah's Eric Weddle, voted Defensive Player of the Year in the Midwest Conference, scores in the first quarter with a six-yard run. A kick from Louie Sakoda gives Utah a half-time lead of 7–0. A few close calls for the Falcons bring roars from the crowd but lead nowhere, and the temperature falls below freezing. It is a wicked, damp cold that penetrates the soles of shoes and makes toes feel brittle as icicles, about to snap off. Burrowing in the pockets of their pea coats, the cadets' hands clutch packets of hand warmers.

At half-time, Ted Rosander, one of four seniors who work with the birds, strides out to the center of the stadium, the bright lights and the roar of the crowd making it seem almost like daylight. Up on the stadium roof, above the press box, stands Waterfield-Copeland, his back to the stadium.

Banshee rests on his arm, shielded by his body from the crowd below. The bird is only five months old, named for her tendency to scream wildly whenever she wants food. Cadets like Rosander and Waterfield-Copeland have spent three hundred hours training Banshee just to sit on the bulky leather glove. Another three hundred hours have gone into getting her ready to fly tonight. Banshee is not fast in flight—at least, not yet—but she is intelligent and has unsuspected reserves of ingenuity.

Once her trainers had left her alone in a room while they cut up her meal, a freshly killed quail. They left her hooded, tethered by her ankles to the perch. When they returned, the falcon had somehow taken off her hood and undone her leash. She was sitting on the counter, queen of her realm. "We were like 'That bird is smart,'" says Waterfield-Copeland. Could she pull such an inspiring trick tonight and breathe life back into the flagging team?

Rosander looks around the stadium and up toward the roof. Although the bird has rehearsed in the stadium, the stands were always empty then. This is the first time she will fly for spectators. When Rosander gives the word—"weathering"—Waterfield-Copeland removes Banshee's hood. Rosander circles the lure around himself and gives the signal over the walkie-talkie: "spinning." At that, Waterfield-Copeland turns so that Banshee, whose eyesight is ten times as sharp as perfect human vision, can glimpse the lure below.

With 27,611 pairs of eyes upon her in the stands, Banshee hops off his arm and takes off, rising high, her wings spread in giant half arcs from her body. The falcon circles the stands, swooping in a wide spiral that dips and soars, slicing the light with her awesome power. At forty ounces, with a two-foot wing span, she can reach a speed of 90 to 180 miles an hour. She makes three passes, coming down for the lure each time and rising under the blinding bright lights.

Once she flies too wide and close to the stands. The spectators sit up in alarm, their backs instinctively pressing against the seats. The last time, Rosander calls her name and throws the lure high for her to catch. She misses the bag, following it instead to rest in the middle of the field. She looks at the little bag as if they were strangers at a bus stop and then twists her head quizzically toward Rosander. An involuntary, collective "Aww" emanates from the crowd. A few minutes later, Banshee is on Rosander's arm, tearing into the still warm innards of a quail—its feathers, flesh, and blood hanging from the falcon's mouth.

On the field, the Falcons have not given up—to the chagrin of the freezing cadets. All the action is packed into the final quarter. The Falcons complete a six-yard pass and tie the score at 7–7, when Utah's Weddle brings in a four-yard run. With four minutes left in the game, the Falcons tear out another touchdown, tying the score at 14–14. For the cadets freezing in the stands, this raises the unbearable prospect of going into overtime.

Air Force calls a time-out as Utah's Sakoda prepares to go for a thirty-seven-yard field goal. The cadets around me wish him well. "If they make it, our football players are getting a Christmas break instead of a bowl. It's a win-win for everybody," says one firstie. "I like it."

"If they miss, I think I'll cry," his friend answers.

They don't. Utah wins, 17–14, and goes on to victory in the Armed Forces Bowl that season, defeating the University of Tulsa. Air Force sinks deeper into its worst losing streak in decades, with more losses than wins for three years straight.

The Utah game turns out to be one of the last for Falcons coach Fisher DeBerry, who made a career of recruiting players that had been over-looked by his rivals and mining greatness in them to build a winning team. Less than a month later, DeBerry announces his retirement, three years before his contract is due to run out. The Falcons coach for twenty-three years, DeBerry denies being forced out but takes no questions from the press, which links his departure to his refusal to replace two assistant coaches in a bid to reverse the team's disastrous record.

Americans who know nothing about football, know of DeBerry. A devout Christian, DeBerry had famously stretched a banner across the Falcons locker room in 2004 that read in part, "I am a Christian first and last . . . I am a member of Team Jesus Christ . . . I wear the colors of the cross." Provided by the Fellowship of Christian Athletes, a national group that urges athletes to promote Christianity through sports, the banner featured what the group calls the "Competitor's Creed." DeBerry also led the Falcons in pre- and post-game prayers to the "Master Coach." Though he took down the banner after two days and ceased the locker room prayers on orders from the academy's athletic director, Hans Mueh, the coach's concessions hardly resolved the issue.

Speaking at an academy symposium in early 2005, DeBerry, who was the highest paid figure at the Air Force Academy, did not rule out resuming the prayers in the future. He told Pam Zubeck and Todd Jacobsen, reporters for the *Colorado Springs Gazette*, that religion—or, apparently, Christianity—is "what we're all about in Falcon football."

DeBerry also stirred allegations of racism, after attributing the Falcons' 48–10 loss to Texas Christian University in October 2005 to the high number of black players on the opposing team. He said, "Afro-American kids can run very, very well. That doesn't mean that Caucasian kids and other descents can't run, but it's very obvious to me they run extremely well." The remarks earned DeBerry an official reprimand, and he offered an apology, saying, "I never intended to hurt anyone."

But neither of these two issues would threaten DeBerry's future as a coach. The clash that ultimately leads him to walk away after twenty-three years comes down to moments like tonight—a string of losses, a broken spirit, and what to do about them.

As the crowd starts moving toward the exits, mentally charting the shortest distance to a warm spot, the cadets suddenly stop as the band strikes up the air force song. The first two verses and the fourth verse are all rousing, redolent of the adventure and joy of flight. As the song heads into the third stanza, however, the music grows solemn, and the cadets around me sing softly, their heads lowered.

It is a verse for airmen fallen in battle.

"Welcome to the PT Challenge!" booms Matthew Schlitter, a firstie from Squadron 28. He is standing in an athletic field, laying down the laws of this year's Commandant's Challenge for physical fitness. He details the precise route the cadets must follow—a sprint around the field, sit-ups, push-ups, and such—and warns that any straying will add a thirty-minute penalty to the squadron's completion time. "All who start have to finish. Any fallout results in automatic failure for the entire squadron."

"I am so psyched," says Kevin Pastoor, a slender, intense junior. Around him, the cadets are warming up, stretching their hamstrings and bouncing their knees with the soles of their feet together.

For the mile-long sprint, Major Mac joins the cadets. Then the freshmen must do a cumulative 2,010 sit-ups—for their class year. The sophomores do 2,009 push-ups. For the sit-ups, the cadets are not allowed to hold each other's feet, so the freshmen arrange themselves facing each other, with ankles interlocking. They do twenty-five at a time, then stop to rest.

Nick Mercurio stands over them. "Get your legs as close together as possible, then you don't have to go up as far," he tells them. Collette Bannister, a two-degree and Elizabeth Simpson's roommate, counts them off. "Seventy-eight, seventy-nine, eighty, eighty-one. Keep it up, guys. Good job, Bulldawgs!"

Just then Major Mac comes back, his face pink. "Good run," he says, bouncing on the balls of his feet. "Good run."

At the next obstacle, Barry O'Neal Loggins, Jr., a senior, stands over a rectangle of dirt and grass with wooden planks on his right. He faces the doolies, who are clustered to one side. "These are anti–land mine . . . ," Loggins begins, looking down at a clipboard. He cracks a half smile and shakes his head, looking at the ground. "I'll just call 'em boards," he says.

The freshmen must use the boards to transport everybody to the other side of the rectangle. Because there are a limited number of boards, they have to find a way to get the boards back to the first shore to ferry everybody. The cadets are allowed hand and arm signals but are barred from speaking to one another. If they speak, they get a thirty-second penalty, and they must complete the entire event in less than twenty minutes. Just as the doolies begin to understand the rules—after four warnings to stay quiet—a smoke bomb explodes nearby, rattling the freshmen and filling their lungs with biting, acrid smoke.

With David Urban as their leader, four cadets balance themselves on one board and reach down for another to place in front of them. "Safety violation," Loggins barks. "Only two people on a board." They start all over again.

This time, Urban takes only two cadets across, maneuvering the boards so that only two are standing on a single board at a time. This seems to work.

Beyond this exercise, Urban is making his way through the academy on shaky ground. An e-mail I sent to him in October initially went unanswered, then I received a cryptic response saying that he was "involved in a situation" and could not speak to me. Two weeks later, I received another e-mail, this time from Captain Uriah Orland in public affairs, warning that I should avoid e-mailing, calling, or speaking to Urban for the moment, for he is no longer "a cadet in good standing" and so "may not represent the academy in any capacity."

Urban has become a ghost of a cadet, moving around me without greeting or nod, as if we are invisible to each other. Some higher-ups hint at an honor violation, a stunning turnaround for a young man who was homeschooled to build a moat around his character. Could he have been caught cheating? I wonder. Urban had been confident, only a month earlier, that he would need no help meeting the academy's tough course load.

"Let's go," calls Lorenz Madarang, a two-degree from Squadron 13. "Learn from your mistakes."

At 7:30 a.m. on Monday, the halls are silent as the Bulldawg cadets line the walls, standing at parade rest with their arms behind their backs. As David Andrews, a senior from Squadron 2, arrives to inspect them, the cadets draw themselves up to attention. He walks by each one, looking for anything out of place.

He surveys Blake Turnquist and points toward his two sleeves and a pants pocket with a pen. "Wrinkled here, here, here," he says. Turnquist gives a slight nod, acknowledging the criticism.

Andrews goes down the line, giving each cadet feedback.

Christopher Yarlett: "Same thing. Wrinkled there."

Nicole Elliott: "That's good."

Rhonda Meeker: A nod. "All right."

Syed Javaid: "Collar's curled. Goes down at the corner."

Michael Tanner: "Shouldn't there be a patch there?"—indicating Tanner's chest. Andrews points to a loose thread. "Cable on the sleeve, and that's it."

Miles-Tyson Blocker: "Good."

Eric Gobrecht: "Good."

Theodore Ornelas: "Good."

Alan Rodriguez: "Good."

Casey Michelle Johnson: "Wrinkled here on the same spot"—indicating her pocket. After he passes, Johnson rolls her eyes, then smiles, as if amazed that something so minor could be taken so seriously.

Andrews pivots into Elizabeth Simpson's room. She stands at attention, watching him. He runs a finger along the top of the medicine chest.

"Neat," he says. He walks toward the windows, looks into a few dresser drawers, where the underwear and T-shirts are stacked in perfect columns, and peruses the rows of books above her desk. "Looks good to me. I see nothing wrong with it," he says, and turns to leave.

Afterward, Simpson is relieved. She and Bannister had cleaned gobs of leaves from the gutter outside their window the night before. Each discrepancy would have cost five points. "They could have failed our room," she says, looking around. I was mystified: to me, the room was so clean it bordered on sterile. (Mental note to self: *Never* invite them to my house.) Simpson tilts her head, looking toward an errant red ribbon hanging outside the spine of a book on her shelf. "They could always hit you for something like that," she says. "This is a chance for cadets to screw each other or to say, 'Your room is just like ours.'"

Simpson is suffering through crushing headaches, for which the air force doctors can find neither the cause nor a cure. The pain practically paralyzes her, confining her to her room for hours at a time. Her greatest dread, she reports, is that the headaches might disqualify her from pilot training.

Back at the squadron's security desk, Andrews tallies up the results. Seventeen discrepancies. He subtracts, divides, and pronounces his verdict: 97.6 percent. He turns to Peppers. "Can you live with that?" he asks.

"Yes, sir," Peppers says, squaring his shoulders and letting himself smile. The score is, of course, outstanding. "Thank you very much."

That is not the final verdict on Squadron 13's performance in the Commandant's Challenge. Although the Bulldawgs wrap up the first few events and land in only ninth place, they climb up from there, ultimately coming in fourth place out of forty. Only the top two squadrons get plaudits, but the performance is more than respectable. Besides, the cadets tell themselves, it is all about the journey.

Part Four

THE DARK AGES

21 | Flyboy

As the rest of Squadron 13 turns its thoughts to Thanksgiving break, Trent Redburn,* a three-degree and a self-described flyboy, bounces on his feet. He swipes a hand over his forehead and smiles, showing teeth aligned like soldiers, as he turns to me. "What's important enough to get in your book?" he asks, in what is, hands down, the most direct bid for attention I'd heard since arriving.

After four months of training and seventy-five flights, Redburn has just been approved as a flight instructor, able to take up passengers, and he will begin teaching other cadets to fly the academy's fleet of gliders next semester. He is jubilant, offering rides like a new father giving out cigars. He confesses offering one to Master Sergeant Mark Winter, the military trainer assigned to Squadron 13.

Redburn, who hails from the mountains nearby, had already earned a pilot's license during his four years at a midwestern boarding school that he'd attended on scholarship. He had originally gone there to play hockey, and he caddied on golf courses to earn money for piloting lessons and flight time.

Upon arriving at the Air Force Academy, Redburn realized he would not make his mark in hockey. Last summer, he took the academy's course in basic gliding. Getting back in the air, seeing the gorgeous Rockies so close, he felt smitten, so he applied for the instructors' training course. The academy relies almost exclusively on cadets teaching other cadets how to fly, training forty new instructors each semester.

The only planes the cadets learn on at the academy are gliders. The serious equipment—the hot dog, high-powered jets and bombers, the cargo planes and helicopters—are for after graduation. For most cadets, glider

---

*Not his real name.

training here at the academy represents their first exposure to piloting an aircraft of any kind. They do up to two hundred flights a day, fifteen thousand a year, from sunrise to sunset.

Redburn had to adjust to flying solely on air and wind power. A plane with an engine is more straightforward; it gives the pilot a sense of power at his or her back. To take off, gain altitude, and land, the craft requires a given set of skills, modified slightly for the conditions on any given day. To gain speed in a conventional plane, for example, Redburn would just make the engine go faster, much like driving a car.

Flying with no engine, however—trusting your life to what is, essentially, a souped-up kite—is something else entirely, demanding a deeper understanding of aerodynamics and, arguably, more self-confidence. At the start, the pilot must concentrate on flying in perfect synchronicity behind the lead plane, which initially tows the glider on a rope fastened under its nose.

When he flies the glider, Redburn feels tied not only to the plane ahead of him but to the elements: tracking the oscillations in wind and heat and the placement of clouds and fog. Once the rope is released, the glider works thermals, or pockets of hot air. It rides the wind that comes off the sides of hills and ridges and the strong westerly winds that come in over the mountains, called mountain waves. In a glider, the only way to pick up speed is for the pilot to dip the nose of the plane toward the ground, but it is just as crucial to know when to pick up.

"Obviously, you have to worry about altitude and stuff like that," Redburn says.

On a chill morning, there is still snow on the ground as we head out to the airfield. Redburn stops in the main taxiway to circle the car slowly, and he peers down at the tarmac for anything that might tear into a glider's tires. He has never actually found anything, and he is not entirely sure what he's looking for. "A rock. A wrench off a truck?" he suggests.

We head to the single-story building that is used for classroom instruction and traffic control, and within a few minutes, Redburn is once again circling and inspecting. This time, it is one of the academy's twelve yellow sailplanes, known to the air force as a TG-10B, and to civilians as a L-23 Super Blanik. It is long and thin, it weighs less than a thousand pounds, and it seats only two people. Plane and passengers together cannot exceed eleven hundred pounds. The sailplane does not look especially flimsy—if your idea of sufficient protection for jumping off a cliff is, say, a paraglide.

Redburn checks the wheels, the air brakes, the canopy, and the emergency transmitter for locating the plane in case we disappear. He explains the array of dials: one measures our speed climbing the sky, another measures our altitude, and a third—the G-meter—shows the push and pull of gravity during turbulence or aerobatics. There is only one instrument that is actually digital: an all-purpose panel that gives the same information as the dials, and then some, like GPS coordinates.

In the middle is a yellow handle, which Redburn, sitting behind me, will pull when he wants to release our glider from the single prop plane that tows us up. He points to a bolt on the underside of the plane, known as the Jesus pin, and chuckles when asked why: "Because it saves the airplane." The term dates back to the Vietnam War, when pilots nicknamed the bolt that held the rotor to the body of their UH-1 Iroquois helicopters the "Jesus nut": if it failed, the only thing left to do was to sputter, "Oh, Jesus!"

We buckle ourselves into the glider's seats, one in front of the other, like a tandem bicycle, and start rolling down the runway. Two hundred feet of rope tie us to the plane ahead as it lifts us up. With the only rumble beneath coming from the tires over the taxiway, we rise. It takes ten minutes to rise three thousand feet. Since the airfield sits at sixty-five hundred feet, our altitude will be just under ten thousand feet.

Redburn, behind me, is using a stick to tighten slack in the rope that connects us to the lead plane. Another stick shifts the nose to control the altitude. Rudders, which his feet are working, clack behind me, manipulating the glider's movements from side to side. In the middle of explaining what he is doing, Redburn looks over to his right, down to a mountain with snow covering it like icing. He turns to a taller, more massive mountain in the distance. "I live on top of that," he says. He points out another, closer mountain, called Eagle Peak—a popular climbing spot among cadets.

At ninety-five hundred feet, he pulls the handle, releasing us from the tow plane. The plane ahead banks left and down, heading for the airfield. We turn right and climb higher, to ten thousand feet, where we ride the air. "Now we're just soaring," Redburn says. The glider whooshes through the air, steady and smooth, giving us a bird's-eye view of the place I have been watching up close all year.

Redburn is talking about spinning the plane, so that one wing goes down toward the other and dips down. Then the pilot brings the plane back up. "You want to see one?" he asks.

"Yeah."

The plane starts turning, and we are facing the ground. A few minutes ago, Redburn had done his checks knowledgeably and thoroughly and had come across as someone who knows the glider intimately. It's hard not to feel vulnerable, however, not to imagine that one strong, unexpected gust—our personal tsunami from God, for instance, or last night's dinner repeating on Redburn—could send us hurtling to earth. I feel myself being sucked back into the cockpit, the effect of the positive Gs.

"You must have a lot of confidence," I say, once we are flying horizontally again.

"Yes, absolutely," Redburn shouts over the air that is rushing in through the windows.

"You have to have a lot of trust, too."

"Absolutely."

"Outside of this, you're a trusting person?"

"Well, right now I'll say I trust myself when I fly the plane."

In what now seems like another lifetime, I once parachuted outside Rheims, the part of France that gives the world champagne. Having moved to Europe without knowing a soul, I was hankering for a kind of roller coaster, something that would crank up the fear and shake loose a feeling growing inside, hard and disconsolate. I had imagined that parachuting would be silent and peaceful, like floating on the ocean, but now I remember the terror of falling toward earth before pulling the cord and the surprising roar as my body ripped open the wind.

"I'll show you another thing we watch for—spiral dives," Redburn is saying. When students practice steep turns, they can sometimes lose control and start spiraling toward the ground. He winds the plane up, we start spinning, the ground comes closer each second—and then he recovers the plane, arcing it away from disaster.

My half-digested breakfast is starting its nauseating crawl from stomach to throat. Ahead, to the right, is Falcon Stadium. The chances are excellent that my Cheerios will end up back in the bowl, this time at, say, the fifty-yard line?

"You can shut that window if you're cold," Redburn says from the back. I leave it open, pitching my head toward the fresh air as he banks toward the airfield, bringing the glider in for a mostly smooth landing. Afterward, he mentions in passing that he had been worried about the landing because clouds blocked his line of sight back to the runway.

During World War II, gliders played some critical roles: quietly landing the 101st Airborne Division at Normandy, for example, and dropping Allied soldiers in the Nazi-occupied Netherlands. Now they are no longer used in combat. In an age when bombers with pilots on board are giving way to remote-controlled drones, gliders seem quaint and archaic—the aviation equivalent of the electric typewriter. Wouldn't an X-Box do more to hone the skills these cadets will need to fight in today's wars?

For future pilots, however, the glider course serves as a low-tech, relatively low-cost introduction to flight, a first pass that allows the cadets and the air force to test whether pilot training for helicopters or jets is right for them. This year, for the first time, the academy gave every Basic a chance to ride in a glider during the first five weeks. Even some upperclassmen have not yet had the chance to go up.

"Whatever they do after they leave here," says Lieutenant Colonel Steve Dutkus, who is in charge of the training program, "the experience of learning to fly a glider helps them understand the mind-set of the pilots they're working with. It's an awesome opportunity for them to find out what the operational side of the air force is about." One cadet who is learning to fly is headed for intelligence work after graduation. "He'll be the best intel officer, because he understands the mind-set of pilots, thanks to his experience here."

Dutkus contends that the glider program represents the closest experience to active-duty leadership that is offered at the academy. Aviation is inherently dangerous, putting one cadet's life in the hands of another. "Perhaps marching a squadron on the terrazzo can't compare with what we do here," he says.

The instruction closely mimics undergraduate pilot training, the initial year-long program for academy graduates and others on track to become pilots. From there, future pilots go on to more advanced training in their assigned aircraft. As teachers, Redburn and the others belong to the Ninety-fourth Flying Training Squadron, so they get on-the-ground exposure themselves, following the same rules, guidelines, and networks as pilots on active duty. "We already have a sense of how to use the radios and how to fly." That, Redburn adds, is something he can get only here. Having done both civilian training to fly powered aircraft and military training on planes with no engines, Redburn favors the low-tech version, arguing that it's gotten him used to operating in a military environment.

What could an X-Box teach him about ensuring somebody else's safety up in the air while completing a mission, or about having the presence of mind to steer a plane to safety when a student freezes up or starts diving toward the ground?

Truth be told, the air force is, with each passing year, shifting heavily to relying more on remote-controlled weapons systems than on planes flown by pilots. The officer who was in charge of Squadron 13 the year before, having trained to fly B-1 bombers, left to control unmanned drones from a computer terminal in Nevada.

Redburn plans to major in mechanical engineering, and he aims to become a fighter pilot. He feels confident that his scores of hours teaching cadets to fly, demonstrating his "dedication at the airfield," will give him a leg up in the competition, and he does not worry about getting diverted to war by remote control.

He hopes to land a slot at Sheppard Air Force Base in Texas, home to the Euro-NATO Joint Jet Pilot Training Program, after graduation. The program was once devoted solely to producing fighter pilots. These days, it is training pilots who ultimately go into a broader array of jobs, controlling and operating everything from bombers to special operations platforms to the flying robots of modern warfare.

22 | Reaching High and Scaling Back

In the weeks between Thanksgiving and final exams in December, Rhonda Meeker begins weighing the wisdom of her choice of major: aeronautical engineering. As a freshman, she does not have to declare her major this early. She can easily wait another year or more. After all, she has only just turned eighteen. However, she has heard that it is a great advantage to choose early, in order to avoid packing her schedule with tech-heavy courses down the line. She also likes the idea of understanding the aircraft she hopes to fly from the inside out.

"Even if I don't get a pilot's slot," she'd said at the start of the year, "I figure, you'd always be able to get a job with aeronautical engineering. If I could be a part of that, I'd have a pretty secure job field."

Reality has intruded since then. Meeker is struggling through her first encounter with calculus, a bedrock course for aeronautical engineering. Despite turning up for extra instruction twice a week, either with her own professor or another one who has free time, she is barely making it. In class, she can keep up, following each step as the professor goes through a given equation, but she feels marooned when she tries to solve problems on her own. She credits her roommate, Nicole Elliott, "a math genius," with saving her from failure.

"I want to be persistent and stick it out, but I want to be realistic," Meeker says. She loves chemistry and is now thinking of making that her major.

In high school, Meeker had convinced herself that she needed a 3.0 grade point average to get into the academy, and she remembers panicking when she got a B in advanced placement physics. It was just on the line. Now she has lowered her sights, adopting the cadet mantra, "2.0 and go," as her own. Anything below a C average means academic probation; from there, Bs look just fine. She expects to pull an A in Spanish; Bs in English, chemistry, and engineering; and a C in calculus.

"I don't claim intelligence, by any means," she says. "I'm just persistent."

Meeker is also energetic. Her day begins at 5:20 a.m. and is long: straightening her room, calling minutes by 6 a.m. under the direction of Trent Redburn (who, others report, is especially tough on her), going to classes, participating in honor guard (which drills for two and a half hours a day and then eats dinner together), doing her homework, and studying *Contrails*, her little red book. Every other Friday night, she cleans her room thoroughly, wiping down surfaces, straightening drawers and bookshelves, and organizing her closet for the biweekly Saturday morning inspection.

On Veterans Day, Meeker parades through downtown Colorado Springs with the rest of the honor guard, shifting and twirling her rifle in elaborate sequences synchronized to the second and handed down to the cadets for thirty years. "Honor Guard, Honor Guard, stop here," Meeker hears the children in the city call. "Do your thing for us here."

"Everybody went dead silent while they watched us," she recalls later. "Then they would clap. I remember this one kid; he said, 'Dad, that was so awesome.'"

For Meeker, the attraction of honor guard is based not on personality or popularity—two areas where she runs into trouble—but on a fanatical dedication to the military and its traditions. The honor guard represents the nation's mettle and might at official ceremonies; it stands continuous watch over the Tomb of the Unknown Soldier at Arlington Cemetery, and it wraps the dead in dignity and meaning. There is no room for error.

Strangely enough, it was Zach Taylor and Brad Bernard who had urged Meeker to apply for honor guard. "I talked her into it," Bernard says. "In basic, she was left out. The girls didn't like her." Honor guard was not something that Bernard would ever consider for himself. He is not even sure he is 100 percent here, and at times he seems to be watching himself from off to the side somewhere, skeptical about his own efforts.

Honor guard stands at the opposite end of the spectrum. Bernard's classmates, as cynical as undergraduates anywhere, look down on it because "you're, like, super cadet. They take this place to the max," he explains. Given the distance between the guard's credo and Bernard's own attitude, his suggestion to Meeker must have been inspired, bordering on genius, or a callous prank. "I think she's found something," he says. "They understand her, and she understands them."

The harder and more secretive the training, the more Meeker values it. Although the doolies must ordinarily spew hours of arcane details from *Contrails* along with the personal histories of the upperclassmen in their squadrons, honor guard demands that they learn even more, down to the names of the brothers and sisters of their trainers and drill mates.

"It's a lot more than friends," Meeker says. The members are more like a family. They get together during the week and on weekends, visiting one another's sponsor families, the civilians who informally adopt the cadets during their time in Colorado Springs and host them for weekends and holidays. She is looking forward to competing in the Southern California Invitational Drill Meet in spring, a vast gathering in Huntington Beach of drill teams from across the country.

Meeker has already taken part of her Spanish final, for which she spoke extemporaneously about a picture for two minutes. The illustration showed a man and a boy speaking to a woman at an airport. The story Meeker invented hints at her own trajectory, rising from the margins to build a better life: "They were saying good-bye to the mother, who is a flight attendant but is training to be a pilot so she could earn more money to send her son to school. They felt bad, she felt bad to be away from them, but she had to do it."

Meeker pauses, looking at her knees for a moment. "It's not so important what you say, they just want to hear how you speak."

In her engineering class, she is part of a team that builds a rocket glider, an assignment that had flummoxed her at the semester's start. She could not fathom how she would do it: craft a booster and a rocket whose wings would emerge after launch, with sensors for a remote control that would guide it toward a given target. She had never done anything like this.

As Christmas approaches, she surprises herself. Her team builds the rocket launcher first, then the glider. "Then we put them together," she says. "I did a lot of the paperwork. Not so much hands-on, but that's okay. I learned something." As part of her final, she still has to give a twenty-minute briefing on how the rocket works.

Going into her exams, Meeker has worked out a schedule for studying four to five hours a night. There is only one day between the end of classes and the start of finals, but she has heard that finals are a lighthearted time.

"We take only a few each day, so the rest of the time, people are studying, playing. People are running around like crazy, playing in the snow, going out to dinner."

Meeker has two exams on Friday and two on Saturday, with the last ending at 10 p.m. Come Sunday morning, she will be on a bus to the Denver airport, heading home for Christmas.

23 | Running Man

The photo on Brad Bernard's desk shows him with a group of his football buddies from the academy prep school last year. They are smiling in their jerseys, their broad shoulders touching. Of the group, only two are still at the academy: Bernard and one other—and that other is not his former roommate, Zach Taylor, a football pal who put in his papers and never came back after winter break.

"He hated this place with a passion," Bernard reports, looking toward the empty bed as though a piece of his roommate, the guy he thought would make it through with him, was still there, listening.

The room, though, is scrubbed clean of Taylor, who lost no time in getting on with his life. The last time they spoke, Taylor was planning to attend community college and wait tables to pay for tuition. He hoped to eventually transfer to Texas Tech University.

Taylor's departure beckons like an open window with sheets tied end to end for his friend's escape. Bernard thinks wistfully of Taylor attending a civilian university, where he can let his socks pile up or party all night without facing hell for it. "He's loving life," Bernard says miserably. "He said he's never been happier."

Too openly for his own good, perhaps, Bernard wonders why he is still at the academy. He certainly is not loving life, and he is not doing what he came here to do. Recruited to play football, he has been off the team ever since he broke his shoulder during practice. The injury happened a year after he had torn his hamstrings at the prep school. Before that, he broke his foot. Bernard wonders if maybe the game was trying to tell him something: that his body wasn't meant for this abuse.

"I didn't quit football," he says, shaking his head. "Football quit me."

At Mitchell Hall, he has traded the football dining table for the track table, with its light blue tablecloth and healthy menu: food that is grilled, not fried; wheat bread, not white; and fruit instead of cake for dessert. He has already shed 17 pounds and is down to 233 pounds, and he hopes to lose another 10. He is running more than three miles a day and finds that he likes track, with its emphasis on striving to top his personal best, more than football. "It's more individual, a different kind of training," he says.

But a change in sport has not changed his feelings about the academy, which he finds steeped in pointless ritual and power games that are bent on breaking his spirit.

"I'm not happy. I'm looking at trying to get out," Bernard says. He is collecting Form 10s like baseball cards. This form—"probably one of the most ridiculous things" at the academy, in his mind—documents a variety of seemingly petty infractions, and the accumulation of forms translates into a lifetime of punishment. Each one means hours of confinement, sitting at his desk in service dress, with coat and tie, his feet planted on the floor. He does his time on Friday night and Saturday morning, and he should be studying during it. Instead, he cruises eBay for things he cannot afford to buy.

He got one Form 10 for walking up the wrong stairwell. As a freshman, he is restricted to walking up the stairs at the far ends of the corridor.

"This one I got yesterday," he says, flicking another paper on his desk, "I got caught carrying my book bag on my shoulder." The rules here demand that doolies carry their bags in their hands, not on their shoulders.

He finds these added hardships gratuitous, even absurd. The upperclassmen in his squadron suspect that his mistakes are intentional, a sign that he just can't be bothered to take their authority, or even the rules, seriously, and they wonder where this will lead. His disregard is an electrical charge; it drives them to ride him even harder.

The latest Form 10 came courtesy of Jamal Harrison, who spied him in a stairwell carrying his pack on his shoulder. The week before, Harrison knew, Bernard had been written up for the same infraction.

"Any other day of the week, I wouldn't have thought two seconds about it," Harrison says, "but I'm walking out, I'm thinking, 'Oh, that's a pretty big guy. He must be a football player.' And I thought, 'Football player. That is Bernard with a backpack on his shoulder.' So, you know, I go up to his face, and I call him, and I catch him." Bernard, Harrison recalls, took a step back and shook his head, as if marveling at the absurdity of it. "I said, 'What are you doing, man?' I wasn't mean. I wasn't yelling. I wasn't screaming."

Bernard did not argue with Harrison. "I know that's inappropriate decorum," he told the upperclassman. "I just wasn't thinking. I made a bad decision."

Harrison let him go on his way but promised to stop by Bernard's room that night. When he did, Bernard shocked him. He apologized and actually sounded sincere. Harrison was moved. He asked how it happened, and Bernard told him he'd been making an honest effort not to carry his pack over his shoulder. Between the last time he was caught doing it and the moment Harrison had seen him, the athlete claimed, he had been faithfully carrying his backpack in his hand.

Harrison believed him and offered encouragement. "I definitely see a change. Keep working on it, and you'll be fine," Harrison told him, but he didn't feel comfortable overlooking the incident.

Although the offense should have cost Bernard ten demerits and confinement to campus until the sentence was served, Harrison, moved by Bernard's remorse, hit him with only four demerits. Nevertheless, as the punishment passed up the cadet chain of command, Bernard's sentence grew from four to nine demerits. Enough demerits could lower his military performance average, which was already precarious, and lead to probation.

Some cadets have a hard time because of rumor or preconceived notions. They make a mistake early, and it follows them all year, wherever they go. But Bernard comes by the antagonism honestly: he earns it anew each day.

Still, Harrison is hopeful about Bernard. "I think he might be an example of one of those guys who comes in here, kind of iffy, kind of shady," he says, tilting his head. "He's starting to straighten out a little bit. I think he'll be all right."

Unlike his fellow four-digs, Bernard does not bother to hide his discontent. But his ambivalence is not so unusual. At one point or another, virtually all the cadets I speak to confess to wondering—usually when they are feeling particularly alone, abused, homesick, or buried under a drift of bad grades—whether they belong here. Some almost leave the academy, either by dropping out or by nearly getting kicked out for poor grades or for violating the honor code. Others, like Casey Jane Barrett and Taylor, let go willingly and start their undergraduate education over again.

If getting into the academy is difficult, getting out is not easy, either. Given the investment, by the taxpayers and by the institution itself, the academy does not let go without a fight. It becomes a kind of automatic pitcher, offering uncertain cadets chance after chance to take a swing at staying. A cadet who wants to leave must meet with virtually every person up and down the chain of command who is involved in his or her life: element leader, flight leader, squadron leader, the officer in charge, coaches, academic advisers, a therapist, and so on.

Matthew Takanen, a soft-spoken, thoughtful senior from Cincinnati who is squadron commander for spring semester, jokes that during his freshman year, if the cadets had had to sign a sheet affirming their desire to remain at the academy each day, there would have been no Class of 2007.

"I wouldn't be here," he says, laughing, "but the fact was that the paperwork was so long that I was just like 'I'll just see how it is tomorrow.'"

Captain Uriah Orland, a spokesman for the academy, says that there are so many speed bumps on the road out for cadets because once they leave, there is rarely a road back in. "They want to make sure that it's the decision that you want to make, as opposed to having a bad day. It's not like University of Colorado where it's like, 'Oh, I don't want to go this semester.' Here the decision is final."

The cadets who decide to leave have usually come for the wrong reasons, Takanen says: they were proud to get in; they wanted to please their parents; they were recruited to play football by coaches who downplayed the military training involved; or their parents went here. The first year, especially, is so arduous that it becomes a test of resolve.

Major Robert MacKenzie, who is in charge of Squadron 13, considers Bernard to be typical of many freshmen in his uncertainty.

"He's still not sure what the future's going to hold," the major says, "but he's come back and he'll go through the semester, and he'll make a decision." Taylor had been doing okay academically, but he had an attitude, MacKenzie felt, that suggested he would never make a stellar contribution to the service. In Bernard, though, MacKenzie thinks he sees something more.

Beyond the outward indifference and the corners that Bernard skirts, beyond his defiance of the rules, MacKenzie sees somebody who genuinely connects with his fellow cadets, who is fundamentally honest about who he is, and who does not bother sucking up. He sees the potential for Bernard to just possibly become a strong leader.

It is a potential that Bernard himself does not recognize. With money such a problem at home, its lack is all that he sees, and he thinks it is poverty that keeps him here.

"I'm not sentimental. This place is free. If it cost money, I wouldn't still be here," he says. He doesn't see how he could leave the academy. "I wouldn't have any money or anywhere to go."

If Bernard seriously wants to leave the academy, however, the reluctant cadet has more options than he admits to himself. Having graduated from a public high school in Georgia with decent grades, he would still be eligible for a HOPE scholarship, a state program that uses the proceeds from lottery sales to cover full tuition and hundreds of dollars in fees at state colleges and universities. He would only have to reestablish a year's residency in Georgia to be eligible.

Taylor, for example, does not end up waiting tables to pay for community college. After registering at a junior college, he contacts his high school football coach, who tells him he still has one day before the deadline to sign up for spring semester at Texas Tech University, which had wanted him for football. Thus Taylor starts classes at Texas Tech a month after leaving the academy.

Like Barrett's parents with their daughter, Taylor's parents oppose his decision to drop out of the academy and blame him for wasting the opportunity. They refuse to pay for him to attend another university, he says, but he still finds generous aid. His stint at the prep school and the academy have made him a member of the active-duty military, which makes him eligible for a waiver of tuition and some fees under a Texas state law known as the Hazlewood Act. Taylor also receives grants earmarked for veterans to cover his housing and other costs. He is lucky enough to find a well-paying job on campus, calling alumni to ask them for donations. He borrows only two thousand dollars a semester to cover his expenses.

Although both Taylor and Bernard gripe that they hate the academy, their backgrounds are different: Taylor's family has some money, and even though they are not paying his way now, he knows that help would arrive if he were ever desperate. Bernard does not carry that kind of insurance.

When Bernard looks toward the future, he sees himself as a "five and dive": somebody who puts in the five-year minimum of military service and then bolts. Viewed one way, his hopes are self-serving, even cynical: to land a slot in acquisitions, where he can make contacts and ease into a good job after leaving the service.

"It's not the most desirable air force job," he admits. Given his starting point, though, such a future would represent a great leap, allowing him to build a comfortable life for himself and the family he may one day have.

The disappearance of his football pals does not surprise Bernard. Even with the breaks the academy gives athletes, between the course work and the military standards, he argues, it just demands too much.

Forty days before Recognition, the spring training exercise, the indignities intensify as the upperclassmen beat the doolies constantly. As an athlete, Bernard gets a pass—further fueling the animosity he feels from his peers and even more so from the upperclassmen.

"They don't realize we're training every day," he says. "They think I'm out there sipping Coke and eating pizzas. I still pretty much hate it here," he adds, raising one shoulder and shaking his head. "Recognition is only a few weeks away, though. Life'll be a lot better once we get past Recognition."

Bernard glances out the window, thankful for the January snow piled high. "That's good for us," he says. Snow means that doolies don't have to jog between buildings but may walk. Snow means not sticking to the marble strips edging the vast terrazzo, a route that lengthens every trip and reminds them, with each step, of their marginal status in the academy's life.

24 | Taylor's Walk

Although Zach Taylor formally quit the academy on his way out for winter break, he had set his sights on leaving months before. It was at the end of basic training, an ordeal that ran longer and harder than he'd expected. As a football player, Taylor had been promised he wouldn't have to go through basic training but would be pulled out midway through it.

That never happened. Not only was he there, it was doubly painful for him. He showed up just after his wrist, broken in a game at the prep school, had come out of its cast and his hand was still in a brace. He received no break for the injury; instead, the cadre hollered at him for shirking. It took a special waiver just for him to be allowed to do push-ups with his right hand balled into a fist instead of flat on the ground.

It wasn't so much the physical demands that soured his appetite for the place; Taylor was in better shape than most of the other freshmen, so he handled the sit-ups, the squats, and the marching well enough. It was the constant hammering and the ossified hierarchy, the sense that he'd been hoodwinked. A few weeks of crushing criticism was bad enough, but the prospect of an entire year with his head on the anvil was more than Taylor had signed on for. He leaned over to Becky Gleason, another recruited athlete, on the last day of basic training. "I'm not going to stay," he said.

Nevertheless, it took him four months to lay the groundwork for leaving. Now, when he arrives at Texas Tech, he feels suspended between two worlds. He had fled the academy's regimentation, but now he finds that he wants to dress down the ROTC kids when their uniforms are not perfectly aligned.

Much as Casey Jane Barrett had found, the accolades and congratulations that had showered Taylor upon his recruitment become icy daggers when he announced his decision to leave. He left the academy feeling depleted, emotionally battered by his training.

At the prep school, the training had been tough, but it was done entirely by enlisted officers, so it had seemed more professional and rational. There was nothing gratuitous in its harshness. Despite the new layers of oversight, training at the academy was still mostly run by older cadets, so it sometimes felt more arbitrary, even cruel. He recalls cadets from another flight, not his, whose cadre during Beast forced them to go from steaming to icy showers and spend ten seconds under each. Getting over the experience once he left was not easy.

"It really brought down my confidence." Taylor's hair is still buzz-cut short, and his build is lean. He smiles, and he does not mind acting goofy or saying what he thinks. His Facebook profile photo for a while is a cartoon face pasted on Elvis Presley's shoulders, with a 1970s hairdo in jet black and a hairline that reaches almost to the eyebrows.

Taylor had been recruited to play football for the academy as a receiver from Northwest High in Justin, Texas. (Its claim to fame: "Where Justin boots are made.") It was the boy's only offer from a Division I school. He had never really thought seriously about the military as a career. His head was all football.

The academy's recruiter, he says, played up the football and glossed over the military commitment involved: he told Taylor that he would spend most of his time on the game, that he would be pulled out of basic training halfway through it. Nobody expected athletes to be supermen, bringing glory on the field and meeting the same academic and military standards as ordinary students; help and understanding would lighten their load.

Moreover, in junior year, a thirty-thousand-dollar government loan would come his way, he was told. Lots of cadets spent the money on sleek Corvettes or other fancy cars, the recruiter said. Taylor has come to feel that the entire process "was corrupt. I had friends who were recruited who didn't even know they were going through basic training," he says.

At basic training for prep school, Taylor had lost twenty-five pounds, and he never had the chance to gain it back—an early sign that the academic and military training would shape his life more than the recruiter had let on. As at the academy, the students at the prep school had to sit tall at mealtime, staring at the eagle on the rim of each plate.

At the prep school, dining decorum—the insistence on precise formulas for passing and eating food—had not been an issue. Nevertheless, the students had only seven minutes to eat—or, rather, inhale—each meal during basic training. No matter how much Taylor stuffed into his mouth in seven minutes, he was hungry again twenty minutes later. He once blew ten dollars buying a granola bar from another kid. "I was that hungry," he says.

Playing football at the prep school, Taylor had been injured again and again. Aside from the broken wrist, cuts on his knees left him with staph infections. Promises aside, the load was never any easier on him for being an athlete. "It was really military first," he says.

He began to research his options and discovered a way out, with the Hazlewood Act easing his way. If he could only stick it out for eighteen months, or through the end of the first semester at the academy, then he would be counted as a veteran and could get financial aid to attend another public college or university.

He put in his time at the gym and on the field, playing a range of positions: receiver, running back, and corner back. "I feel like they really didn't care about us," he says. "I didn't really know what the officer commitment was all about. It was something I didn't really want to do. I didn't want to graduate and be told how I would live my life, where I was going to go."

Feeling cheated by the academy, Taylor did not hesitate to cheat at the academy. Ten minutes before each week's exam on *Contrails*, the pocket encyclopedia of factoids about the air force and the academy, Taylor would get the answers to the test. An upperclassman would post them on the Internet, and some freshmen used a program that figured out the passwords to access that week's answers.

"Certain people would send messages," he says, "and others would pass them out. I would get a copy of the answers, and I would memorize them. I got the answers to the test ten minutes before the test, every time."

Taylor did not usually even look at the questions. He just memorized the answers. Then, when four-digs lined up in the corridors for their weekly knowledge exams, he would write the answers. He never acted greedy or stupid, answering every answer correctly, like some of the other students he knew. Instead, he would make a show of looking stumped and would throw in wildly wrong responses now and then to avoid arousing suspicion.

"I would stand there and act like I was thinking about it and then write the answers," he says. "I would purposely mess up on a few of the questions." He was satisfied to get a 70. "All I needed to do was pass," he says.

Taylor did not feel guilty about cheating. During the year, he and the other athletes were at practice until dinnertime, so they never had time to study and memorize the little red books as their classmates did. Nevertheless, they faced the same tests as their classmates each week. The information they were supposed to know seemed largely inconsequential to Taylor. If they flunked the tests, they were not allowed to go out all weekend. Even the upperclassmen who were in charge of their training would have to stay in.

"It didn't really bother me," Taylor says. "They give you the book, and they don't really tell you what parts to study or know. It's pretty ridiculous. Pretty unnecessary." He adds that he never cheated on any tests that involved a course he was taking.

"I feel like I was lied to by my recruiting coach," he says. "Not lied to," he corrects himself, "but misled pretty badly."

Ragged from his time at the prep school and the academy, where he had dropped to 165 pounds, Taylor bucks expectations at Texas Tech and doesn't play football. "I was all banged up," he says later. He doesn't want to play much of anything.

"I guess it's like a process: freshman year they cut you down, and then after that, in sophomore and junior year, they build you up again. I was never there for the build-you-up part. I was just there for the tear-you-down part. I had to build myself back up."

25 | The Four-Dig Slide

To the known reasons Zach Taylor is glad he quit the Air Force Academy comes another, almost as a bonus, six weeks after he leaves: A cadet denounces the cheating operation that Taylor and countless classmates had relied on to pass the weekly knowledge exams, setting off an investigation into its operation and cadet involvement that consumes most of spring semester. The inquiry would most likely have included Taylor, forcing him to make painful choices.

"It's a good thing I left when I did," Taylor says with relief. He might have gone out in shame, otherwise. The investigators, the cadets on the academy's honor board, could have pressured him so much that he would have either lied outright or turned in his friends.

Taylor can see the avalanche coming. Every week, he learns of more and more cadets who begin cheating on the exams—not just athletes like him, who felt entitled and overloaded, but classmates who never played on any team.

The majority of cadets first caught cheating are athletes, who are busy training while others are free to study. To most of them, the ethical dilemma is minor. It is simply a matter of meeting all the expectations that are placed on their shoulders.

"I don't see how athletes would pass that test without some kind of help," Taylor says. Not all the athletes participated, he adds. Some wanted to live by the honor code. Over time, however, two things happened to make the discovery of the answer sharing all but inevitable: the students who were cheating sparked suspicion by answering every question correctly, time after time, and the circle of cadets that was sharing the answers widened to include nonathletes.

"You had to know somebody who knew the answers," Taylor says. "It wasn't just being an athlete." After a while, it became an academy version of *Six Degrees of Separation*, where many cadets knew somebody who knew somebody who could get the answers. He suspects that the majority of doolies could have gotten their hands on the answers.

More than two dozen cadets are caught sharing answers, at first. The cadets, all of them four-digs, face possible expulsion for violating the honor code, a cornerstone of academy life that is as old as the academy's first graduating class.

The doolies had sworn to uphold the code on Acceptance Day a few months before. "We will not lie, steal or cheat, nor tolerate among us anyone who does. Furthermore, I resolve to do my duty and to live honorably, so help me God," they had pledged as their parents watched. As doolies, they are new to the code; if they confess and cooperate with the investigation, they will most likely get off with punishment and probation. A sophomore, or three-degree, might also survive a cheating violation. But the same offense committed by a two-degree or a firstie would likely put an end to the cadet's career.

The scandal also sideswipes the academy's campaign to rehabilitate itself in the public eye; once again, its standing is lowered before parents and the taxpaying public, demoralizing the cadets and the academy leadership. Pranksters take down the words at the heart of the honor code, from an inscription on a granite overpass known as the honor wall. What is left is meaningless, empty spaces open to improvisation: "We will not _____, _____ or _____, nor tolerate among us anyone who does."

As scandals go, the discovery of a cheating ring is less messy than the sexual assault scandal of 2003, which targeted not just the assailants but also the leadership, for punishing the alleged rape victims because their behavior had violated academy rules against drinking or fraternization. Cheating among cadets is also less politically volatile an issue than religious coercion by Christian fundamentalists, which had dogged the previous superintendent of the academy, Lieutenant General John Rosa.

This scandal is straightforward and uncontroversial: swiping the answers to an exam is in direct violation of the honor code. It's also familiar. Cheating is like a buoy that bobs up from time to time in the flow of the academy's history. Just two years ago, 19 doolies had been disciplined—either given probation or kicked out—for cheating on the same kind of exam. In the biggest single incident, 109 cadets had resigned in 1965 for cheating or for not informing on classmates who had cheated. Since the academy's start, the equivalent of an entire class, some 1,200 cadets, had resigned over cheating and other violations of the honor code.

Cheating scandals have brought notoriety to the academy's doorstep maybe half a dozen times. Taylor believes that the discovery of cheating might be unusual, but the practice is not. In light of the demands on the four-digs, particularly the athletes, he considers cheating to be an essential part of academy life. Doolies who fail the tests of military knowledge may not leave campus the following weekend, and two failures mean that the upperclassmen in charge of the cadets' training may not leave, either. This creates enormous incentives for the upperclassmen to quietly slip the doolies some help. It is almost like travel insurance.

"I think that in some way every year they found a way to get the answers," Taylor says.

Apparently learning from the mistakes of their predecessors, Lieutenant General John Regni and Brigadier General Susan Desjardins strike a refreshingly open tone when the revelations of cheating break. They make no attempt to cover up the problem. The academy's spokesman, Johnny Whitaker, a retired colonel who is an academy graduate himself, talks to local and national reporters in a tone of frank dismay.

"The fact that they made this choice, knowing full well from the first day what the consequences are, that they still choose to do this is very disturbing," he tells Tom Roeder, a reporter for the *Colorado Springs Gazette*. "Our mission is to create officers of integrity and character. It all begins with the honor code."

Whitaker also discloses that earlier in the month, the academy had banned forty-three cadets from using the Internet after they were discovered viewing or downloading pornography online. The candor helps to blunt criticism. More important, it spares the academy death by a hundred scoops, with each new sin that is uncovered prompting another news cycle of notoriety.

Although the Class of 2010 started out with the highest grade point average of the four classes then at the academy, by the end of first semester, the four-digs have the lowest average grades of any class in the last two decades and the most cadets, one in five, on academic probation. The disparity is not necessarily the result of rampant grade inflation by high schools across the country, with overhyped cadets collapsing before the more rigorous coursework of the academy. The slide might also be caused by the many invitations to play that are available to today's cadets.

Recalling his own career as a cadet in Squadron 13, Captain Uriah Orland, a 2002 graduate, says that cadets then had an easier time concentrating on course work.

"We weren't allowed to have phones, CDs, music players, or anything that distracted us," he recalls.

Soon after the scandal breaks, General Regni summons all forty-three hundred cadets to Mitchell Hall, where they stand at parade rest for a lengthy dressing-down. Like previous superintendents, Regni blames the current problem on "a few bad apples," but in a barrage of severe rhetorical questions, he presses the cadets to look deep into their characters.

"Is this about respect?" Regni asks the cadets. "Is it about dignity? Is it about core values? Is it about ethics? Is it about honor? Is it about pride in yourself, your academy, and your profession?"

That weekend, he orders the entire cadet corps to remain on campus, banning all manner of distractions, from cell phones to movie players. On Saturday, the cadets do a major housecleaning and get a one-time amnesty to turn in contraband. In Squadron 13, two hamsters have to hit the road.

"It's too bad, but I think they found a better home," says Justin Goodin, a four-dig who is Bernard's new roommate.

The following day, the cadets meet with their classmates and then with their entire squadron for three hours after lunch to talk about what had happened and why, and to figure out how to improve their academic performance without resorting to cheating.

General Regni also wants them to think hard about the honor code. If the cadets are ignoring it, is it serving any function? Should it be toughened? Should it be scrapped altogether? The latter has happened before. In 1984, the superintendent, Lieutenant General Winfield W. Scott, Jr., had suspended the honor code after nineteen cadets were expelled for cheating on a physics exam. Scott believed that there was a general apathy among the cadets for the honor code and that it would be better to have no code at all than to have one that was ignored.

Instead, the cadets lived by the Uniform Code of Military Justice, just as they would in the active-duty air force. After some time, he put the question to a vote. The cadets opted for a return of the honor code, adding the second sentence at that time: "Furthermore, I resolve to do my duty and to live honorably."

The toughest part of living under the honor code is not its demand that the cadets, who physically walk in straight lines nearly all of first year, resist the temptation to skirt moral corners. Rather, it is the code's demand that they inform on their friends or classmates who stumble.

Bettina C. Erzen, the chief of honor education at the academy, says that turning in a friend runs counter to the bond that cadets are supposed to feel for their classmates.

"We come here and you tell us we have to watch out for our buddies," the cadets tell her. "Now you're telling me I might have to turn my buddy in."

That contradiction poses an almost insurmountable challenge, she acknowledges. "We tell the cadets, 'If you see your buddy go down that path, call them on it, so you don't have to report them for the honor code violation.' We try to get them to understand you're here for the greater good. A real friend is not going to put you in a position where you have to turn them in."

Erzen pauses a moment, as if hearing the words herself as a cadet, measuring the call to honor against the threat of isolation and worse for informing on a fellow cadet. There is not much to fall back on.

"They voluntarily take this oath," she offers. However, the pledge is not really voluntary; abstaining would be a quick ticket out of the academy.

So far, at least, no Bulldawgs have been named in the scandal—a relief to Major Robert MacKenzie. Still grappling to understand the origins of the cheating ring and the free fall in grade point averages of the new cadets, MacKenzie says he does not see the current crop of doolies as inherently different from his own class, which graduated in 1992. Nor does Captain Orland, ten years later.

"We all wanted to be officers," Orland says. "We all wanted to be committed to something bigger than ourselves." He glances at Major MacKenzie's door as the cadets bustle through the hallway, four-digs along the walls and upperclassmen commanding the center of the corridor. "We all wanted something better than the rest of society."

26 | Of Love and Pain

As the academy descends into the Dark Ages—the weeks between the return from winter break and spring Recognition, when the nights are longest and the training most intense—Rhonda Meeker makes her way through classes ahead of honor guard practice that afternoon. Her hair is growing out, pulled into a low ponytail behind her neck, curled like a baby's fist.

In her engineering mechanics class, she calculates the right position for a crowbar to leverage three hundred pounds of supplies onto a C-130 cargo plane. In world civilizations, she learns about a German explorer who stumbled upon the ancient kingdom of Zimbabwe and a different kind of leverage. His presumption—that Africans were not smart enough to have designed such a grand palace, so Europeans must have been there long ago, became the justification for white rule throughout the continent.

The professor, Alan Osur, a Vietnam veteran with wavy hair going grey, gives the students hypothetical missions, hoping to train their minds to ask the right questions. The first is a joint operation with the Moroccan military, and the issues are mostly prosaic and cultural: What is the climate in the region? Are there any traditions or taboos, like offering your left hand in greeting, that you need to watch out for? The second is entering the lawless, lethal anarchy of Somalia.

"You want to know all the different ways you can get into trouble," Osur warns. "I mean, you really have to be realistic. You want to know the environment. What's the political nature of that environment? What's the religion? What about the clothes you're going to wear?"

"The first question I have when I go to a different country: Can I drink the water? A very important question." Osur says, walking around the room. "I spent a year in Thailand during the Vietnam War. We could drink it on base, but we couldn't drink it off base. And also, we had bottled water. In Bangkok, when we held a glass of water up to the light, there were bugs at the bottom."

"No way," a student blurts out in disgust.

Osur nods, his lips pressed together. "You've got to just be aware of that," he says. He warns them not to count on commanding officers or orders to give them this kind of important background orientation before shipping them out. "You have to think about other people, other cultures, and not generalize."

Meeker does not say much during class.

Her grades last semester landed as she expected: an A in Spanish; Bs in English, chemistry, and engineering; and a C in calculus, giving her a B average. When she went home for the holidays, it was to a new place, which did not have a space she could call her own. Meeker's parents had moved into a retirement community, and she stayed in a guest room. She spent a week visiting with her best friend. Long before classes resumed, she felt ready to come back.

Back in class, her foot taps the metal bar under her chair like a metronome set to presto. She is worried that she will not have time to dress for honor guard, to which she hurries at sunset. The drill team's camaraderie is tight, the training legendary for its intensity and ruthlessness. It is normally kept under wraps and closed to outsiders, but today they have agreed to let me watch.

"There are some things you'll see that you'll want to know why do you do that," Meeker warns me ahead of practice, "and there won't be any answer." Sometimes, the cadre drop the four-degrees for five hundred push-ups, or they have to do "trips"—running with their rifles across the grass at the center of the terrazzo, up the hill at the far end and back in less than two minutes.

At highly advanced levels, they might drill in a circle, tossing rifles fixed with sharp bayonets past a cadet who stands in the center, unmoving. The exercise emphasizes the dependence of each member on the others, the degree to which their lives are intertwined. There is no room for doubt or mistrust. The team must be perfectly attuned, each to the others, to pull off such maneuvers without landing in the emergency room.

Meeker says there is no rationale behind these strange binding rituals but then offers one. Against the backdrop of her turbulent upbringing and her yearning to fit in, it is not hard to understand her choice.

"It's showing that we'll give whatever it takes, whether it's five hundred push-ups or a run up the hill. A lot of what we do is showing through our actions how dedicated we are to the will, the discipline, to learning how to do it right," she says. "And to showing the team that we love them and that we care for them."

Fat snowflakes are falling as she crosses the terrazzo and ducks into an unheated meeting room, where the lights are dim and floor-to-ceiling windows do little to keep out the icy chill. She joins four other doolies and twice as many cadre. Although this is a club, there is no laughter or small talk. Ordinarily, they practice outside, no matter how frigid the temperature, but the snow makes that impractical. Instead, today they drill in this room, which offers shelter, scant light, and only as much warmth as they generate through their work. Christopher A. Wolff, the two-degree in charge of training SMACKs for honor guard, says the practice itself heats up their bodies.

Meeker and the other freshmen grab M-1 rifles bandaged in white tape. The tape makes the weapons easier to grip during the elaborate moves ahead. On the cadets' heads are dull black helmet liners shaped like soup bowls, and for a moment I imagine them straggling off a World War II battlefield. They warm up with a few simple drills, their hands clutching, climbing, and twisting their rifles. Since there are more upperclassmen than freshmen in the room, few mistakes go unnoticed. The trainers surround the freshmen as they practice, pouncing on their slipups.

"Hoove," bellows Ryan Holets, a three-degree. "Double trouble." The sequence, which the four-digs began learning at their last practice, involves an intricate series of perfectly coordinated moves of increasing difficulty. It starts with spinning the rifle overhand, once clockwise and then counterclockwise, followed by tossing the rifle in the air, first for one full spin high above the head and then two full spins. The effect suggests a pinwheel that changes rotations, then spins free of its base, flying up and returning to its starting point. These wheels are heavy rifles, however, not weightless paper or plastic, and they must be acrobatic—twirling, flying, and stopping at precisely the right position at exactly the right moment.

That is what the maneuver should ultimately look like, but there is a world of trial and pain between that dazzling precision and where Meeker and her comrades are today. As they go through the drill, they count each of the sequence's twenty-one steps: "Cock, spin, catch. Pause, spin, throw back." Despite the count, they are still each working the moves out individually; they falter and quickly fall out of sync.

"I'm losing my patience," booms Ryan Wiese, a two-degree. "Why don't you try pumping together? Why don't you try doing what you're supposed to do? Where's your commitment?"

They begin the sequence again, their rifles spinning, but when they are supposed to toss their weapons, Nick Wright, a four-dig, drops his rifle to the floor. His face is stricken, as if he has wrestled a buddy and broken his neck by mistake. Three trainers surround him, berating him at the same time.

"Get down!" shouts Wolff, ordering Wright's teammates to hit the floor for yet more push-ups.

"We gave you another chance, and what did you do with it? Nothing!" Wright stands there, humiliated, powerless to help.

Holets glares at Wright. "We care about the details," he hollers. "We want everything out. We don't slough through anything. What's the standard, Wright?"

"The standard is perfection," Wright answers hoarsely. He is breathing heavily, watching his teammates with their hands flat on the floor, pumping up and down.

"It's all on you, Wright," says Holets. "Imagine that you're not on the front anymore. You have only one opportunity." For raising or lowering the flag, crossing sabers for a wedding arch, or escorting a coffin, there are no second chances. A sequence is either right or you've failed.

"Why is it we have four cadre on you every day?" Holets adds. "I find it ironic that your name is Wright."

"I'll leave it up to you," Wolff tells the group. "Do you want to actually drill, or do you want to stay down?" He orders them up.

"Double trouble. Hoove!"

They repeat the sequence, their hands raw, their breath forming clouds in the half-light. In a few minutes, the cadre stop them again, ordering them back down for more push-ups.

As they rise and fall, Wolff suspects one of the SMACKs, Thomas Posey, of staying down too long. "Why were you lying on the ground?" he hollers over him.

"Sir, I was not lying on the ground," Posey replies. "Sir, I went down for a push-up and I hit the ground. I was not lying on the ground."

"Obviously, you were, Posey," Wolff snaps. "Stop BS-ing me. Start upholding the standards."

"You know what mediocrity is, right?" Wiese demands.

"Yes, sir!" the group answers.

"You're letting it slip in," Wiese declares. "It takes a hold of your team. You get complacent. Why? Why are you complacent?"

There is only silence. Each second stretches as if endless, like a road to the horizon.

"Someone give me an answer!" Wiese booms.

Chris Allen, a freshman, volunteers that his teammates are becoming frustrated with the difficulty of the routine.

"Usually, when we get frustrated, we try harder," Wiese tells them. "That's not what I'm looking at. I'm seeing you surrender. Do you hear me, Allen? I don't want to see that. I want to see effort! Get up. Get the mediocrity out of your system."

The year that Wolff entered the academy, one hundred freshmen had tried out for honor guard at the start of the school year. Less than a fifth of them survived to spring Recognition, when those who have succeeded formally join the elite group. Until then, they are mere candidates for honor guard; their status is equivalent of that of basic cadets back in July.

An internal conflict between the honor guard and the saber drill team had boiled over at the start of this year, crippling recruitment. As a result, fewer than twenty freshmen from the Class of 2010 tried out for honor guard. This meager number, however, has not made the group any more reluctant to boot out candidates who don't fit in. Rather, the attrition and elimination rates for the Class of 2010 are the same as for the classes that started out with a hundred students. As a result, instead of contributing fifteen to twenty members to the honor guard—the typical contingent from a class of thirteen hundred—the Class of 2010 already has the smallest honor guard contingent in the academy's history, and Recognition is still more than six weeks away.

To my eyes, their practice looks like basic training on speed: the unrelenting criticism and punishments, the imbalance of power, the jittery tension of marching on a volcano's rim, not knowing which misstep will burn you. But Wolff insists the experiences are very different. "The point of basic training is a haze for you to survive," he says. "You're focused on yourself and making it through. Honor guard is supposed to be a challenge that forces people to grow together, to rely on one another and trust one another—to know they can do these jobs and details and know one hundred percent that they can rely on the person next to them.

"If you take rifle drill, it's our goal to be the very best when we go to competition. If you're doing a complicated maneuver, you have to depend on the person next to you to be where they're supposed to be, to catch it just right.

"We have to get up at 5 a.m. to raise the flag sometimes. If you don't have that sort of commitment to your teammates, you might not get up, you might just as well sleep in. You don't want to fail the people around you. If you end up neglecting your duties, it reflects poorly on the military. It ends up looking like crap, and in the public's eye, what does that say about the military?"

The honor guard candidates eat dinner together to build up that bond, weaving their lives together like any family, meal by meal. After eating, the cadre tell the freshmen to relax, and they ask how they're progressing as a team. "We're interested in things that we can't see," Wolff explains.

Nathan Nordby, a junior who is training the freshmen, pipes up. Two days ago, someone at the table confided that a teammate had discussed growing up without a father in his life—something he thought was hurting his performance on the team.

"It was important to him. It was important to us," says Nordby. "We concluded that talking it over shows your ability to care for each other as a family. That we are valued. We are important. They are part of something. They're more than just themselves."

There are many reasons that cadets decide to try out for honor guard. Some want to show how tough or dedicated they are. Some think they cut a sharp figure and like the attention of the parades. Some, like Meeker, are awed by the precision and pizzazz of the drills, or they are looking for a family to hold them close.

In the crucible of nightly practice, those reasons tend to deepen and change or else slip away. The intensity and sheer pain of the daily drills elbow out the superficial attraction and become a barometer of the cadets' devotion to the group. When candidates for honor guard are kicked out, especially in freshman year, it is often because their teammates believe that they are not entirely committed or because the chemistry is off.

"It's not about popularity," Meeker says. "It's about what's involved in getting recognized in honor guard. It's definitely a vibe that most cadets respond to. Some don't want to be around it at all."

Fingers stinging, muscles aching, Meeker and her fellow hopefuls from the Class of 2010 march off to dinner at Mitchell Hall in their helmets of another age, the sound of their footsteps swallowed by the snow. Under the bright lights of the terrazzo and a full moon, the snowflakes fall as if illuminated from inside. The cadets seem farther away than they really are, locked in a bubble of their making. The only sound is a plaintive jody led by another SMACK, Julie Warren:

> Don't cry for me
> I don't want your sympathy
> I'm an airborne ranger
> That's all I'll ever be.

Part Five

INTO THE LIGHT

27 | On the Runway

The countdown to life after the academy begins one hundred nights before graduation, with a formal bash known as Hundred's Night or "dining in." Firsties don their dress blues and gather at Mitchell Hall. On the tables are white linens and cloth napkins. Gold banners and balloons decorate the hall. Cider sparkles in the stemware, and generals have flown in to wax wise.

Tonight, after dinner with their classmates, after the speeches and the toasts and the memories that trip off one another like interlocking gears, each firstie will receive a certificate. On it is a road map, announcing in elegant calligraphy where the air force will send him or her from here.

As they come in to dinner, the firsties already know the training or the job they will be doing after graduation. Tonight, however, they discover where they will do it. Their assignments will be the result of a process known here as "rack and stack," meshing the hopes of cadets against their performance and the needs of the military. They've been evaluated—ranked by their academic, military, and, to a lesser extent, athletic standing. Then the air force matches the cadets against one another, with the stronger performers in the more competitive fields most likely to get one of their top three choices for a first assignment.

There are wild cards: firsties have no idea how much in demand their particular request are, so cadets who are not particularly strong can still get their first request if nobody else is asking for it. The needs of the air force trump all and can send cadets far from their first choices. Even knowing that, however, the firsties have an unspoken sense that the fancy certificates couch a judgment of sorts on their four years at the academy.

Around the room are giant projection screens flashing a collective version of "This Is Your Life," a slide show featuring milestones of the Class of 2007: their first day standing on the painted footsteps, scenes from basic training, Acceptance Day, and Combat Survival Training. It is not quite four years ago that the earliest of these pictures were shot, but to the firsties' eyes now, the doolies that they were seem clueless as new immigrants, overwhelmed by this harsh culture.

The pictures take them by surprise. At the time, the new arrivals were so caught up in these experiences that they scarcely noticed anybody snapping photos. Poised on the border between their past and the future, the firsties are surrounded by scenes of a comedy in which their greener selves are the stars, a reality show in which they had, by virtue of surviving to sit in this room tonight, all won.

Watching his classmates on the giant screens, Michael Tanner remembers himself four years ago, his hands gripping a thick rope stretched over a muddy trench. He inched his body across the rope, his hands rubbed raw and all his strength concentrated on not letting go. "I got all the way through that obstacle without getting wet," he says, his eyes narrowing and a corner of his mouth lifting, "and the cadre were like 'Get back, Tanner. Do it again. You're going in.'" The table around him erupts in laughter.

Christin Schulte recalls her spin at Combat Survival Training. She had a perfect record, she quips to her fellow Bulldawg grads: missing her target every time.

"If she were shooting a real round, I bet she would have hit something," says Robert Santos, who is sitting next to her.

"I've never shot a live machine gun," Schulte answers, laughing.

Then Santos sees himself up there, training with two classmates who ended up alongside him in Squadron 13. I ask him about his own spin at training Basics in boot camp eight months earlier, when he seemed to play the irascible, pitiless drill sergeant, wielding sarcasm like a machete.

"Yeah, well, the thing is, you kind of just . . . ," he begins, and thinks a moment. "If you gotta be mean, you gotta have fun with it, you can't be, like, malicious," he says. "I just tried to have a good time with it. You know, the more over the top you are, the more the Basics remember you and have great stories in the end. Like those are the cadre I remember. I don't remember the cadre that was kind of like 'Oh, whatever. I'm not going to say anything.' No personality. The guys that were over the top, and really pushed us and challenged us, you know, those were the ones I have stories about that I told my folks afterwards."

Each upperclass cadet has a picture in mind of the ideal cadre, whose outlines are drawn through his or her own experience as a Basic. For Santos, the image was mean and salty, even sneering, but tough enough to take whatever punishment he dished out. He is not sure he got it right, but he figures he will find out this weekend.

Hundred's Night is a release not just for the graduates but also for the four-digs they tried to torment into shape. Tonight, when the firsties head out for drinks with friends or leave for the weekend, the doolies get to take over the firsties' rooms. Their goal is to make each firstie's room barely recognizable, to trash it or seal it up or turn it into a movie set that plays off something the SMACKs know about the firstie who lives there. The greater the upheaval, the greater the love. The cadre who have earned no respect or affection come back to pristine rooms.

"If you can get it right, then the four-degrees will remember you, and they come back to haunt you on a night like this," Santos says. "God knows, they have enough material."

Watching the screens, he remembers his own cadre, a "tag team" whose sole purpose amounted to demolishing any sense of self-worth SMACKs came in with.

"It was a black belt in karate and a body builder," Santos recalls. "These two guys would just destroy us. Like, this guy could do—at the time, he could do more one-arm pushups than I could do with both hands. Like this guy was just covered with muscle. And the black belt karate guy made us do these crazy karate drills, and the two of them just took us down to the field one day. I mean, they weren't just characters, they were over the top.

"We just ran a drag, and of course they're hardly breaking a sweat, right? And then you have the random guy with a blow horn, blaring, 'This is not the voice of the God.' We were like, 'Argh!' But it was fun, you know, like, after we were done, we did the cadre skit at the end and we were, like, making fun of them and stuff. They just had this God complex and it was just really funny. It wasn't funny at the time, but it was funny afterward," Santos says.

Grace Anderson recalls her first exposure to academy life. She had just finished her junior year in high school, and she came out for a summer seminar that offered high school students a taste of academy life. Her main worry was a guy-crazy roommate from an all-girls high school.

The roommate was horrified by the no-frills regimen she'd unwittingly signed on for, even for just a few weeks. "She took forty-five minutes to put on her makeup, and she never made her bed," Anderson says. "She couldn't get out the door." Because they were supposed to demonstrate teamwork, Anderson had to wait while the girl perfected her look. Anderson, her hair pulled back in a neat bun, feigns exasperation, as if she were still there, and it is easy to imagine her pacing the room, gravitating toward the door and pulling herself back in, almost against her will. "I was late every day," she says. By the end of the program, Anderson was afraid that the girl had sabotaged her chances of getting in, on the grounds of chronic lateness.

"She put on her BDU [battle dress uniform] the first time," Anderson says, pulling her hand ahead of her body and curling back her torso, launching into an impersonation of the girl from another planet. "They look so baggy," she whines, and she pauses for effect. "They want us to look like boys!" she says, to waves of laughter.

"I remember her," Tanner throws in. He had been at the summer seminar, too. He and Anderson have known each other for five years now.

Anderson nods at him, then shakes her head. The girl had come with her posse, a group of her friends from high school, none of whom had the least interest in the academy as a college destination. "They just wanted to meet guys," she says.

Coming here tonight, Anderson feels elated and nervous at the same time. She just learned that she has qualified for pilot training, thanks to a waiver for a vision problem. She thought she'd have to go for her second choice, navigation, and she didn't know which bases did undergraduate pilot training. Master Sergeant Mark Winter assured her that morning that he had her assignment in hand, but he would not tell her where it is.

Santos remembers the chaplain's picnic, the big afternoon party that rewards the academy's nearly thirteen hundred SMACKs for making it through the six weeks of Beast. When Santos went through Beast, his cadre taunted the Basics by telling them that the chaplains had canceled the picnic that year.

"Wow, they busted you guys," Anderson says.

Santos remembers the cadre's explanations: "The chaplains don't care about you enough to have the picnic. The weather's too bad. It's too hot."

There were other significant moments that shaped the firsties' experiences at the academy, but those found no representation in the pictures fading in and out, nor did they come up in the animated conversation: a cascade of women accused fellow cadets of rape during this class's doolie year, followed by complaints of religious coercion. The incidents produce a complex brew of emotions among the graduates: sadness that they'd missed out on important hallmarks of an academy education such as Recognition, resentment for the victims for somehow bringing the injuries on themselves, and loyalty to their alma mater under attack.

Santos watches the Basics up on the screen going through the assault course, the most grueling of all the trials the doolies endure at boot camp. "We were on there the day that all the interceptors fell off of the obstacle course because they got all dehydrated, remember? So we had to have the hydration cars, or whatever."

Tanner and Schulte laugh at the joke, but there is more to Santos's memory.

Without the medics, who'd gone off to treat the injured cadets, the cadre ordered "low-intensity training" on the assault course. "So then we were kind of like standing there, and then the assault course cadres are like 'Okay, you're going to low-crawl the entire course for all two hours.' It was, like terrible. It was the worst day of my entire life."

Santos mentions a fellow graduate, Chris Campbell, a "wing-staff dude, really smart. He got all cut up. You know that water? He got, like, some scarlet fever."

The firsties around Santos laugh—everything that turns up in the rearview mirror looks safely distant tonight—but Santos is not laughing. He is suddenly not just retelling a story but thinking about what happened.

"I'm not even joking. It was bad, because we got all cut up, you know, having to low-crawl for two hours. It was not a fun time," he says, his eyes resting on his wine glass, soon to be raised in a toast to their accomplishments.

I find myself remembering something that Russ Ragon, an Evangelical Presbyterian chaplain, had told me a few weeks earlier about the psychic cost paid by the people who were filling the room tonight. They have been slammed up against their own vulnerability and mortality and have discovered themselves "capable of experiencing failure at any moment. Every cadet who makes it through here," Ragon said, "has experienced a tremendous amount of pain."

A lengthy speech by a many-starred general offers jokes and advice on how to succeed in the active-duty military: turn up fifteen minutes early for appointments; don't just bring problems to your superiors, come armed with solutions; seize opportunities when they arise; and so on.

Then General John Regni, the academy superintendent, appears on the giant screens. Shoulders squared, military decorations arrayed like a multicolored bar code on his chest, he tells them that he has been detained by bad weather on the East Coast. He quips that he is now the only thing standing between them and graduation. With the squadron officers standing nearby, ready to hand out the certificates, Regni launches into a history of Hundred's Night, which he traces back to West Point in 1871. He too offers what he calls "tongue-in-cheek words of advice."

"Orders will soon be in hand, and graduation is really, really going to happen," he tells them. The room erupts in whoops and whistles, and the sounds seem to dart across the roomful of tables and spiral off the cavernous ceilings. The three women at one table—Casey Johnson, Schulte, and Anderson—steal looks at one another and smile, laughing quietly, their eyes wide. The anticipation is almost too much, and Regni finally says the words they have been listening for all night: "Okay, give out the envelopes."

Within seconds, the seniors' next posts are in their hands, and the excitement explodes as the cadets laugh and fling their arms over one another's shoulders and hold up their certificates to compare assignments.

"I can't believe it," Santos exclaims. He throws his head back and laughs. He is headed to Eglin Air Force Base on the coast of the Florida panhandle, one of the air force's largest and busiest sites and a major testing ground for nonnuclear weapons. "I got my first choice!"

Jeremy Putz, his roommate, draws Peterson Air Force Base, down the road from the academy, where he will be doing management. "My lifestyle is not going to change at all," he says, smiling ruefully. Putz, who took a year off to learn Russian in Moscow, had not even put in for Peterson, so the assignment comes as a surprise.

Santos is beyond relieved; he is thrilled. "I had myself all psyched," he tells his friends. "I never thought I'd get my first choice." In fact, Santos is lined up to graduate with academic honors. He turns to Anderson, whose certificate says she will be doing pilot training at Pensacola, Florida.

"Awesome!" he says. "How far is—"

"I have no idea," Anderson says, laughing, before the question is out of his mouth.

"Me, neither," he answers, laughing along with her. Tanner is headed to Eglin as well.

Johnson, who is from California and is on track for pilot training, draws Edwards Air Force Base. "I'm going home," she shouts gleefully, over the excited din.

Matthew Takanen, the squadron commander who will leave the academy as one of a handful of distinguished graduates, does not share in the euphoria or flash his assignment around. He looks quietly down at the paper, then up, his eyes unfocused, and then down again. Coming here tonight, he knew that he'd been approved for pilot training and was hoping for Sheppard Air Force Base in Wichita Falls, Texas. That assignment, which would be for Euro-NATO Joint Jet Pilot Training, is the most coveted at the academy this year; it's seen as a virtual guarantee that the pilots will one day control the cockpit of a jet fighter or a bomber.

Instead, Takanen's assignment is to Whiting Naval Air Station in Florida. He has no idea what his prospects for getting a fighter or a bomber will be at Whiting.

The air force, of course, has far more pilot slots than the navy does, and there are certain presumptions about the pilot training that one receives from another branch of the military, explains Captain Uriah Orland. As an Air Force Academy graduate, Takanen would have ranked high in the pecking order to fly the plane of his choice at any air force base. He wouldn't have that standing at a naval station; he'd be relegated to fly whatever craft was left after the navy pilots made their choices.

When it was over, he would come back to the air force, only then to begin building up a network of friends and allies in his own branch. He would return as something of an outsider, somebody who'd gone out and played for the other team. Never mind that it wasn't his choice.

Takanen is unaware of all these assumptions, some of which fellow graduates who train with other branches later dismiss as groundless. He is bothered, instead, by not knowing what the assignment means for his future as a pilot. He does not realize it, because their certificates read differently, but he has actually drawn the same posting as Anderson. He bites his lip, and goes over to Major Robert MacKenzie, checking what is in his hand against the master list in the major's folder. There is no mistake.

The assignment is not necessarily a reflection of some shortcoming on the firstie's part: Takanen is a star, ranking in the top 10 percent of his class for a combined academic, military, and athletic average. In the course of anyone's career, there are bound to be postings of uncertain desirability. Tonight, he's drawn his. He pastes a smile on his face and poses for pictures with Santos and Tanner, each holding up his certificate.

Takanen had always known that Sheppard was a long shot. Beyond that, "I didn't know what I wanted," he says, his voice taut as a wire, barely audible over the joyful cacophony.

28 | Doolies Rising

After their formal dinner, the firsties stop back at their dorms for a quick change of clothes. Now, as they stream out of their rooms to celebrate their impending moves over drinks, it becomes party time for the doolies, too. As a blizzard whips snow over the roads and the mountains, doolies up and down the corridors spill the mind-boggling cache of materials for mischief that they packed in the night before.

Borrowing cars from upperclassmen, they'd gone shopping, filling carts to overflowing at Wal-Mart, just outside the academy's south gate, and piling supplies high on flatbed trolleys at Home Depot. They'd collected golf balls and brightly colored beach towels, sacks of sand and boxes of heavy black garbage bags, plastic wrap, cement blocks and mortar, rolls of chicken wire, Jell-O in all colors, and scores of other oddball items that will come together by the end of the night into a coherent statement that can definitely be called payback.

For the SMACKs, each of the forty days leading up to Recognition presents a different hardship, which either steels them or wears them down before the final marathon trial of their doolie year. Once again, they are waking early, dropping for push-ups for minor mistakes, and getting shouted down. Each day in the approach of Recognition belongs to a different squadron. Today, Squadron 28 blocks the stairwells, forcing the rest to dodge or go around its members to get to class. In the midst of this, Hundred's Night hands doolies their first and only license to poke back at the firsties who have been pounding them all year.

Tonight, the firsties' dorm rooms become blank slates, backdrops for scenes crafted by the doolies' overworked imaginations, using the mountains of doodads they've collected. The chance to wreak havoc on the upperclassmen, role models and architects of their original misery, moves the doolies to impossible feats of ingenuity, unmoored by natural laws like gravity or equilibrium. In the language of their new culture, in which toughness is venerated, the more beloved the firstie, and the greater the gratitude of the doolies, the more outrageous will be the upheaval in his or her space.

In the run-up to this night, the doolies divided up the graduating class, sorting out who among them would target which firsties. The SMACKs studied up on the firsties' histories, characters, foibles, loves, and hobbies and then designed the scenes they are now about to inflict on each firstie's room.

For a reason no one can explain, the metal captains' beds—perfect stages once the mattresses are pulled out—inspire an inordinate number of SMACKs to fill them with water, almost never successfully. They create beach scenes and swimming pools, jungles and snake pits, miniature golf courses and mazes, and the perennial favorite, fish tanks in the clothes drawers. In a squadron upstairs, somebody pops 150 pounds of popcorn.

Through the efforts of Rhonda Meeker, Megan Biles, and Rebecca Rasweiler-Richter, Connie Chung's room becomes the backdrop for an island paradise. Chung is headed for Vandenberg Air Force Base in Santa Barbara, California. A cardboard cutout of a hula dancer sways over her bed, which is adorned with tiki torches and bunches of tropical flowers. Across the room, a blue and yellow parrot doll swings on a perch, croaking in a mechanical voice, "Sitting on the dock of the bay . . ."

Chung's clothes drawers prove irresistible. The SMACKs are intent on filling them with water, and they experiment with different liners: thin plastic sheeting, like the kind used to package vegetables, or garbage bags taped together. They are on their fourth try, this time taping plastic wrap over the holes in the corners of the drawers. The carpet is covered with white towels to soak up the water, and near the door they have created a miniature island with blue plastic sheeting and polished white stones.

Biles cuts small fish out of lavender paper. "I have lots of blue," she says. "Maybe I'll make bubbles out of it."

Meeker smiles and cocks her head. "Sweet," she replies.

For the four-digs, this is their first break from school and training in twelve days, and they have laid in a stash of junk food for the night: miniature chocolate bars, potato chips, and lime cola drinks. They are dressed in green battle pants. Meeker wears a black T-shirt with a quote from Proverbs 20:30, which David Urban had quoted to me months earlier: "And wounds cleanse away all evil."

Earlier in the day, I had received a mysterious message from Meeker, passed through the officer in charge, Major Robert MacKenzie. "She's going through some personal issues and wants to take a break from talking about things," he said. Her sudden unwillingness to engage in anything more than small talk is mystifying, and given her turbulent start and yearning for acceptance, it worries me.

Through others, I learn that Meeker has lost her place on honor guard, and with it, the substitute family she was building for herself. Her drill mates got together to vote her off, says Christopher Wolff, the two-degree in charge of training her group. "They felt her heart was not in the team, that she was in it for the wrong reasons."

Only four cadets from the Class of 2010 remain on the honor guard—the smallest contingent of any class in the academy's history—but Wolff does not second-guess the decision to shed Meeker or any of the others who do not make it through. "We encourage them to trim the fat, get rid of people. We expect them to become a family.'"

Now, building Chung's paradise, Meeker jokes about whether she will ever make it to graduation. Biles glances her way. "If you stay, you'll make it," she tells her.

Down the hall, in Mike Tanner's room, which he shares with Alan Rodriguez, a tall, easygoing firstie, David Urban and Chris Flynn circle clear plastic wrap over the uniforms hanging in the closet. They have twelve rolls on hand, which they seal tightly over the uniforms, crossing the sleeves in front as if they are straitjackets. Then they go for the rolling desk chairs.

"They said they wanted their stuff protected," says Flynn, with a smile not entirely free of malice. "We said, 'All right.'"

They move the massive desk units, with bookcases above, to form a barricade a few feet into the room, so the only way for Tanner and Rodriguez to enter is on their knees, through the opening under the desk. However, they won't be able to go anywhere: Urban and Flynn cram two hundred small paper cups in rows across the floor, filling each cup with water.

Tanner also has a penchant for language, so Urban and Flynn have brought nine sheets of poster board they will blanket with words. "Contractions—that's the one thing Tanner really takes on," says Urban. He cannot abide them, at least when they're uttered by four-digs. He also hates acronyms. Urban and Flynn tack the poster board on the wall over Tanner's bed and cover it with the offending contractions: *can't*, *it'll*, *weren't*, *isn't*, *you're*, *he'll*, *we'd*, and so on, into informal infinity.

Flynn is on probation for his low score in physical training, the fruit of "living a life of playing computer games." Three days a week, he goes for mandatory reconditioning in the gym.

Firsties getting assignments on Hundred's Night: (left to right) Michael Tanner, Robert Santos, and Matthew Takanen.

Christopher Flynn and David Urban wrapped the room in plastic, from uniforms to desk chairs.

Adam Brunderman, top left, and John T. Rice try to create a beach scene in the well of Matt Adams's bed. Eventually, they go for GI Joe in a sand trap.

One room gets the cement dungeon treatment.

A bed turned into a lake of red Jell-O, dripping into the drawers.

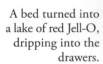

Cups of water cover the floor.

Urban is still working his way through an apparent honor violation and is not yet permitted to speak about it. He is also shaky academically. His confidence from having studied at a community college turned out to be overblown. It did not give him a foundation for the academics here; it was more like a trap door that fell out from under him almost instantly. He is on academic probation.

As the roommates start filling scores of balloons with helium, Calvin Hunter, a cadet from Jamaica and, at twenty-three, the oldest doolie in the squadron, comes marching down the hallway, a one-man band with drums, knees rising high in caricature. Hunter, who became an American citizen the previous year, has served at Luke Air Force Base in Arizona. He hopes to one day fly an F-15E or an F-22 Raptor. The doolies drop their projects to check out the racket—it sounds like a parade coming their way—and their laughter fills the corridor.

Adam Brunderman, a SMACK from Virginia, peers out of a room, then ducks back in. The room belongs to Matthew Adams, a fanatic for extreme sports who is headed to Misawa Air Base Station in Japan. Brunderman, along with John T. Rice and Daniel Hickox, is trying to create a beach scene on top of Adams's bed. They pull off the mattress and cover the well with trash bags taped together. In one end they pour buckets of water, and in the other end they pour sand. It's a clever concept, but the execution is something else.

Crouching by the dripping bed, they all suddenly realize that the beds are not waterproof. "We lined half of it, then put a wall of sand, thinking the sand would keep the water in place," Brunderman explains. "Then the water started seeping through the sand, and I'm like 'You know what? Law of equilibrium, equaling out.'"

"At least we took out the drawers first," he adds, his thumb swiping his nose. "Sometimes you get caught up in the moment." He raises an eyebrow and a corner of his mouth, turning to Hickox and Rice. "Do we have any caulk?" he asks.

Rice thinks he has a solution: "Let's make a solid wall, dry it very quickly, and put down the tape" along the edge.

Brunderman leans back on his heels and suggests starting over. "Let's move it to a drawer." He walks out of the room and rubs his neck. "Not good," he says under his breath.

The crew starts over, emptying out the water, hoping to dry the space and give the duct tape another go. More quickly than they can work, however, the water starts dripping again through the bed.

"Darn these paper towels," says Brunderman. "They aren't absorbent enough."

Jamal Harrison, who will be a firstie next year, stops in and shakes his head, amused by their dilemma. "It's like performing an operation," he says, tilting his head in mock seriousness.

Across the hall, Brad Bernard sits the night out, serving time. With each day, he stacks up more punishments, most recently for closing the door to his room while he worked on remedial chemistry. Although both he and his roommate were busted for the same offense, as a recidivist, Bernard's sentence is worse: thirty hours stuck at his desk. "I'm supposed to know that you're not allowed to do that," he says. Eventually, he gets his sentence reduced, but he still has hours to serve. Taking a break, he strolls the hall in his bathrobe, dropping into Adams's room to survey the mayhem as he munches chocolate chip cookies.

"It's not going to work like that," he tells Brunderman, Rice, and Hickox. They nod glumly. "So what are you going to do to fix it?"

"We don't know," Brunderman says.

"Come on, guys," Bernard exhorts them, like a coach at game time. "You're from the academy!"

"Yeah!" they all shout back, in exaggerated excitement, goofing on themselves as gung-ho jocks. "We're from the academy!"

Down the hall there are rooms crisscrossed with police crime-scene tape, making them impassible, and filled with orange streamers hanging from the ceiling. There are rooms with cement blocks filling the doorway and only a small space left open through which to see the mess inside. In another room, thousands of tiny beads fill the light fixtures, so that a careless attempt to empty them would send beads rolling all over the room.

In Squadron 16, which counts many swimmers, the four-digs use a thick plastic tarp big enough to cover a bed's middle and make it into a small swimming pool, complete with tiny lanes separated by white beads. In another room upstairs, a doolie fills a bed well with liquid red Jell-O and rubber snakes—*Apocalypse Now* in miniature. Then the Jell-O starts leaking. Like a magician spinning plates, he runs frantically to empty the clothes drawers below before the liquid spreads to them.

Ryan "Buzz" Regan, a popular Bulldawg bound for Sheppard Air Force Base in Wichita Falls, Texas, will open his door to a solid wall, made by doolies who push two seven-foot desk and bookshelf units together.

Peter Kaszynski, a SMACK whom Regan has trained, blows up the twentieth of six hundred balloons to fill the space. He, Calvin Hunter, and Brett Killion, from Lubbock, Texas, fill bunches of balloons with shaving cream and tether them with duct tape. Killion, built like a bean-stalk, works with his shirt off. Meeker and the women who are doing Chung's room pop in for a look.

"Killion," Meeker calls, "what's this? Indecent exposure to a reporter."

He steps back, and looks at her briefly. "You can get me a shirt over there or something," he says.

"Yeah. Actually, I'd love to."

What doesn't she want me to see? I wonder.

Six hundred balloons, 150 pounds of popcorn, and two hundred paper cups—in each room, the SMACKs bring their ambitions of overwhelming the firsties with upheaval, which will take hours to clean up when they come back. In each case, when the doolies create the outsized scenes they've envisioned, the rooms seem to dwarf their accomplishment. The paper cups form an island but fail to cover the floors wall-to-wall. Even the massive bags of popcorn do not look like all that much once they are dumped out in the room.

In the room shared by Ben Smith and Jonathan Elliott, the straight-arrow son of missionaries who'd been in charge of training the four-digs for much of the year, the doolies create a "love shack," complete with a blowup doll. They push the beds together and tape white paper napkins together into a heart-shaped quilt. They scatter stuffed animals and shower the bed with confetti in rainbow colors.

Robert Santos, who finds country music unbearable, gets a western scene and speakers piping country tunes that he cannot turn off, because they are wired from the room next door.

Lucas VanTassel, who performed in *The Thorn*, the Passion Play extrava-ganza at New Life Church, gets the dramatic black and orange posters for the play plastered over his walls. VanTassel had played an angel in the production, which used Cirque du Soleil staging and pyrotechnics to dramatize the crucifixion and resurrection. The show attracts more than twenty thousand spectators a year. The doolies dangle fake hundred-dollar bills from the ceiling, a nod to VanTassel's assignment in finance, and fill his lights with countless tiny orange beads.

The doolies remake Lance Watson's room into a gym. Watson, the first cadre to train the doolies upon their arrival, lifts weights daily. The doolies virtually empty the weight room downstairs and bring up all the equipment. They take out the furniture, lining up benches, barbells, and free weights where his bed had stood.

In Casey Johnson's room, two doolies tape garbage bags together over the mattress well, which they are about to fill with Jell-O. Captain Uriah Orland mentions the swimmers in Squadron 16, pointing out that they might have extra plastic sheeting to help these doolies with the inevitable leaks.

"Thanks," the two doolies say, and go back to their duct tape. "Let's open the window," says one, glancing at the snow frosting the glass. "Then it will gel fast."

None of the doolies hits a firstie with the ultimate insult of a spotless room, ready for Saturday morning inspection, or SAMI. A room left alone would be like an untouched soul, pure and disconnected from the life of the squadron. On a practical level, there are still two weeks from the safe harbor that lies beyond Recognition, and nobody here is looking to pick a fight with a firstie by excluding his or her room from the fun. "They would have to be pretty bad to get a SAMI room," says Flynn.

There are, however, firstie Bulldawgs who can choose not to play, either because they do not feel particularly close to the freshmen, or because they'd just as soon avoid the clean-up. Two upper-class cadets in one room, Travis Wittick and Aaron Barrow, tack a note on their door. "4 Digs," Wittick has written, "we love you guys, but Aaron and I *don't* want our room decorated."

Elliott does not find the love shack funny. He takes the scene as a sign of disrespect, done in poor taste. It isn't even original, he notes. Every year, whoever is training the doolies in Squadron 13 gets the love-shack treatment.

"I also understand they've got a bunch of rooms they've got to do," he says later. "They've got upperclassmen they looked up to because they were a shoulder to cry on or they were nicer to them."

Back in Adams's room, Hickox and Rice seem to have wandered off, leaving Brunderman to his own devices. Noticing Adams's golf clubs in a corner, Brunderman forgets about water sports and instead builds a sand trap on top of the bed. A GI Joe statue in battle dress stands in one corner, a foot planted in each of Adams's giant brown and white Oxford-style golf shoes, gripping a putter that stretches across the bed, about to strike a ball. The sand is littered with golf tees. On the floor, Brunderman encases Adams's black flip-flops in quick drying cement.

"Well," Brunderman says, taking a step back and folding his arms over his chest, "it works for me."

29 | Harrison's Moment

As a two-degree, Jamal Harrison has no direct role in the excitement and release of Hundred's Night: he is neither dining in nor filling balloons with shaving cream. However, the postings that go out that evening, assigning firsties to military bases and graduate schools across the globe, effectively line the most senior cadets for leaving come May, and right behind them stand two-degrees like Harrison and his pal in Squadron 13, Miles-Tyson Blocker. For them, graduation is first coming into focus.

"Looking back, there's so much I love, so many great stories and people," Harrison says over dinner at a restaurant off the academy grounds. It is the same place he'd eaten at the night before he entered the academy as a Basic. In a few months, his fiancée, Emily, will come in for Ring Dance, the formal dinner where the two-degrees get their class rings. "I still don't think it's hit me: I'm going to be a senior."

Others track his passage with interest. Much to Harrison's surprise, Major Robert MacKenzie taps him to serve as flight commander for the coming summer, in charge of the first phase of basic training for the new cadets who will enter Squadron 13—the same job Lance Watson held last summer. It is a sorely welcome vote of confidence in light of Harrison's campaign to rehabilitate himself after his near-death experience last year, pulling himself up from a 0.8 grade point average.

Although upperclassmen often vie for coveted leadership positions, making their interests known to the officers in charge and grooming themselves for the honor, Harrison has done none of that. He is not a glory hound. He doesn't strut or put his classmates down.

"Sometimes people need that spotlight to show what they can do," MacKenzie says. "He has all the potential to step up and be recognized."

The upperclassmen in Squadron 13 adore Major Mac, who puts his trust in them. His faith stands in stark contrast to his predecessor, who was subsequently dispatched to Nellis Air Force Base in Nevada. The cadets blamed her for controlling their squadron too closely, openly criticizing them, and they had grown disaffected and cynical.

Major MacKenzie is the opposite, shrinking his own place so the cadets can take charge. He doesn't run Squadron 13 as much as mentor and guide it, occasionally hosting barbecues and parties to celebrate its milestones and stepping in only in dire cases.

Although the military is, by nature, a hierarchy, MacKenzie has an informal, egalitarian streak. At training exercises, he sweats alongside his cadets, running a mile or helping them navigate their way out of the wilderness. The rectangular conference table in his room has no head, no position of control. The short side that would be its head sits snugly against the front of his desk. The only places to sit at the table are on each of the long sides.

Harrison is not MacKenzie's first choice for flight commander, but the other cadets he was considering, like Collette Bannister, are being snapped up for more exalted posts. Bannister is slated for squadron commander and is in line for language training. MacKenzie likes Harrison's sincerity and steadiness and the example he sets for the younger cadets. Despite the strains that Harrison has faced in the last year, which the officer knows only too well, the cadet exudes a sense of dignity and professionalism.

"Even with everybody else available, he's still a good choice," the major says. "I think he'll do a great job. He carries himself with the same demeanor twenty-four hours a day. It's not like he turns it on and off. I think he'll hold his freshmen to high standards." After a year of skidding grades among the four-degrees and a cheating scandal that showed elaborate planning and sophistication, Harrison will send a message of honor and fairness to the squadron's newest cadets. "He'll be fantastic to set the bar where we need it to be," MacKenzie declares.

Harrison is now making the same kinds of calculations as MacKenzie about the cadets in the class below him, deciding whom he'll recruit to help run basic training. He combs through his experiences in basic training, once as an incoming cadet and more recently as a cadre working Beast. He will pick his staff from cadets who are now three-degrees. They've been in Squadron 13 for just a few months, so he knows them only superficially. He'll ask around and learn what he can that way, but has to make his choices from the admittedly vague impressions he's built up watching these three-degrees from a distance.

Harrison brings a strong sense of priorities with him in putting together a staff. The cadre he most admired as a Basic were not the ones who shouted over the terrified faces of the new kids, playing God and steamrolling the sense out of them. The ones he tried to emulate were tough and able to get a job done, but "they knew when it was time to check up on their people and see how they're doing—aside from the numbers, aside from how well they make a bed—to see how they were each doing as a person."

"I kind of tried to find that role working basic last year," Harrison recalls. "Keep an eye on people, looking for the warning signs." I remember how he and Blocker had quietly encouraged Rhonda Meeker not to give up, after her outburst on the assault course had booby-trapped her path through basic training and beyond.

It is also crucial, Harrison believes, to have at least one female cadet on his staff. Women, he has noticed, have an especially rough transition as they start out at the academy. He remembers walking down the hallway where the women were clustered in the dorm, ten minutes before taps, during basic training.

"I'd look in the room, and there'd be two people in there, and they'd both be just crying. Just crying, really crying," he says, reaching for a glass of water. "And I'd walk down the hall and look in the next room, and there's more women crying. It really opened my eyes to see that."

By the time Second Beast arrived, with the march out to Jacks, Harrison had told Blocker, who was just coming on for the training, to look out for the women, especially; they were having a tough time. He never completely understood why so many were so miserable. What he heard was

"'Well, I can't get along with the rest of the girls in the squadron.'" Now, he says, "I'm not sure if that's stereotypical girl behavior or whatever, but I'd go down the hall and keep hearing it, so I'm seeing a common thread."

With his straight shoulders, his wire-rimmed glasses, and his square jaw, Harrison comes across as a man who would sooner confront a fellow cadet who slips than walk away. He cannot abide the sliding scale of rectitude, in which cronyism trumps what is right. He wants John Langley, a smart and encouraging three-degree, to work basic training on his staff.

"He works very well under pressure," Harrison explains, "and he's not afraid to uphold standards. Because something that I see a lot around the academy is, 'I'm your friend, so I'm not going to tell you that your button's unbuttoned.' Or 'I'm not going to tell that you didn't go to breakfast.' And he's a straight shooter. He's a rules and standards guy, and you need that during basic."

Langley is not available, however, so Harrison sends an e-mail seeking volunteers to work First Beast. Only six cadets come forward. He is now sifting through the names, putting together his team.

Before next year's doolies are inducted, there are still this year's to usher fully into the fold. That will happen at Recognition. In this final haze-a-thon, the doolies will emerge as full-fledged cadets, never to be beaten again. However, for the upperclassmen of Harrison's year, who lost Recognition in the glare of the sexual assault scandal, the approach of this year's event brews an uneasy mix of feelings. Alongside their pride in the cadets who've risen to the challenge and their suspicion of the slackers, there is also a bitterness and a strange nostalgia in Harrison's classmates for the moments like this that were lost to them.

Harrison takes a philosophical approach. "If I can give them a good Recognition," he says, "it must not have affected me too much."

30 | Closing the Circle

Miles-Tyson Blocker mentally starts packing for Japan as his best friend, Jamal Harrison, puts together his team to train the next crop of high school graduates who will come through Squadron 13. Blocker, who has a minor in Japanese, lands an assignment that is probably the closest thing on offer to a paid vacation: four weeks in Kanazawa, living with a family that speaks no English, to improve his Japanese.

He will leave just after Ring Dance, the ultraformal party a few days before graduation where he and the other two-degrees will get their class rings. Blocker can imagine no other college or university besides the academy that would arrange the same opportunity for language immersion, at no cost to him. He will even continue to receive his salary while he learns.

Blocker, who is slender and long-limbed, raises an eyebrow and looks sideways when asked about his hyphenated first name. "My mom," he says. He speaks in the squadron's rec room, where cadets stop for a snack or a drink or a game of foosball. It was "an eighties thing. Names." His friends mostly drop his mother's nod to the notorious heavyweight champion, Mike Tyson, to whom he is not related, and just call him Miles.

Aside from the fact that he is part African American, Blocker bears virtually no resemblance to the boxer. He is soft-spoken, measured, and not given to violence or ranting. Around the squadron, Blocker takes seriously his charge to bring up the four-digs; he corrects and kids them, but he also stands up for them behind the scenes, and he tries to keep them from dropping out.

He defines himself as somewhat liberal, but that is a relative term in the overwhelmingly conservative institution. When he thinks about his own road getting here, he suspects that affirmative action might have opened the way for him. Nevertheless, Blocker says, he is "not really a fan" of the practice, which offends his sense of fairness. He believes that minority students should compete on an equal footing with white applicants, and he feels that affirmative action does not do this, that it involves lowering standards to fill a quota.

"Even Martin Luther King said people should be judged not by the color of their skin, but by their character. They're doing the exact opposite, but it's the same kind of discrimination," he insists. "I hate that."

In fact, there is no evidence that the academy, where roughly 7 to 8 percent of cadets are legacies of parents who attended service academies, lowers its standards to admit African Americans, who account for only 5 percent of the student body in Blocker's year, and 6 percent in more recent years. According to the admissions office, black cadets are virtually indistinguishable from white cadets in their success at the academy. About 74 percent of cadets of either race graduate within four years. (In this regard, Air Force Academy cadets are markedly more successful than their counterparts at public civilian universities, where just 56 percent of non-Hispanic whites and 38 percent of blacks earn their diplomas in four years.)

Blocker himself is a one-man rainbow coalition—black and white, Native American and Japanese. He sees himself as the product of a "color-blind" environment, one that taught him not to focus on race in judging people.

As a teenager, Blocker attended a highly competitive high school in Riverside, California, whose top graduates went off to Ivy League universities. He was not one of them, however. His early childhood had been chaotic; his mother tended to her own dramas and left her children to largely fend for themselves, he said.

From the age of eight, Blocker had to wake up early to get himself and his younger sister fed and dressed. He cooked meals for both of them on his own. At some point, he recalls, he and his sister looked at each other and realized that they could not count on their mother to rear them. "'Mom's crazy,'" he recalls telling his sister, who was four at the time. "'Mom'll probably feed us. Maybe. But we gotta find a way out.' Me and my sister stuck together," he adds.

When he was fourteen, some friends who'd known his mother since high school, Daniel and Lorena Bull, took Blocker and his sister into their home. Dan was an air force veteran, a former enlisted man who was paralyzed in action. Lorena worked as a dietitian. The couple sheltered, clothed, and fed Blocker and his sister, and his mother's absences stretched longer and longer. At that time, she was studying to become a truck driver.

"The more my mom kept being away, the closer we got to Dan and Lorena," he says. The couple was stable and loving, "wise to the point where we trusted them." They paid Blocker's way in extracurricular programs. He studied martial arts, joined the school band, and became a member of the highly competitive California All-State Band. The couple became the children's legal guardians, setting off a feud with his blood relatives.

The Air Force Academy was the sole four-year college he applied to as a high school senior. Blocker craved the order and security of a military academy, but he veered away from the army or the navy, the branches of the service associated with other family members. Now he slaps his head at the audacity of applying to only the academy and a community college.

"I know! That's so stupid, now that I look back on it," he exclaims. Left on his own for so long, Blocker yearned to belong to something larger, which would give meaning and purpose to his work while also taking care of him. "The structure," he recalls. "I wanted that so bad." His grades put him just barely in the top 10 percent of his class, and his SAT scores were not stupendous. It was only because of his guardians' help in building up his application with extracurricular activities, he believes—tae kwon do to show his athletic ability, marching band to show his leadership—that he even made it in.

All of this cost money, and here is where class and race can play an outsized role. "This place favors the person who does a lot of stuff, and it costs money," Blocker says. "If my mom had been taking care of me, I wouldn't have been able to do tae kwon do. I wouldn't have been able to do band to the extent I wanted. I would probably have had to work a job. I wouldn't have been able to join the California All-State Band. Every little thing on my application counted for getting me in."

His admission to the academy humbled Blocker—and not in the faux-modest way that politicians and actors use the word to magnify their glory after a victory. Blocker truly felt unworthy. Academy officials had initially tracked him for a year at the prep school, but then allowed him to enter the academy directly when a few slots opened before the start of the school year. Imagining that his white classmates must have all been brilliant, he worked doubly hard to prove himself. "I'd better earn my keep here," Blocker recalls thinking. He studied incessantly. He joined the Drum and Bugle Corps, the band that plays at parades and football games, and that's where he became fast friends with Harrison.

The effort paid off, catapulting Blocker to the top 10 percent of his class, with a 3.7 grade point average after his first two years. As he heads into his firstie year at the academy, Blocker is a case study in the academy as a launch pad of social mobility. For a time, he thought of applying to medical school, but he has moved away from that. His grades in organic chemistry were poor, and the practicing physicians he sought out made for an unhappy lot. "They seemed exhausted all the time," he notes. Instead, he put in for airfield operations or intelligence, and he is headed for airfield operations.

Blocker's sense of inferiority lasted, he now thinks, for two years, about the time we met the previous summer. His hankering for the childhood he never had, however, has endured far longer. "When you're cooking for your sister at eight or nine? Oof," he says, leaning back in a desk chair and exhaling audibly. "You just want to be a kid. And I'm so glad I got to be a kid. I reveled in it, and I still kind of revel in it right now."

He loves "the small things of being immature and having fun": foosball, paintball, laser tag, arcade games, and Guitar Hero. "Cartoons. I want cartoons," he croons, like a kid calling for ice cream. He once was reprimanded for playing foosball after taps, but he couldn't help himself. "I'm afraid that's going to stick with me for the rest of my life. I don't care," he admits.

What Blocker values most is the chance to influence younger cadets, he says, and he also watches out for them. He would love to be the first cadre that the Basics encounter on the bus ride from Doolittle Hall, the one who blasts them with the sudden orders to sit up straight and start looking like airmen.

Despite the flaws—the flare-ups over cheating or drugs, the rumors of athletes keeping an apartment off-base for partying—Blocker sees the academy as a place for strivers who can take failure and keep pumping under pressure. Those are the kids he seeks out, and he tries to help them through the tumult of their first year.

"I really would like to serve people who don't look at this as just a job," he says. "It's not a school. It's not a frat party house. It's not camp." To him it is a belief system.

On paper, Miles-Tyson Blocker and Rhonda Meeker seem like psychic twins: both cadets at the academy, both survivors of chaotic childhoods, both rescued by friends or relatives who came forward when their natural parents failed. Both are drawn, almost irresistibly, to the structure and security of the military. Both are idealistic, yearning to hitch their youth and talents to a greater cause. The similarities may explain Blocker's efforts to help Meeker make it through her tumultuous year, to try to keep her on track, to lend a shoulder or an ear when few others bothered.

"The main difference between me and [Rhonda] is that she has an abrasive personality," he says. "She believes highly in her views, to the point where she insults other people. She needs to be open to other people's perspectives and not change them and not discount them."

Blocker's roommate cannot abide Meeker. Once, when she dropped in on them playing a video game, she stated bluntly, "Video games are a waste of time," seemingly oblivious to the offense she was giving.

With the semester almost over, Blocker's coming journey to Japan closes a circle. His grandmother came to the United States from Japan after World War II because she had married a black marine. She wanted her children to succeed in her new home, so spoke to them in broken English rather than in her mother tongue. For most of her life, none of her children or grandchildren could speak to her in her first language. That legacy, she presumed, was lost to the generations that flowed from her.

When Blocker started learning Japanese, he called her. She was seventy years old, and her grandson was on his way to becoming an officer and—at the time—considering medical school. "I love you," he told her in Japanese. "Your food is tasty."

She laughed, elated and joyful, and as she responded, her voice climbed with emotion. "She couldn't contain herself," Blocker recalls.

When he goes home to Dan and Lorena, after he returns from Japan, he will stop by to mow his grandma's lawn, as he always does. As usual, there will be no grass. He will push and pull the mower over odd patches of weeds in the front yard. Nothing has grown there in years. At some point his grandma will run out to him, bringing lemonade and offering to help with the weeds. She will talk about seeds and perhaps try to plant something she has picked up, flowers or squash plants. Maybe, someday, something will grow.

31 | The Beast Rears Again

Each of the forty days that usher in Recognition brings new trials, new humiliations, and more to learn for the academy's four-digs, heightening their anticipation for the grand finale of their year's training in late March.

The cadre who are running the assault course, the hardest trial in Recognition, cast themselves as descendants of the three hundred Spartans in the Battle of Thermopylae in 480 BC. The doolies, as their superintendent reminds them, trace their roots back to the ancient Greek *doulos*, or slaves.

After classes today, four-digs reported to Mitchell Hall for the official start of Recognition. Now the doolies are back in their rooms when the cadre start banging on their doors and hollering madly, like a posttraumatic flashback of basic training.

"Let's go! Move!" Trent Redburn, the flight instructor, shouts, louder and more urgently than any of his classmates who are rounding up the four-digs. As a training clerk, he has been responsible for summoning some of Squadron 13's doolies to the halls and training them before breakfast. Up and down the hall he goes, hammering on the doors. "You are the last people to get this door open. Move! Move! Move!"

In the hallways, the upperclassmen have unscrewed the lightbulbs to heighten the disorientation of the doolies at this dawn of Recognition. *"2010, strength within!"* the four-digs holler together, until all of them are there.

With the off-kilter guitar riffs of Hoobastank's "Crawling in the Dark" blasting from the loudspeakers, Redburn orders them down for push-ups, with two push-ups counting only as one. He has them run in place with their knees raised high while they recite the U.S. Military Code of Conduct. He keeps up with them as they run up and down seventy flights of stairs.

Matt Takanen, the firstie in charge of the squadron for the semester, chuckles at the whirlwind and steps back. "I've never seen them run so fast," he says.

Katie Fabbri, a three-degree, orders them to do slow flutter kicks, lying on their backs and raising their feet six inches from the floor, while Lorenz Madarang, a two-degree, matches them kick for kick. "It is the soldier, not the campus organizer, who gives us the freedom to demonstrate," Madarang calls out, in a slightly off quote of Charles M. Province's poem "It Is the Soldier." Madarang does not stop the kicks, even as the veins bulge in his temples and his legs tremble with the effort.

The doolies' faces turn red, and sweat runs down the sides of their heads and their necks. Some can barely move their legs. "Recover," Madarang finally calls, giving them a one-minute break for water.

"You all are resting," Jamal Harrison says gamely, over their panting. "I'm resting, too."

They break up, going into different rooms to train in small groups. One room, called hell, is filled with smoke and heat from a jerry-rigged humidifier and has a skull on the ground by the door. Strobe lights make everything in the room flicker, disconnecting one moment from the next, while the twisted strains of punk band Flogging Molly rake their ears. David Urban and two other four-degrees crawl into the room. Upperclassmen, their faces painted in camouflage, order them through scores of push-ups, flutter kicks, and high kicks while calling out the code of conduct.

Another room is called heaven; it has Oreo cookies. Upperclassmen who are watching a movie on television invite the four-digs to relax and talk about themselves. But few doolies are foolish enough to be taken in by this show of kindness. Stretching out while their buddies are getting beaten outside would undoubtedly not get them to heaven tonight.

After two bouts of high-stress training, the doolies are sent back to their rooms. They think that the training is over, for now, and that they should relax. They have only to slip into their bathrobes and shower.

However, John Cox notices that the closet door in his room is ajar. He leans against it, signaling his roommates, Jonathan Benson and Austin Westbrook, to be silent. He suspects that someone is inside. In fact, there are upperclassmen crouching in each of the four-dig rooms, listening for any incriminating remarks that could fuel further punishment. Flattened by fatigue, most doolies think the worst is over, at least until tomorrow morning, but on signal, the upperclassmen fling open the doors and spring out, like monsters from the deep rising in a bathtub. They shout at the doolies to raise their knees, hit the floor, get out there, and do it now.

"You cannot contain me!" Madarang hollers in superhero bravado, pushing Cox out of the way to leap from the closet. At first, the roommates smile, pleased at their minor victory in figuring out the surprise. It is no joke, though. Briefings and pep talks aside, this is the high-intensity, mind-twisting start of Recognition—a surreal redux of basic training, boiled down and concentrated into forty-eight hours.

If final exams test what the students have learned academically, Recognition is the proving ground for their physical, military, and mental training. It is the cadre's last chance to beat, berate, and humiliate the doolies into shape, their last chance to weed out what they see as the cheats, the fakes, and slackers. The doolies are told that it is the crowning training exercise of their four-degree year, aimed at pounding the ego out of them to fuse them into a larger military identity. That has been the purpose of everything they have done since arriving here eight months ago. But it is also the final ring of hell they must travel through before they become full cadets, to be counted as equals among their peers.

Tonight's "shock and awe" kickoff of basic training, in the words of the commandant of cadets, Brigadier General Susan Desjardins, hits the unsuspecting four-digs with successive waves of training from the cadre in their squadrons. As each class finishes with them, the doolies presume they are done, only to find the next year's class roaring at them after what turns out to be but a brief pause in the evening's ordeal.

The more seasoned cadets call this round robin of beating "Meet the Classes." Half of the exercises the doolies are ordered to do—a lengthy list that includes push-ups, hip rotations, abdominal crunches, running, leg lifts, and jumping jacks—carry no restrictions and can last as long as the cadre like. The other half—which include box jumps, lunges, jumping in place with knees high, carrying their buddies, and reverse curls—may go on for only two minutes at a stretch, and then the doolies get a break of sixty seconds.

Before the training begins, the cadre get together and agree on a list of doolies who bear extra attention. At the top of that list is Brad Bernard, who seems, to them, to make sport of sidestepping the rules. He's racked up so many infractions that he seems perennially confined to the dorm, as much a partner to his desk as the chair or the lamp.

Elizabeth Simpson, the two-degree who serves as the squadron's representative on the honor board, is all but fed up with Bernard. "He flat out said he doesn't want to do this, he doesn't want to do that. 'I'm only here to play football.' And so, you know, it's like, 'Well, why *are* you here?' I want him to, like, care." She stands near her room, scanning the hallway, echoing the shouts of the upperclassmen and the doolies counting their way through sit-ups.

"Because you're not going to put out, we don't want you here, you know. There're enough things going on where we don't need that going on as well," Simpson says firmly.

The training is just beginning when Bernard sees his first sign of trouble ahead. His training does not begin like anyone else's. "Bernard," a three-degree calls sweetly outside his door, as the others are being shouted into the hall. The upperclassman's voice creeps like a beautiful, hungry vine climbing the walls, crawling under the door. "Come out, now. You can't hide. We know you're in there."

As Bernard starts to strain under the exercises, Simpson is at his face. "Your classmates are not breaking. You are breaking," she hollers. All year, Bernard has skipped much of the physical training and military exercises. Ostensibly, he was instead training first for football and then for track. "You have been at it only two minutes, and you're breaking," Simpson yells. "We want to see you breaking." Bernard's face is flaming like the red-hot inside of a furnace.

"You can't do it because you've been shirking all year long," Simpson shouts. *"This is your last chance!"*

Andrew Cooper, a three-degree with a narrow face and curly dark hair, orders the doolies to recite "Invictus" by William Ernest Henley. A few of the four-digs, exhausted, speak up in flat voices. Benson fears the night might never end. "Under the bludgeonings of chance / My head is bloody, but unbowed . . ."

Cooper turns on his heels and glowers. What is this milquetoast rendering of a poem that counted as the personal anthem of countless warriors? It is clear that not all the four-degrees are reciting the quote, even though he ordered them a month ago to memorize it. Some are moving their lips, counting on their classmates to carry them.

"You guys can't keep your bearing, and you have no discipline to learn quotes," Cooper says, his lip curling. "What makes you think you have the right to get trained?"

This is the second year since Recognition has resumed, as the academy tiptoes back toward traditions it had suspended after the sexual assault reports of 2003. In shutting down Recognition, the academy struck at a ritual that crystallized the vast disparity between the all-powerful upperclassmen and the lowly SMACKs, which, the leaders feared, might have set the stage for abuse.

For the cadets of the Classes of 2007 and 2008, however, the loss of Recognition was a grievous slight, an injury worse than any abuse they might endure if it went forward. The absence of Recognition reminded them, whenever they thought of their class year, of the sexual assault scandal. Grace Anderson, a firstie, remembers traveling her doolie year, when she was obliged to wear the uniform of the beleaguered academy. Strangers would come up to her to ask if she had been raped. She lived for the moment she could travel in her civilian clothes—one more perk reserved for doolies after Recognition.

But restoring Recognition without the master-slave scenario and the threat of punishment at its core seems almost unimaginable, to many cadets. The whole point of Recognition is for the fully trained cadets to accept the initiates as equals, worthy of respect. What would such a test look like now? For many officers and cadets, what feels right is what feels familiar. Doolies share the belief that the tougher the experience, the prouder they can stand afterward.

Perhaps what the academy's cadets need is the equivalent of forty years in the desert, for one generation to die off so a new one can move on, unshackled by memory. In academy life, this process would take four years, as an entirely new class would come in and create a new kind of Recognition, based less on hazing and more on proving oneself under stress. As it is, though, the hiatus lasts only two years, so the belief in beating cadets to exhaustion and playing with their minds remains strong.

Going into Recognition, the freshmen sit down for dinner and the briefing that kicks off the event in Mitchell Hall. All around the cavernous two-acre room, the doolies are sounding off, answering questions from the cadre like human foghorns, going through the code of conduct and singing the air force song.

Redburn comes across the hall to fetch me from the table I am watching. "This'll be fun," he says gamely, as we make our way through the sea of cadets reciting military knowledge.

When we reach the other side of the room, Bernard is standing at attention, apart from the others. Redburn, who is shorter and thinner than Bernard, stands inches from his face, blasting him for a torn pants pocket. "How do you not check yourself?" he sceams, seemingly enraged. "Where's your pride?"

"No excuse, Sir," Bernard hollers. Then Redburn turns away. He looks at me and smiles, showing teeth. "Pretty neat, huh?"

The outburst is so extravagant that I can't focus on what he is saying now about being on the lookout for Bernard to make excuses and getting him to think about why he is at the academy. The point is valid: the cadets are here to mold their characters, and attention to detail is important. Better Bernard should learn it over a torn pocket than on a battlefield or in a plane.

But something bothers me. Bernard is already standing out when Redburn brings me over; the upperclassman has already berated him for the mistake once. The second time is just for me. Redburn's smile tells me the infraction isn't the point. It is about his pleasure in wielding such power.

I suddenly remember Redburn's strange greeting last semester: "What's important enough to get in your book?" I move away, uneasy about his performance and the possibility that his thirst for attention is ratcheting up the pain for the people I am here only to describe.

In bringing back Recognition, General Desjardins is trying to strike an elusive balance between professionalism and tradition, tightening the guidelines for training the SMACKs, setting limits for the most taxing exercises, and spelling out what kinds of criticism fall out of bounds. But the result feels tentative, as if the tide of history and hormones could wash it all away in just a few years.

The next day, the doolies line the hallways around the Cadet Quarters desk, the anchor for each of the squadrons. Matthew Stillman, the two-degree, sits on top of the tall counter, his black boots dangling, reading dozens of questions on the year's supreme test of military knowledge. He asks first for the "primary function" of the A10/OA-10 Thunderbolt II, the first twin-engine jets built for the air force to support ground forces.

"What year was the Cessna C37 B-3? Name one important country that uses the C-37 to train its pilots."

"What is the payload of the Minuteman?"

"What is German Field Marshal Erwin Rommel's quote on war?"

"What is the primary function of the Maverick?"

As the questions come quickly, the four-digs who know the answers write feverishly, until one of the more arcane questions brings them up short. Rebecca Gleason, a recruited swimmer from the western suburbs of St. Louis, seems to be suffering through the exam; she looks intensely at the floor, her mouth open and her face red. She writes something, then looks at it and shakes her head, as if in private conversation with her exam.

Bernard stands by the window, answering only a handful of questions. He squints to see the badges held up for one question, and he runs his hand over his scalp, as if trying to rouse his brain. He does not even hazard a guess on seventeen of the fifty questions. If he gets everything he answered right, he will still score only a 64.

Aside from the military quiz, for which an enthusiasm for teamwork could land the students before the honor board, today's panoply of obstacles and exercises are the real soul of Recognition, and these are aimed at driving home for the doolies the importance of watching out for one another. They begin with a leadership course and go through a spirit-crushing assault course and other exercises, none of which an individual could complete alone. They end the day back in the dorms, which have been transformed into a surreal theater that opens vistas on the consequences of their choices. One room is a "liberal café," where they are attacked for belonging to the military. In another, they attend their own funerals.

Soon after their knowledge test, the doolies gather in the field house for the leadership course: a series of exercises that seem to be more about cooperating than taking charge. In the first part, the doolies break up into groups and consider an elaborate scenario: You are alone, trapped in two feet of snow on a wooded mountainside after a helicopter crash has killed your pilot. What will you do to survive?

At first, they answer the question individually. They must rank the following list of twelve items in order of their importance for survival: signal flares, a hatchet, a ball of twine, a pocketknife, snowshoes, cross-country ski equipment, sedatives, a rechargeable flashlight, a loaded rifle, a cooking pot, a fishing line and hooks, and a disposable lighter.

After answering the question individually, the cadets gather in a circle on the floor to reach a consensus on the right order.

"The first thing is to keep warm," says Rhonda Meeker, suggesting that the hatchet should be at the top of the list. "You'll need the cooking pot to melt snow so you'll have water."

"Sedatives?" asks Bernard.

"That's the last thing," says Adam Brunderman.

"That's what I'd want," Bernard counters.

"That's what you'd want, but . . ."

"Sedatives. Dead last," Meeker says, ending the discussion.

The answers are scored by adding up the number of points between an item's position on each student's list and its proper place in the order. Working alone, Urban gets a score of 44. Meeker gets a 22 on her own. As a group, they score far better: 18. The correct order is lighter, pot, hatchet, snowshoes, flares, twine, flashlight, pocketknife, rifle, skis, fishing line, and sedatives.

What is particularly striking about the moment, what distinguishes it from a similar exchange at any civilian campus, is the absence of any pretense to consider all ideas as valid, worthy of discussion, if not consideration. The idea that sedatives might be more important than a flashlight or a pocketknife is so absurd that it dies instantly.

The cadre Paul Tracy tells them how crucial it is to know your people and to take good care of them. Meeker, munching on an energy bar, talks about an instructor, a major, who told her class last semester about his mother's death ten years earlier. His commanding officer denied him leave to attend her funeral, instead telling him to "suck it up."

"I don't want to comment on a specific case," Tracy says, "but if you can accommodate your people, you should."

The doolies of Squadron 13 break up into groups once again. Meeker and Justin Goodin are blindfolded and led to one area of the gym, where the cadre have laid out an island of paper squares. Standing on one side, Meeker and Goodin must make their way to the other side stepping only on the squares. They must rely on the rest of the squadron to guide them to the finish line.

Nearly everybody helps Goodin, leaving Meeker to wander nearly alone; only one teammate talks her over the patchwork of squares. Goodin takes big steps, then baby steps, and then a combination of half steps, working his way in straight lines around the perimeter.

"Sidestep more with your right foot," one of his teammates calls. "Make more room," another advises. "Push your foot over." Toward the end, Bernard stands on the other side of a mess of papers with his arms opened wide. "Just jump as far as you can," he tells Goodin, bracing himself to catch his classmate. Meeker hears a single voice telling her how to move across the field; it does not offer to steady her when she lands.

Afterward, Tracy criticizes the group for its disorder and disproportion. "How many people were helping you out?" he asks Meeker. Of course, since she was blindfolded, she doesn't know, so he answers his own question. "Only two or three." Then he turns to Goodin. "And how many people were helping you out? Pretty much the entire group, right? So we had one guy helping her and everyone else helping you."

He tells them that all that help was confusing. The group should have designated one person to speak, and the instructions to the blindfolded cadets should have been straightforward and simple. "This is what we're going to do. This is where we're going. This is how you're going to get there," Tracy instructs, leaning toward them. The course is meant to educate, not intimidate. The criticism comes across as helpful, without accusation or the suggestion of punishment ahead.

Before it is over, the doolies redeem themselves. Tracy breaks them up into two groups, asking people in each group questions about someone on the opposing team. Officially, the person who gives the wrong answer should hit the floor for push-ups, along with his or her teammates. The real goal of the exercise, however, is to get both groups to see themselves as part of a single team and for all the students to share the pain of each individual. To Tracy's surprise, Squadron 13 seems already to do that coming in.

In Meeker's isolation and strange silence, I wonder who is sharing her pain.

On a hillside by the athletic fields, the doolies of Squadron 13 are divided into teams. Firsties hurl questions like hand grenades, and each wrong answer leads to an onslaught of abuse.

Jocelyn Mitnaul, the cadre in charge, asks them what year Doolittle Hall was built. Peter Kaszynski volunteers a wrong answer, 1961, then compounds the mistake by addressing Mitnaul as "sir."

"Use your head and think about what you're saying," she hollers, ordering the group to walk like crabs over twenty yards—forward and backward. They move clumsily, especially when they try going backward. She is unconvinced.

"I can tell when they're not trying," she says. "It's not about fitness. It's about commitment." Then she turns to the stumbling doolies and blasts them. "Earn your props and wings!"

"What is the plane on display in the northwest corner of the terrazzo?" a second cadre asks a group of four doolie Bulldawgs, one of them Bernard. Dan Hickox knows the answer: a General Dynamics F-16 Fighting Falcon, built to defend against ground and air attacks. The group gets a pass.

"Hold on. Be strong. 'Cause when it's on, it's on," advises the cadre.

"How many rooms in Vandy Hall?" a third cadre asks.

The group huddles and comes up with an answer: "One thousand four hundred and fifty, sir," they holler in unison.

"That's completely wrong!" he shouts, ordering them to do push-ups. They have already done one round, but these push-ups are diabolical: two count only as one, with the SMACKs seldom knowing how many repetitions they will have to do.

"Good job. Get up. Take a drink," Mitnaul says eventually. The doolies suck on the tubes from their CamelBaks.

Mitnaul orders them on their backs, where they must keep their hands behind their heads and touch opposing knees with their elbows while keeping the other leg completely straight. They keep on until Mitnaul blows her whistle, then they move on to yet another station, where they do jumping jacks. Bernard is by now crimson and grimacing, struggling to continue.

"That was weak," Mitnaul says afterward. The doolies must start all over again.

Bernard is flailing, hardly able to raise his arms. His teeth are bared, locked together in concentration. He struggles to keep pace as best he can.

Later that day, Miles-Tyson Blocker tells me that the last twenty-four hours have brought out qualities in Bernard that he doubted the young cadet even possessed. "Throughout the year, he was mediocre, to say the most. But right now, I see that he's trying hard, looking out for his classmates."

Perhaps the intensity of the event is breaking down the athlete's facade of nonchalance, or perhaps he is beginning to realize that his future is not in pro football. Blocker looks away, as if watching a scroll unfurling of Bernard's months of bucking the system.

"I hope that he's not just putting on a show. I really hope he's reaching inside, like everybody else is."

Before beginning the assault course, the cadets empty their pockets and drop their essentials into a pile: badges, gloves, *Contrails*. Chris Valine, the upperclassman in charge of the course, gives them a chilling introduction to what lies ahead:

> I know you remember what it was like during BCT [Basic Cadet Training]. But in case you forgot, let me remind you. You will feel tired, you will want to quit, and you will feel pain. But know this: If you do not try and if you quit, you will not pass. There is no knowledge on this course. There are no levels, and cheat codes won't help you do any better. Your level-forty warlord powers and demon spells will have no effect here today. You will suffer to become a member of my cadet wing. Your days of being weak are over. My cadre are the biggest, strongest, meanest cadets you will ever met. We are ruthless. We are heartless, and our sole purpose is to make you feel pain and suffering today. We are direct descendants of the three hundred Spartans, training our whole lives for this day, to bring pain and suffering into your life. I know you feel it—that feeling in your stomach you felt during BCT. Only this time, you know what's coming. And there's nothing you can do about it. Nothing's going to stop what's going to happen.

The four-digs listen, their bodies tensing, their eyes wide with alarm. Unbeknown to them, Valine is actually reading from a speech taped to his microphone. Now he utters the dreaded phrase that unleashes a free-for-all dash to bring down the doolies, reminiscent of their first assembly at Arnold Hall:

"Assault-course cadre, fall out and make corrections!"

The field explodes in screams from the upperclassmen, with criticisms of the SMACKs flying—about their slowness, their sloth, their fitness.

Across the field, the doolies are doing sit-ups, push-ups, squats, and kicks. The voice of one upper-class cadet rises above the cacophony. "Do not hit me," he shouts. "Do not touch me."

In exercises in hand-to-hand combat, the cadets learn to kill without weapons, using the balls of their feet and their elbows to slay an enemy. "Your thighs are parallel to the ground, your back is straight, shoulders back. Look your enemy in the eye. Look proud," says Brad Seifert, a two-degree, shifting from side to side. "Your power is in the legs. Every movement should initiate in your legs. Lift the elbow. Strike!"

In small groups, the doolies of Squadron 13 practice destroying an enemy, attacking with their elbows, their hands, and their feet. Throughout, the cadre shout over them:

"Get your butt down!"

"Bend your legs!"

"I'm not a trigonometrist, but I know that's not ninety degrees."

"Get them down to the ground!"

"Strike him! Go for the collarbone!"

At the next area, an upperclassman announces: "Welcome to Suck. I'm the mayor. Let's go!"

He has them jump over fourteen-inch-high barriers and crouch upon falling, a move they would use to avoid a hand grenade. Then he orders them to bear-crawl up a hill in groups of four each. It is remarkably difficult to do this crawl uphill: the cadets must keep their knees straight, carrying the entire weight of their bodies in their arms and their feet. Every ten seconds, another group hits the ground, with the cadre shouting on top of them:

"Spread out! Get your knees up!"

"Keep moving! Get your hands off the ground!"

"Get your knees up. You all look like gummy bears to me!"

The four-digs climb the last bit walking, with their hands crossed behind their heads. Gleason is barely able to drag herself up. Her face is red, her mouth open in exhaustion. She tries to raise her hands, but they cannot go, and they fall to her sides. Bernard turns up alongside Gleason, helping her up the hill. He knows that his fellow four-digs, like the upperclassmen, believe he has sailed through the year while they suffered. They doubt that he deserves to be recognized this weekend, and they would just as soon see him go. Going up that hill, he feels a burst of energy, so he hurries over to Gleason, eager to show effort.

Also running the course is Major Robert MacKenzie. The four-digs say that his presence is a great motivator, but the upperclassmen use him largely for the power of embarrassment. "Hey, how does it make you feel to know there's a guy your father's age who's doing this better than you?" taunts one of the cadre. "He's got kids. He doesn't get any sleep, either."

The doolies are still not finished. They grab rifles to practice killing without firing a shot, jabbing and hammering at an enemy. Some are finding unimagined reserves of strength. Megan Biles, the soccer player, is unwavering, her eyes focused and intent as she slams the rifle butt. Others have gone past their limit. Their feet are planted on the field and their hands are on the barrel, but their minds are frayed with fatigue and cannot connect.

"Do it with some passion," a cadre exhorts them. "You're trying to kill someone, not tickle them to death."

Nobody is laughing. Goodin's face is smeared with mud, and dried grass sticks to his mouth and his nose. Chris Flynn's shoulders cave in, as if yearning for earth. He is immobile with fatigue. Bernard materializes at his side, bucking him up.

"Go on, man," he says quietly. "You'll make it."

The doolies are lined up along the walls of the corridor in their dorm. Meeker is in a corner, where a short leg meets the long hallway. Like everybody, she is tense and exhausted by the day's unfolding ordeal. She does not see Redburn coming from behind her. He whips around, catching her by surprise and hollering something in her face. He is volcanic and unstoppable.

Meeker's lower lip trembles, and her eyes well up, but she does not cry or say anything. The blast is so sudden and loud that nobody can even make out Redburn's words. The sophomore steps back and smiles, nodding, satisfied that he has brought Meeker to the brink.

Erin Moubry, a fellow two-degree, shoots a look at him and then at me, as if in Morse code: "D-o-n'-t—y-o-u—s-e-e—y-o-u'-r-e—b-e-i-n-g—w-a-t-c-h-e-d-?-?-?-?-?-?-?-?-?" She draws Redburn away. His classmates hurry him off to a room like their wayward brother.

Later, when I think back to the hallway after he left, I know that the doolies were all standing at attention. Meeker's shoulders must have been back, her spine straight and her chin high, but that is not how I see her when I remember this moment. I see her shoulders coming together like parentheses, her back curled as though her head were too heavy. I see an invisible shell over her.

Weeks later, as the year winds down, Redburn brings up his ambush of Meeker. "That was so not me," he says. "My friends came over to me afterward and said, 'We thought you didn't even know how to yell.'"

That night, the cadre transform the dorms into theme rooms, each becoming the stage for a different nightmare. In one, the doolies are called before a Recognition board and must argue the case for why they should be allowed to stay at the academy and graduate. They drop in on a "liberal café," whose patrons attack them as homophobic "baby killers." They get shot down, taken prisoner of war, die under interrogation, and attend their own funerals. Together, the rooms form a coherent story, aimed at provoking the academy's newest cadets into thinking hard about the choice to become an officer.

The four-digs, their nerves raw from the day's all-out assault on their endurance, move from one scene to another like hostages; they are led through the halls single file by the upperclassmen, red blindfolds tied at the backs of their heads. Their hands rest on the shoulders of the class-mates ahead of them. The halls are filled with the sound track from *Black Hawk Down*, a reminder of the military fiasco in Somalia more than ten years earlier. They do not know where they are going or what their friends are going through.

As the doolies enter the men's bathroom, the cadre swarm over them, hollering in foreign languages and forcing them to kneel down. When their blindfolds are pulled off, they see an infernal vision: Exposed electrical cords hang from the lights, and the shower stalls are splashed with "blood." The walls are black, covered with plastic garbage bags, and hay covers the floors like sawdust in a slaughterhouse.

They see a torturer hollering over an airman on his knees, a bloody tourniquet around his head. The interrogator, being played by Ben Smith, is shouting questions and insults in Chinese. Another interrogator holds a gun to the airman's head, demanding that he give up the day's work codes. In response to their hollering, the American prisoner is shouting, "I will give no information. I will never forget that I am an American, dedicated to the principles which make my country free. I am prepared to give my life, if necessary." His words, which are almost drowned out by his jailers, are the only words whose meaning the cadets can make out clearly. The hollering ends when one of his captors shoots the pilot in the head. The room goes black. The blindfolds are put back on.

When the blindfolds come off again, Adam Brunderman is sitting in a room with a coffin in front of him. A normally easygoing guy from northern Virginia, Brunderman now sees his picture propped in a corner and hears someone playing taps for him. Kate Fabbri is standing at the head of the coffin in a short black skirt and a black blouse, weeping.

An upperclassman in the corner tells what happened: Brunderman was shot down in Afghanistan at the age of twenty-five. He'd graduated with academic and athletic honors from the academy and had gone on to pilot training in Pensacola. He'd married a local girl, Alison, and they'd had two children. Kate Fabbri, playing his widow, accepts the folded flag.

To prepare the funeral service, Kevin Pastoor has called Brunderman's family and has gathered information on his background: his father, John A. Brunderman, a colonel in the air force; his mother, Cindy; and his brother, Eric. As the mournful strains of taps fill the room, the blindfold goes back on, and Brunderman is led across the hall, to an extreme change of mood.

After they leave, the upperclassmen laugh. "Hey, I'm not sure I'd want my widow walking around in that," one kids Fabbri, tilting his chin at her skirt. She laughs and shakes her head.

In the next room, two firsties are dressed like buffoons, wearing ties with bright orange pumpkins on them over T-shirts. One initially speaks like an emcee on Latino television, the other in a Chinese accent.

"In my country, when we tell jokes we don't laugh. That disrespect ancestors," one says in broken English. He honks a bicycle horn. "What you get when you cross an elephant and a rhino? Elephino." Honk, honk. "Two peanuts walk into a bar. One was a-salted." Silence for a second. Then the cadets actually erupt in laughter.

The room is casual; cushions are thrown around, and there are cookies for the taking. The three-degrees who are in charge of this scene, Aaron Barrow and Reed Wildman, explain that it is a "reflection room": a place for the doolies to decompress before ending the night and to talk about why they are here.

Brunderman says he's a military brat who saw the academy as the surest way to get a pilot slot. That was his reason for coming here at first. "But after basic training, a couple of months hanging out with these guys, it is all about them."

Frank Mercurio, who lives down the hall from Brunderman, nods. "Ever since I can remember, I wanted to fly," Says Mercurio, who is not related to the upperclassman Nick Mercurio. He had thought about ROTC, but once he learned about the academy, he dropped that idea. "For some strange reason, I think it's the easy way out. You know you'll have a job after graduation."

Barrow and Wildman ask the cadets to think about the kinds of leaders they hope to become. They tell them to write these descriptions on index cards and drop them in a box on their way out. The two tell the cadets to come back to look at the cards during the course of their careers at the academy. If they are honest with themselves, the two men say, it will be a measure of sorts, a gauge showing whether they are becoming the people they set out to be.

For the doolies, the various scenes, whether harrowing or disturbing, can be cathartic, giving vision and voice to the fears they ordinarily bury about the road ahead and prompting them to think through their presence here. With the nation at war on two fronts, the threat of capture and torture in enemy territory is eminently real for the airmen, soldiers, contractors, and even civilians serving in Iraq or Afghanistan, whose ranks these cadets may join after graduation. If they are ever captured while deployed, the risk they run—of beheading or slaughter, videotaped for the glory of their enemies—is far more terrifying than anything they see tonight. The night can also be taken as another round of hazing on the road to Recognition, more creative and intense, poking at their psyches instead of their bodies this time.

There is something about the episodes that seems unmoored in time, disconnected from the life of the nation. At that moment, the rest of the country is struggling with the issue of torture in Abu Ghraib prison and the practice of flying suspected terrorists to secret CIA prisons or to third-party countries for interrogation and torture.

The "liberal café" seems like a page from the Recognition 1968 handbook. As the cadets play out these scenes, popular sentiment in the United States is shifting against the war in Iraq, but without a military draft, the urgency that brought hundreds of thousands of protesters to the streets during the Vietnam War is nowhere being heard.

Casting liberals as a budding cadet's opponent also sends an unmistakable signal about the political culture at the academy, whose cadets tend to the right of college students around the country. In fact, libertarians could just as easily have served as their adversaries in the café. They have also been early and vocal critics of the war in Iraq. But libertarians are ideologically closer to conservatives.

"All the people who are conservative are more open about being conservative," Blocker explains. "All the people who are liberal keep their mouths shut. I'm one of those people who keep their political affiliations to themselves. If you're in a different political boat, people get angry."

The theatrics, however, do get the four-digs thinking. Urban, who has also watched his own funeral, begins reconsidering his relationship with a girl back home in Texas and the kind of life he'd be asking her to share. His roommate, Flynn, says that he'd been vaguely aware that the bombs he would drop, directly or indirectly, could end up killing innocent civilians alongside their intended targets, but he had never really thought much about it before. The criticism that the military does not accept people who are openly gay is valid, they both state, but beyond their pay grade. "Those are the rules for us," Flynn tells the straw men at the cafe, "but we don't make the rules. That's up to you and everyone else."

Word has gotten out that the four-digs have found the schedule for Recognition. With it, they'll have an idea of what to expect and when each event will end—important psychological advantages in the grueling campaign to pound them down. When the upperclassmen investigate, however, asking questions during Recognition's Saturday morning inspection, or SAMI, nobody will say how they got it.

Redburn is pressing Cox to give it up. "I hope it was worth it," he tells him, "so that you know you only had to put out for an hour and a half during this training session or that one. We all heard [Meeker] say, 'I can't try right now because we have the assault course this afternoon.'" He shakes his head in derision. "That one was great."

Ryan Regan, the cadet commander of Recognition for Squadron 13, calls across the room to Bernard, who is standing at attention. "Bernard! You know the schedule better than I do," he hollers, then comes up close, asking for the schedule. Bernard looks at him but does not move. "Man, nobody remembers," Regan says. "This is like Watergate. Like Monica Lewinsky."

When Westbrook is asked, he refuses to answer, saying, "It's an improper question. Sir, the answer would require me to incriminate somebody."

Actually, Regan says in an aside, an improper question is one to which the person asking it already knows the answer and is only trying to trick the cadet into self-incrimination. In this instance, Regan truly does not know where the schedule is, so the question is permitted.

Nobody is in the mood to spoil Recognition over the incident, though, even after they find a printout on top of some papers in Bernard's desk drawer. "It is pretty serious," Regan says, "but we're just, we're really just coming down on them.

The doolies work for hours preparing for the inspection, sweeping, mopping, shining, and stacking their clothes in perfect order. Still, it's not perfect enough.

In Bernard's room, there is gum on a bedpost. Christin Schulte, a firstie, finds it and shows it to Harrison, who looks at Bernard and says nothing. Like Blocker, Harrison thinks that some spark of sincerity and concern may be glinting in Bernard for his fellow cadets—but there's that gum. "I feel like I have to go wash my hands now," Schulte says in disgust, and she walks away.

Up and down the halls, shoes are not shiny enough, clothes aren't sufficiently neat, and there's sand by the edge of the floor—"It's a beach back here," an upperclassman calls out. Once the cadre are finished grading the rooms, they trash them—emptying drawers and bookshelves, throwing mattresses down on the floor, tossing blankets in corners.

RECOGNITION

Push-ups.
Thomas "Brad"
Bernard at left.

Squats, from left:
Thomas "Brad"
Bernard, Peter
Kaszynski, David
Ostrom, and Daniel
Hickox.

Four-digs go through the dorms blindfolded, where upperclassmen
have designed scenes they might encounter in combat.

In the capping event of Recognition, cadets run to the Cathedral Rock, about two miles from their dorms.

They haul back a heavy log they decorate back in the dorm.

At Cathedral Rock, from left: David Urban, Peter Sohm, Samuel Pang, Jonathan Benson, Christopher Flynn.

David Urban and Christopher Flynn in their dorm room, dressed for Recognition.

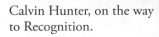

Calvin Hunter, on the way to Recognition.

Four-digs facing the windows, as upperclassmen prepare to pin props and wings on the younger cadets, now accepted as equals.

Adam Brunderman and Megan Biles.

Jamal Harrison pinning the prop and wings on Thomas "Brad" Bernard.

"Okay," Redburn barks at Westbrook, Benson, and Cox. "You have ten minutes to get this into SAMI order!"

Instead of fixing their rooms, the academy's twelve hundred doolies head out for a two-mile run with the firsties to Cathedral Rock, a cropping of white granite towers. The worst of the year's myriad punishments is over, and they are euphoric, exhausted from the run, and laughing. "Yeah!" they holler in triumph, fragments of their joy spiraling up the hill, away from them, like tissue-paper airplanes. They down icy sodas from a cooler and fall over one another's shoulders.

"You mean I can't get in trouble anymore?" Meeker calls out, laughing, her eyes wide with disbelief.

"I can't believe we made it!" someone in the middle of a crowd squeals. "Done. Done. Done. Done! Done!"

At Cathedral Rock, the doolies pick up a heavy log, emblazoned with their squadron's plaque, and haul it back together to their dorm rooms at Vandenberg Hall. Bernard grabs a piece of the heavy log, which, he lets on, is not made of metal or wood, as it appears. "Recycled trash," he says, with a half smile.

I ask how the training was for him, with the upperclassmen riding him so hard. "Do you think they wanted you to make it?"

"The academy?" he asks. "Yeah. My squad mates?" Bernard looks around and shakes his head, pursing his lips. Over the last few days, the cadre have come down on him like Niagara Falls, determined to pound him either into shape or out of the academy. Then Bernard tells me something astonishing about the torrent of invective: he heard none of it.

"I can take yelling," he says. "It doesn't bother me. I grew up in a rough family." His parents' marriage fell apart when he was in high school. The breakup was violent, ugly enough to send his father, a former football player, to jail. His father also went to jail for drunk driving, Bernard says. Now Bernard mentally shuts down when the shouting starts; he retreats to an inner bunker and does not listen. "I can just block it out pretty easily."

What bothers him more, he says, is knowing that not only the upper-classmen but also many of his own classmates believe that he didn't earn his place throughout the year and perhaps did not deserve to be recognized as a fully prepared cadet. That's why he stepped up to help his squad mates when he saw them flagging.

"The truth is," Bernard says, "I wanted to do that during basic training, too, but I wasn't in good enough shape then. I was having trouble myself." He is still ambivalent, unsure whether he belongs here. He worries about the war in Iraq and presumes that it will still be going on when he graduates.

But two things motivate him to stay. First is his determination not to become his father, who is out of jail and is trying to eke out a living in sales. The second is economic: getting out of the house and not relying on his mother to pay his way. "She always worried about how she was going to get me to college," he says. "This was God's plan for me."

As Squadron 13's doolies approach the academy, they pass by several grey-haired couples, who are sitting on a bench near the ramp alongside the chapel. They are some of the sponsor families who adopt the cadets for a year.

"We've graduated seven cadets," Pat Wilson, a sponsor, says proudly. Those cadets are now scattered across the globe: one flies F-16s in South Korea, another flies a B-52 bomber out of Guam, and a third is flying F-15s in Iraq.

"This is the first year I don't have a freshman," Wilson says.

Just then, Squadron 13 marches past. "Hi, Mom!" Bernard calls out. She does now.

Back at the dorms, the doolies discover that the upperclassmen have cleaned their rooms spotless in their absence; this is the first sign that their year of suffering is over. The doolies change into their dress uniforms, double rows of brass buttons marching up their chests and blue stripes climbing the sides of their white pants.

This is the moment of their formal Recognition. The doolies gather in an unused rec room just around the corner of the long hallway, where the lights are low. Along the walls, the upperclassmen stand at parade rest in the semidarkness.

Going through the alphabet, a two-degree, Boyd Fritzsche, hollers out the names of all the cadets who started basic training last summer. Those who are here emerge upon hearing their names, to march down the center of the hall. The march is a barometer of their performance: the upperclassmen salute the cadets they've come to respect through the course of the year. Toward the cadets who have failed to earn their esteem, the upperclassmen remain still or even turn their backs, in a show of disapproval.

"Casey Jane Barrett," Fritzsche calls. Barrett had left the academy just as classes were getting under way.

"Recognition denied!" booms Matt Stillman. A door slams down the hall, and then the corridor is quiet for a moment. I wonder if Barrett, hundreds of miles away in Ventura, feels something at the instant her name rings out, some ripple from the life she didn't choose.

"Cadet Fourth Class Jonathan M. Benson!"

Benson marches slowly down the hall, suppressing a smile. Coming from the bright rec room, he cannot make out the identities of the upperclassmen who are watching him, but he sees hands go up to salute him.

"Recognition granted!"

"Cadet Fourth Class Thomas B. Bernard."

Here and there, scattered hands go up in salute. Most of Bernard's squad mates do not move.

At the end of the hallway stand Major MacKenzie and Master Sergeant Mark Winter, waiting to congratulate the doolies. On a table are brass plaques engraved with their names, mounted on wood that is shaped like a dog bone. I had watched Redburn make the stencil and carve the wood for these in the wood shop. Now they gleam.

"Cadet Fourth Class Christopher P. Flynn."

Flynn, of Biloxi, Mississippi, sees the hands fly up as he passes, and he smiles with a flush of pride.

"Cadet Fourth Class Rhonda Meeker!"

Meeker turns the corner, unsmiling, her eyes straight ahead. A whole row of upperclassmen fails to salute her, but a few others do, including Harrison, Blocker, and Fabbri.

"Cadet Fourth Class Samuel H. Pang!"

"Recognition granted!" As Pang, who suffered more than most, perhaps because of his slight build, makes his way down the line, the upperclassmen salute him. "Good job, Pang," one says softly as he passes.

Fritzsche summons another cadet, who bailed out early in the year. There are no steps approaching. "Piece of shit," somebody rasps, as the door slams. As the names of those who quit echo through the hall, the four-digs look at one another, trying to remember them. For most, they are but dim figures who have faded from sight.

"Cadet Fourth Class David Urban!"

He, like Meeker, is serious as he turns the corner. Here and there, hands go up to honor him. He is associated with violating the honor code, but also with turning himself in: choices that elicit mixed judgments from his squad mates. "Good job," says one upperclassman. Another, a firstie, is not persuaded. "Cheater," he says as Urban passes.

The doolies head down to their squadron's assembly room, off the terrazzo, where the upperclassmen are supposed to pin on their props and wings, the first decorations of their military career. The freshmen stand along the edges, facing the walls as the upperclassmen file in, then turn to face the upperclassmen. The room is silent as Takanen, the senior in charge of the squadron, steps forward, uttering the dreaded words that have lit his fellow upperclassmen's fuses time and again.

"Upperclassmen, fall out! Make corrections!"

Only this time there is no fire. There is no noise at all for a moment. Instead, in unison, the upperclassmen shout back the words that the four-digs have been longing to hear all year.

"Sir, there are no more corrections to be made!"

32 | Urban's Honor

David Urban had missed the weekly test of military knowledge, so now he sat in a room waiting for the makeup exam. A few seats away by the door, an NCO sat silently, a rolled-up piece of paper in his hand. It was early October, the weekend that Air Force would take on Navy at Falcon Stadium. Out in the hallway, a sudden burst of noise, a show of spirit before the football game, made Urban look across at the door. In a glance at the NCO's paper, he spied a column of mostly letters alongside numbers and a single word that stood out in bold print: *True*.

A few minutes later, as Urban took the exam, he came to what turned out to be the test's only true-false question. "I think for the first time ever, I didn't know the answer," he says later, in his first discussion of the incident that had cost him his good standing at the academy. "My mind raced. I put down *True.*"

The instant he did, he realized that he had cheated. Should he stop right there? Throw down his pen? He filled out the rest of the test, afraid of arousing suspicion.

He passed.

He stole back to his room, thinking, "I cheated on a test," and half expecting a knock at his door. "I'm going to get kicked out," he worried, but once he calmed down, he realized that nobody knew he cheated. They would only know if he told them, and only a masochist would do that. True or false?

He went through the rest of the day as if nothing had happened. It was only one answer, five points on a minor test, he rationalized. It wasn't as though he set out to cheat. He couldn't help it if his eyes rested on the paper and his brain came up with the last thing he'd seen. He stood a 50 percent chance of getting the question right even if he hadn't seen anything. It wasn't as though he had gone into the exam planning to cheat. "It means nothing in the long run," he told himself.

Urban's parents had homeschooled him and his nine siblings, sacrificing thousands of hours not so much for academic advancement but to build his character. They didn't trust the "secularists" at their local public schools, and they wanted to protect him from poor choices: drugs, early sex, and the brazen self-indulgence to justify anything he did. He was active in the church and had even done a missionary trip.

Thus, he should know better. True or false?

As he was agonizing over copying a single answer, dozens of his classmates, led by the athletes, were hatching an elaborate system of sharing all the answers to the military knowledge exams, week after week. As a homeschooled kid, Urban carried a reputation of being socially and athletically inept, and got booted from the Ultimate Frisbee team after the others voted him "most likely to suck at sports." The athletes involved in the cheating ring were not studying their *Contrails* at all but merely depending on the answers to come through like a wake-up call, ten minutes ahead of each test. They passed off perfect scores on the exams as their own—geniuses in jockstraps.

By Saturday night, two nights after the test, Urban had let himself off the hook. Why risk his entire future by confessing, when he wasn't even entirely convinced of his own guilt? He could just pledge to himself never to cheat again. That would serve the same purpose, minus the humiliation before his squad mates and his friends, sparing him the risk of losing his college education and his career. "I finally got my conscience to shut up and let me go," he recalls.

However, Urban was not brought up to traffic in shades of grey. On his moral street map, there was right and there was wrong. If he muddled them at the first crossroads he encountered, then all was lost. He had, after all, voluntarily taken the honor oath, pledging never to lie, steal, or cheat. Now, barely two months into classes, he'd already broken his word.

On Sunday night, as Urban was reading his Bible, the spiritual equivalent of calling home, he realized that he could not cover up his mistake. "I don't even know what the passage was that I was reading," he says later. "It just hit me one more time: 'If you let this go, then you're never going to be able to uphold those standards. You will never be able to tell another person to uphold the honor code.' And at that point, I knew that if I didn't speak up, it would be with me for the rest of my life." True.

Thus began Urban's odyssey through the Air Force Academy honor system, and its well-worn path of introspection and punishment, aimed at weeding out liars, thieves, and cheats.

On Monday morning, Urban reported his crime to the NCO who'd administered the exam. He, in turn, took it up the chain of command.

Urban called home and told his mother, who did not believe him at first. His parents were disappointed in him for cheating but impressed that he had turned himself in. Because he'd confessed, there was no need for a hearing.

Two weeks later, however, Urban was sitting before an honor sanctions board. They grilled him for ninety minutes, making him go over what he did and why. He realized he could be tossed from the academy for cheating and that his name could be tainted for the rest of his college career.

"I was nervous about what was going to come out of it," Urban recalls, but he was also at peace with his decision to turn himself in. A week later, he learned that he'd gotten probation—the lightest possible punishment for what he'd done.

Two key factors worked in his favor: Urban had come forward of his own will, and he had been living under the honor system only briefly. Early in the year, Brigadier General Susan Desjardins, the commandant of cadets, had warned them about the importance of coming clean.

Still, Urban was jolted to see how seriously the offense was taken. Because of it, he would have to get special permission to leave the academy and could not represent the academy to outsiders in any capacity. He was barred from most clubs and extracurricular activities. The development of his own character became his extracurricular project for most of freshman year. He was the frog, pinned down for dissection, and the scientist, poking around inside to discover the weaknesses and flaws that led him to steal an answer on a test.

If the honor board was not going to expel the cheater from the academy, it would—in its highly structured, formulaic way—purge the cheater from the cadet. Urban began working with a mentor, deconstructing the components of honor and examining his own behavior.

It would have been easy to dismiss the exercise with cynicism, but in its way, it went to the core of why Urban and countless other young people join the academy. Certainly, many come because it is free, because they dream of flight, or because they are ambitious and spring from military roots. But many also come from idealism, because they reject the social mores of their contemporaries, and because they yearn to better themselves.

"I have a lot of problems with society, with people not taking personal responsibility," Urban says. "That's not a good way to live, if you're not answerable to yourself." In a dozen essays and twenty-five journal entries, Urban evaluated his character and charted his evolving understanding of who he was.

In his first journal entry, he recalled:

The first and only time I ever "stole" something, I was about 6 years old and I took what I think was a toothpick from a store display to mess with and forgot to put it back. I got home and was horrified when I realized that I had just taken it. The memory of that feeling is still with me. I learned about the culture of cheating firsthand at community college. There I saw many people cheating, sometimes openly and blatantly and getting away with it. Every time I saw it happen I got so mad that they were doing it while I was trying to earn my grade. Those experiences taught me to hate cheating.

Given his upbringing, he had not hesitated to raise his hand for the honor oath, but now, he acknowledged, "I have shown in my actions that I am more than capable of cheating."

A few weeks later, he wrote about the shame and loss of face, even as he minimized the significance of his lapse, and he realized that some people would give him points for turning himself in:

When I came forward and admitted that I had cheated on the knowledge test I told the entire squadron that I was a cheater. Despite the fact that it was a small matter on a fairly insignificant test, once I admitted to cheating on that it allows the perception that I could cheat on anything. How many times does a person have to cheat before he is a cheater? How many times does he have to cheat before people think he is a cheater? The answer to both unfortunately and justifiably is the same, once. The fact that I self-reported has in some ways dampened that perception, but even by adding a perception of honesty to my situation people still can keep that idea that I will still cheat. By earning the title of honor cadet I have a stain on my record that will not go away by explaining it away or telling my story to everyone. The only way for me to get rid of that perception is to live in such a way as to eventually remove any doubt from people that I still have that tendency toward cheating. Perception is reality, and the only way to defeat it is to show a new reality that is different from the perception.

In a series of entries, week after week, he ruminated on integrity, humility, moral courage, honesty, and other qualities, rating himself for each on a scale of one to ten. By New Year's, the structure and regimentation of the exercise began to feel hollow and self-serving:

I am copying myself and just changing the subject with each of these journals. . . . Every time I write about something that I have been taught about since I was a child I almost feel whoever reads this cringing. I know that I have character flaws. I see them each time I write. Sometimes they seem small, other times I wonder why I haven't dealt with them sooner. And every time I come away having seen something in a different way and learned something new about myself.

Urban realized that unless he wanted to continue repeating himself, he would have to dig deeper into his character and motivations. "When I did that, I ended up getting a whole lot out of it," he says.

He writes that he lacks humility and is sometimes easily distracted:

[It's] a flaw that goes back to my time before high school when I had no concrete schedules for anything and no strong incentive to get anything done. It developed into a somewhat lazy lifestyle that is only now being truly confronted and corrected.

Before coming here I had a 3.88 GPA over five semesters at the college I was attending. I figured that no matter what, I would be able to keep my grades up enough to stay out of any real trouble academically. And then as I got past the middle of the semester and began to see how far I was from reaching my goals here, and how close I was to academic probation, I began to really get worried. But still because I had allowed myself to build up that opinion I never sought the help I needed to do better. As a result my grades slipped just below 2.0 and now I am on academic probation, which I had thought I would be able to avoid. Looking back I see that the failure was on my part in that I never had the humility to admit my mistakes and seek help to do better.

In an essay on the qualities of a good leader, Urban wrote, "If soldiers cannot trust their leader to be honest, then how can they trust him to lead them the right way? If I never lie but also am not completely open about what is going on, then I have done nothing to earn anyone's trust."

At some point, all the analysis led to a kind of vanity. Many who knew about his confession praised him for telling the truth and setting a good example. For a while, he started to feel pretty swell about himself:

As much as I tried to not let it, the compliments went to my head and I began to think that just maybe I was all that. I kept those thoughts to myself because I knew that they were not right.

The whole time I was struggling to keep myself grounded and to remember that even if everything that was said was true I had still broken the honor code and there is nothing about that to be proud of.

And beyond that, the examination led him to admit his weaknesses, to commit them to paper for all to see. In the middle of his probation, he began attending the same weekly Bible study group as his mentor in the honor program, with whom he regularly discussed his campaign to improve his character. His mentor held tremendous sway at a vulnerable moment in Urban's life, when Urban joined the academy in tearing down his identity and building it up again. But Urban, who comes from a religious home, says he did not feel coerced. Rather, he says, his "walk with God was slipping off" first semester, and with that distance, the values that once felt "really concrete" also began to wash away.

The problem is that while digging I came across more than just buried potential and abilities, I also found poor qualities that had been allowed to hide beneath the surface for years. My procrastination jumped out and slowly ate away at me until I had fallen behind in nearly everything at one point. My lack of responsibility reminded me that it was here as I let things slide by without getting them finished. . . . For the first time in my life I have had to truly work hard for what I have, and through this rehabilitation I had to face just how much work I have to do in my life.

"I guess it's my way of learning," Urban says. "I do something dumb big enough to take a fall, and then I realize 'I don't want to do that again.'"

Urban's personal test of character corresponded to the wider cheating scandal that erupted among the four-digs throughout the academy and that has repercussions for the school as a whole. The ensuing investigation of that cheating ring forces eighteen doolies—none of them from Squadron 13—to leave the academy, and it lands thirteen others on probation. Of some forty cadets who are investigated, nine are cleared for lack of evidence or found innocent by honor boards.

Academy officials pointed to the results as proof that the cadet-run honor system works. Cadets reported the cheating, investigated it, and comprised the honor boards that judged the accused. But the frustrations of the investigation, and the sense that some cadets were gaming the academy—admitting guilt only after it has been independently established—prompts a closer look at the honor process. Should the honor code be shelved for a time, as the academy had done once before? Should it stay the same, or does it need "teeth"?

In a referendum, Urban joined more than 70 percent of his fellow cadets in voting to toughen the honor code. As a result of the vote, the cadets who turn themselves in for violations will probably get a shot at rehabilitation. Those who hide their transgressions or protest their innocence will face mandatory expulsion if they are found guilty.

This is sharply different from the Uniform Code of Military Justice, which lays out crimes and penalties, and from civilian law, with its protection from self-incrimination. Cadets like Urban and Calen Pope, who also voted for the change, see it as an incentive for the cadets to come clean and take greater responsibility for their characters.

"It simplified things," says Pope, a soft-spoken and serious two-degree who is given to quoting the Bible and whom Jamal Harrison tapped for assistant flight commander that summer. "It narrowed the amount of scheming and weighing options that someone accused of an honor violation has to do."

Urban agrees. "It puts it on the cadets to stay clean, not on the honor system," he says. "I like that personal responsibility."

33 | Human Once More

Now that they are formally recognized, accepted as fully trained cadets, the four-digs, who have tried so assiduously to avoid notice all year, begin to emerge as distinct personalities to the upperclassmen. Their first names come back to them like gifts, comforting them and filling the corridors. There is no more fear of running into cadre and perhaps not remembering their names. The four-digs are citizens in a newly borderless world, able to drop in on friends without regard to distance. As summer approaches, the shutters have been thrown open, and the academy begins to feel more like a campus to them.

John T. Rice, a prizewinning farm boy from North Dakota who goes by "J. T.," has kept his head down all year, studied his *Contrails*, and recited its articles without flaw. In his spare time, he likes to make funny astronaut movies in his room, donning a flight suit and a helmet and talking into the camera from his desk. "There's a person behind that four-degree," marvels Miles-Tyson Blocker.

Christopher Flynn, David Urban's roommate who is from an air force family then stationed in Biloxi, Mississippi, is still disoriented, amazed by the change of atmosphere. It is as though the air has lost the electrical charge that kept them on edge all year; they'd gotten so used to its existence that they forgot it was there.

Now Flynn delights in the civility that he's achieved with Recognition. The four-dig asks an upperclassman in the hall what time dinner is tonight, and the upperclassman actually answers—a conversation of equals that would have been unthinkable before Recognition.

"I've been corrected three times for calling them sir," Flynn reports, his eyebrows climbing up in mock shock. "Recognition is awesome!"

Urban pulls out a duffel bag from under his desk that is stuffed with civilian clothes: jeans, shorts, and T-shirts from home. Since Recognition, he is finally allowed to go out in his own clothes. He grabs his favorite black leather jacket and hugs it, closing his eyes.

No longer must the freshmen walk by the walls, bark greetings, recite that day's menu, or state some *Contrail* factoid upon request. Now they command the center of the hall and speak only if they have something to say. Urban is tickled by the confidence that such simple acts give him. He becomes "decently good friends" with his training officer, Ben Smith, a firstie. They attend the same Bible study group.

"I really respected his leadership style," Urban says. "He wasn't really training us to be abusive. He was never hard to be hard. If we messed up and he said something about it, we knew it was serious." Smith is a firstie, roommates with Jonathan Elliott.

"Hey, Ben, when you going to head down to Bible study?" Urban calls down the hall. Urban isn't going there himself at the time. It is more of a shout-out for Jesus. In asking the question, Urban says, "I was standing up for my Christian beliefs."

Others—Flynn and Major Robert MacKenzie—are suggesting that Urban use his experience in honor rehab to consider becoming an honor officer himself. Major MacKenzie credits Urban with internalizing the honor code, adding, "That's what we're looking for." Flynn, in whom Urban had confided just before he turned himself in, takes his room-mate's future in the honor system as a given. "You *know* you're going to become an honor officer," he tells him. Urban squares his shoulders as he recalls the remark, pleased by the prospect.

As the year ends, he feels himself coming full circle. Exactly 358 days after he'd first stood in Clune Arena for his freshman orientation, Urban is back there. He volunteers to take next year's doolies through the academy, *his* academy, as another four-dig had done for him. He shows around an incoming cadet from California and another from Kansas. Urban enters the summer, however, with a grade point average just under 2.0, so he is likely to continue on academic probation.

Rhonda Meeker also glimpses that light, or at least steps halfway from the shadows. She is enjoying her freedom and the camaraderie of her classmates. She seems to be over her wounding break with the honor guard, which she describes as devastating at the time, and is thinking of going in for sharpshooting. "Not like the team," she says. "More like weekend learning."

In looking back over her year, she is sober and thoughtful. She regrets having channeled most of her energy and attention to her personal survival and thinks that she would have done better to direct it at helping her classmates through their trials. She might have felt less isolated when she was down. She's made a handful of friends in the squadron with whom she plans to stay in touch after the four-digs go off to their new squadrons in August.

Although she began the year curious and spontaneous, Meeker is guarded now, worrying about how she sounds and about the academy's image. I ask about her feelings when Trent Redburn pounced on her just before Recognition, and got yanked away by another two-degree, Erin Moubry. What was going through Meeker's mind?

"Crap. He's really mad at me," Meeker says, eyes wide, exaggerating the obvious in a voice that could have come from a children's cartoon.

"Thank you, Cadet Moubry, for pulling him off me." She couldn't make out what Redburn was shouting or whether he targeted her intentionally.

"It doesn't really matter," she says. "It was like ten minutes to Recognition." Ten minutes to becoming fully human again. Nor does she know whether he was genuinely angry or playing to the crowd. "I, I—I couldn't really say. I just know what he did, and if that was acting, cool. If he acted, I'm happy he got your attention.

"It's not an acceptable experience, by any stretch of the imagination," she continues, "but it happened." She looks at the window for a moment. Clouds are gathering like a restless mob, but the thunder hasn't started yet. "I don't even think about it anymore."

Meeker relaxes only after bringing up something that has been weighing on her mind: she fears that I might have picked up "a bad vibe" surrounding her treatment. Although she did feel harassed, she wants to steer me away from of any suspicion of a sexual element.

"I want to make that very clear," she says. "It was not sexual." Her fears take me aback. I hadn't sensed or heard anything from her classmates about sexual assault, so I hadn't brought it up with her.

"Am I missing something?" I ask. Given the conversation, the question is more to myself.

"No," Meeker answers quickly. "I just thought you were going to write it in a sexual way, and I wanted to make sure." She adds that she is worried about the kind of book that might emerge from the year since we'd met. Weeks earlier, on the afternoon of Recognition, we'd spoken for the first time in months, and she said that she did not want to be identified by name. "I'm just starting out," she said. "I need my career clean." Given her turbulent year, I agreed to her request.

The academy is not perfect, Meeker allows. She thinks that the supervisors could use more training, and she hopes to see Combat Survival Training brought back. The three-week program, which cadets do in the summer between their freshman and sophomore years, simulates survival after crashing in wartime. Cadets live in the woods for part of the time and live on field rations, and on chickens and rabbits they receive at the outset, which they must kill and prepare. Some resort to eating grasshoppers and other insects.

Grace Anderson, a firstie and a member of the last class to have done Combat Survival Training before Meeker's arrival, calls the course "one of the most worthwhile things we did" at the academy. The ants, she says, tasted like lemon drops. The program was suspended in 2005. Some cadets suspect it became a casualty of the sexual assault scandal, but air force officials said, rather, that they were weighing whether all cadets needed Combat Survival Training. The training was restored in 2008—too late for Meeker's class to participate.

Beyond Meeker's fear of her and the academy's portrayal is a feeling that so much of what the place means to her, and the changes it set off, came not from the daily drills or the starred events—Beast, Commandant's Challenge, or Saturday morning inspections—but from the spaces in between: stuffing shopping carts with odd scraps to decorate the upper-classmen's rooms; the unexpected joy of tracing any shape she chose as she walked over the terrazzo; or seeing Christmas lights as if for the first time.

"It's loving your parents because they sent you here, it's learning to appreciate your own home," she says.

Meeker has had, by far, the rockiest and most challenging doolie year of any in Squadron 13, hanging on when many would have packed up and gone home. Her classmates would insist that most of her difficulties were self-imposed. She held on tight, however, expressing gratitude that the academy has given her the room to "learn how to be here. The academy is my teacher, letting me have a cry when I need to cry. This is my academy," she says. "I live here. I go to bed and I wake up here."

I ask if she would recommend the academy to her younger sister. Meeker does not hesitate. "If you want to be in the military? The only way to go is up," she says. "Just think about it. Who do they put in the rockets going to space? It's not marines. It's U.S. Air Force."

If there is seemingly no ambivalence in Meeker, Brad Bernard's journey is not nearly so decisive. Unlike Urban, the athlete makes it through the year without any kind of probation—academic, physical, or military—but he still carries the whiff of just crossing the finish line. Bernard ends the year without the goodwill of Jamal Harrison, one of the few upperclassmen who has believed in him even when the evidence gave him little reason to do so.

At Recognition, Harrison and Blocker think that they see Bernard throw himself into the effort and connect with his fellow cadets in a genuine way for the first time. Of his own accord, Harrison pins props and wings on Bernard in a sign of respect. But something, seemingly small, bothers Harrison. During Recognition, Bernard fails to memorize the poem "Invictus," despite repeated warnings by the upperclassmen. Instead, he relies on his classmates to get by.

The lapse gets to Harrison, who tells Bernard, even after Recognition, that he will continue to call him by his last name until he learns the poem. The four-dig is confused. Wasn't this kind of pressure supposed to end with Recognition? One week passes, then two, then three, and Bernard still does not learn the poem. When Harrison asks about it, Bernard tells him that he has too much bearing down on him to study the poem.

"He just kind of shrugged it off, like it wasn't a big deal. Like he'd get around to it," Harrison says, shaking his head and opening his mouth as if tasting something spoiled. "Take two minutes out of your day to learn one line. Take two minutes out of the next day to learn another. You'll learn the poem in no time."

Harrison thinks that Bernard has trampled on his good nature and believes that he is seeing the cadet's true character, only too late. "I took a personal interest in him," Harrison says. "I believed. For me personally, he's my failure for the year."

Bernard carries some of the same doubts about whether he belongs at the academy, but he says, in retrospect, that he would not have left midyear because "I'm not a quitter."

He has little appetite for combat, however, and the news from Iraq worries him. "We're a country at war, and I have a feeling we're going to be at war for the next twenty years," Bernard says.

Harrison feels little sympathy for Bernard's lingering uncertainty. "If that's how he feels, the air force doesn't need him," he declares.

Major MacKenzie is more optimistic. He is headed for a promotion to lieutenant colonel in January, and he and Master Sergeant Mark Winter will spend another year with Squadron 13 before getting new assignments.

MacKenzie agrees that Bernard still has "some work to do on duty and character." However, he's done fine academically, and MacKenzie praises the former football player as having "tremendous leadership potential.

He has charisma, and that could make him a very good leader. The light's at the end of the tunnel."

Bernard actually does not impress even himself much by the end of the year. Academically, he does fine, finishing with a respectable 2.8 grade point average, despite a C– in calculus. "I don't get really freaked out about finals or tests," he confesses.

Bernard ends the year like a guy in a country song. Pockets empty, he's spent his last dollars on a plane ticket to visit his Mom that summer. He has just lifted something too heavy, and his back aches. He breaks up with his girlfriend, an earnest, straight-flying cadet who attended prep school with him, then he patches things up a month later. The fault was all his, he says.

She was struggling to avoid academic probation while he never worried about finals. Add to that Bernard's catalogue of mistakes: "I guess I was manipulating and controlling and disrespectful." In retrospect, he realizes that he did not work as hard as he could have, either at the academy or on the relationship. He leans back in his chair, absently turning an apple in his hands, his royal blue running shorts shimmering in the light.

"I'm good at flying through the loopholes, I guess," Bernard says. His smile lingers a few seconds. He raises the apple to his mouth and bites off a chunk.

34 | Hearing the Silence

As my year following Squadron 13 winds to a close, there are pieces of the picture whose edges are frayed, as if torn from the larger canvas and locked in a safe. How to reconcile Trent Redburn, who is so careful and deliberate on the airfield, with the human roadside bomb he'd shown himself to be in the hallway at Recognition? What of Meeker's abrupt silence, and her fears when she starts talking again? What had prompted her retreat?

It is only well after the year ends that I learn that these questions are connected. Their answers offer clues to the difficulties of tackling some of the academy's most sensitive issues, including the one that had first brought the academy to my attention.

Although Redburn talked of his friends' shock at seeing him holler the day he exploded at an already beaten-down Meeker in the hallway, the truth was more complicated. When he spoke to me and took me up in a glider, Redburn seemed the model cadet, talking about how the academy's honor code was so deeply rooted in his character that he once reported himself to the police after accidentally hitting a stop sign near his house.

He poured his energy into the academy: teaching others to fly, rising early for the thankless task of calling minutes with the four-digs, lining them up in the hallway to drill them with questions and exercises until thirteen minutes before mealtime. He sought out mentors among the active-duty officers.

But the upperclassmen who lived alongside Redburn were wary of him. Whereas I glimpsed momentary outbursts, they saw more. He had lost his first roommate in Squadron 13 after shoving him during a disagreement. He'd resorted to a fistfight on the athletic field over Ultimate Frisbee. A number of his squad mates kept away; they thought he gloried in himself as he climbed the social ladder. They considered him explosive, unpredictable, and well connected.

Major Robert MacKenzie had said that Redburn could make a fine officer but that he had trouble harnessing his energies and his temper. "His only thing is, he needs to control his emotions. He volunteers for anything," MacKenzie had stated, adding that Redburn would grow flustered when plans changed midstream. He's "all thrust, no vector."

The four-digs, many of whom accepted and even admired the hard-body training of Lance Watson at the start of the year, had more mixed reactions to Redburn. As a three-degree, Redburn was himself a recent survivor of doolie year. His ostensible role was to coach and serve as an informal older brother to the SMACKs. Instead, they said, he ratcheted the tension way up from the start, training by shock and intimidation.

Zach Taylor, who'd left the academy midyear, said that on some mornings Redburn and his fellow training clerk would come pounding on the doors and turn morning minutes into a grueling ordeal of physical training; at other times they would not. It was impossible to predict. The two men seemed to revel in shouting down and humiliating the four-degrees.

That in itself did not prompt much concern among Redburn's classmates or higher-ups at the academy. The old-schoolers, who come in all ages, see the kind of harsh training that Redburn and his cotrainer were doing as essential for toughening the cadets, to mentally numb them. Others, however, saw the two as straddling the line. "It wasn't bad enough to be punished for, but they were a little bit excessive, and everybody knew it," Taylor said.

Jonathan Benson, another four-dig, said Redburn "cared about us a lot and invested a lot of time."

That year, Jamal Harrison, the training NCO, took Redburn and his fellow training clerk aside, explaining that they did not have to destroy the four-digs, just train them. Save the high decibels for the really important stuff, he advised. The other cadet dialed down his intensity, but Redburn remained volatile, his classmates said.

Well after the school year had ended, Taylor and others said that there were a handful of freshmen whom Redburn singled out for more criticism and punishment, Most of them were athletes, who were seen as having an easy time because they were usually at practice while the other four-digs were being beaten.

At the top of the list, however, was Rhonda Meeker, who was not an athlete. With her, Redburn's methods seemed to cross the line of accepted practice at the academy—even for the old-school traditionalists.

He once ordered her down for push-ups, but, in an all-but-unheard-of step, he barred her classmates from dropping with her in the customary show of moral support, said the four-digs who were there. "This is just me and her," he had said, and he matched her, push-up for push-up, until she broke, or gave up, humiliated and defeated. The cadet trainers typically avoided isolating the cadets this way, because it risked making the training personal rather than professional, and it ran counter to one of the main purposes of cadet training: to build a group identity.

At other times, Redburn punished Meeker's classmates for her missteps but barred her from taking the punishment alongside them—a classic psychological technique for creating a scapegoat. After enough incidents like this, the classmates naturally came to blame her, finding even more fault with her than Redburn did.

Taylor's assessment of Meeker was typical, among both the four-digs and the upperclassmen that year. "There are some people who got it more than others, but they asked for it," Taylor said. "Some would just give them attitude or not really do things right. They'd be messing up more than other people. I just learned from the prep school: Do what you're told, say what they want to hear, and keep your mouth shut. Otherwise, you end up getting beat more."

Redburn's contempt for Meeker grew as the year wore on, her fellow doolies reported, so he would deride her to the other four-digs when she was not around. Benson recalled training sessions in which Redburn's "strong hatred" of Meeker grew as Recognition approached and in which he talked openly about how much he hated Meeker and wished she would leave the academy.

Given that Meeker was not present at these sessions, the steadily rising pitch of the calumny seemed not so much intended to improve Meeker as to poison the atmosphere and leave her friendless. Asked about this later, Redburn said, "No comment." By the time I saw Redburn lash out at Meeker during Recognition, there could have been no pretense, even in his own mind, that it was for her own good.

There was even more to Redburn's animosity than most of Meeker's classmates realized.

Late in the first semester, Meeker had come forward to Major MacKenzie, reporting that Redburn had made a sexual advance to her—a violation of the academy's rules against fraternization. She said that she had rejected the overture, and as a result Redburn was singling her out in training as retribution.

In an interview after leaving the academy, MacKenzie, by then a lieutenant colonel, said that he had recognized the accusation as one of sexual harassment. He confronted Redburn, who denied expressing any sexual interest in Meeker.

"This is what we're hearing," MacKenzie recalled telling him. "This is what you've been doing. This is where it's wrong." He said he documented the fraternization charge, warning that another accusation would establish a trend and trigger "more substantial action."

"If the victim feels harassed, no matter what the intent was, if it was construed as harassing or unwarranted, then it needs to stop," MacKenzie recalled telling Redburn. "That is sexual harassment of you singling her out."

As a result of the accusation, MacKenzie relieved Redburn of some of his training responsibilities. He also barred him from training four-digs unless another upperclassman was present. "It was humiliating to him, a blow to his ego and his position as an upperclassman," said MacKenzie, but he saw the step as necessary. "We had to take that precaution."

"We tried to reassure [Meeker] and the other females," MacKenzie continued. "It's very important for them to know that we're acting on it." At the same time, he could not completely discount the possibility that Redburn was telling the truth. He tried to balance the accusation and the denial with his charge to train both cadets.

"We can't just punish Redburn," MacKenzie said. "We need to show him where he did wrong. The victim is seventeen or eighteen, and he's only one or two years older. The person who did the acts is learning, too. Those are always tough—the 'he said, she said' incidents. All we can do is support Meeker, but it's tough to totally discredit what he said."

MacKenzie said he thought hard about his response to the accusation, choosing a course to both protect Meeker and teach Redburn. Redburn, however, downplayed the seriousness of the charge when he was asked about it. He said that Meeker's accusation never led to a formal investigation because it was false. He called it "a brief allegation that never went through."

Yet he also contradicted himself, saying initially that he did have personal issues with Meeker but then denying fraternization. "As soon as I started having personal and professional issues with her, she decided to bring fraternization charges against me," Redburn said. "I certainly did not fraternize with [Rhonda Meeker]." He said he did not recall going one-to-one against her in push-ups until she broke, or preventing her from taking punishments alongside her classmates, but he also defended the measure, saying that male cadets were sometimes singled out this way.

"What I remember is that [Rhonda Meeker] was not well liked by a majority of the squadron," Redburn said. He did train Meeker harder than the others, he added, but not because she rejected him or had blown the whistle. "It was because she had no respect for authority. It was never a 'Yes, sir' or 'No, sir.' It was always 'Whatever' for an answer. She was a completely substandard cadet."

In practice, the balancing act translated into a lecture for Redburn and a warning not to train four-digs on his own. In other words, very little changed. Benson and others remembered Redburn training doolies solo right to Recognition. They recalled Redburn's remarks about Meeker growing more venomous as Recognition approached. Redburn himself claimed not to recall having been barred from training doolies on his own. "Mostly, I just stuck to flying after that," he said.

Aside from following the guidance the academy had given her since virtually her first day, to report any suspicion of impropriety, Meeker stuck to Taylor's dictum: she kept her mouth shut, to most of her classmates and certainly to me. I have managed to piece together what happened only through the reports of witnesses and others involved.

After much thought, I have decided to recount these events despite Meeker's refusal to discuss them directly with me. I was able to corroborate the allegations independently, and I believe that her silence and her hostility to even discussing what happened were important elements of the story.

As the year ended, Meeker, who had earlier asked to be given a pseudonym for this book, changed her mind and gave permission for her name to appear. However, I had reservations: she'd had a particularly stormy first year, and I had won her fleeting trust in part by promising that I was not out to torpedo her career before it had a chance to start. Afterward, Meeker withdrew her cooperation and demanded that her name not appear publicly, saying she did not want to risk any damage to her future in the air force. She specifically did not want to discuss her experience with Trent Redburn, and she accused me of wanting to "sensationalize" problems at the academy.

I have granted her that anonymity and have extended it to the cadet she accused, as well. Given the toxic nature of the charges and the fact that her identity is protected, it did not seem fair to name him publicly. For both, the academy is a training ground; the place they go to learn and to make mistakes before they assume far greater responsibilities in the active-duty air force. With the exception of sexual assault allegations and criminal convictions, the cadets' records at the academy are wiped clean upon graduation.

Meeker did confide in a friend, Miles-Tyson Blocker, who told me about the incidents and confessed remorse that he did not do more to help her. He said it was hard to separate out the strands of Meeker's problems during her first calamitous year. Most upperclassmen focused on Meeker, not Redburn, as the cause of her problems.

"She had a rebellious attitude, a free mind," said Blocker. "It was hard to get her to just shut up and color. The whole year was about trying to get her to calm down and get through her four-degree year.

"It was just an incident that was really bad, but it was part of a theme, and pretty much it was like a normal thing. Amongst the upperclassmen, it was like, '[Rhonda] did this' or 'Oh yeah, I would chew her out, too.' When this happened, it was like another thing. You get desensitized to what hazing is."

It was only afterward that Blocker put the pieces together and saw Meeker's treatment as sexual harassment. "Maybe it does take a year, or the realization that it's a theme, or that at the time it happens you may not know," Blocker said. The harassment was a large part of the reason, he explained, that Meeker had stopped talking to me for part of the year.

Blocker said he did not fault then Major MacKenzie or Master Sergeant Mark Winter for giving Redburn the benefit of the doubt, because at that stage it was difficult to discern a pattern. "They figured [Trent] just had a bad day. It happened once and wouldn't happen again. It was a small problem. He could change," Blocker said, adding, "It works for most people."

A year later, Blocker saw Redburn coming down especially harshly on a female four-dig from the next class to come through Squadron 13. He asked around and documented allegations that Redburn had hit other four-digs. He'd allegedly punched one in the stomach on Hundred's Night, in front of the technical sergeant assigned to the squadron (who'd corrected him on the spot), and another doolie said he'd punched him in the chest. At MacKenzie's suggestion, they brought the accusations to the squadron commander review board.

At the time, Blocker said Redburn did not dispute the accusations, but when I asked Redburn about them after graduation—when he was no longer bound by the honor code—he dismissed the accusations as "bogus" and "false," saying, "We went to a big meeting about it, and nothing happened about it."

Upon learning of the investigation, Redburn, a two-degree at the time, nearly came to blows with Blocker, who was then a firstie. Blocker said that Redburn had turned up in his room and ordered, "You. Me. My room." Blocker didn't move. "I'm not going anywhere," he said. Redburn stormed out of the room.

Asked about this, Redburn said he was angry at the way Blocker had gone about the inquiry, without notifying him, and he said it was unfair to judge his four years at the academy on the basis of "two or three issues where I was extremely wronged. People get upset," he insisted. "To take these two moments out of four years and say I have anger management issues . . ." Actually, I hadn't mentioned "anger management issues" at all, although others, including MacKenzie, had when asked about Redburn. I was asking him about something much more serious: allegations that he had systematically used his power to destroy a fledgling cadet who had rejected a sexual advance.

Blocker said that he didn't really grasp the toll that the year had taken on Meeker until the following year, after she and the other four-digs had dispersed to other squadrons. When Blocker told her he was investigating Redburn's treatment of four-digs, "she got pretty emotional about it," he recalled. She said that finally Redburn would get his due.

"It was just him versus her, and he was trying to show his dominance," Blocker continued. "He was trying to show that he had power over her: the training officer that you just rejected in a romantic way is now beating you." Because the whole foundation of training is a form of incessant needling and harassment that they call beating, harassment that is specifically sexual is harder to uproot. "It gets masked," Blocker noted. "You could easily argue it was part of training and not abuse. The lines are really blurry."

In turning down my request to discuss Redburn's treatment of her that year, Meeker, fiercely protective of the academy and concerned for her future, dismissed the harassment as a "one-off" incident, a "personal issue" with no broader meaning in the life of the academy.

The Department of Defense's own investigations suggest otherwise. A survey of the military academies in the spring of 2006, a few months before Meeker's complaint, found that 51 percent of women at the Air Force Academy and up to 60 percent of the women at Annapolis and West Point said that they had been victims of sexual harassment. In a 2003 survey by the department's inspector general, done at the height of the sexual assault scandal, 68 percent of the academy's female cadets said that they had been sexually harassed, and 20 percent reported they'd been victims of sexual assault. Thus, even though Meeker felt isolated, she was not alone.

If her experience was part of a broader phenomenon, so was her reticence in discussing it. The alarming numbers that emerged in these anonymous surveys are in striking contrast to the *officially reported* cases of sexual harassment: only thirty-two incidents, from 2003 to 2006, at *all three service academies combined.*

Since 2003, the academy has taken steps to curb sexual harassment and assault, creating a system that gives the cadets multiple avenues for reporting assault, officially and unofficially. The cadets attend twenty-one hours of briefings on the issue during their four years at the academy, and each squadron has a special counselor, a cadet who is assigned from another squadron, to whom the other cadets can turn to report abuse. Each base, including the academy, has a specially designated sexual assault response coordinator.

Although research and the department's own reports document that where there is sexual harassment, there is an atmosphere for sexual assault as well, in practice the two are dealt with very differently. An accusation of harassment, lacking as it is in hard evidence, leaves more to the personal judgment of the higher-ups. In responding to any accusation, the cadets and the active-duty officers who are weighing a course of action bring their perceptions of the context and the people involved.

After leaving the academy in 2007, Dr. Harold Breakey, who was the sexual assault response coordinator during Meeker's doolie year, said that the academy had taken important steps to aid victims of assault. Nevertheless, the underlying military culture and hierarchy tended to protect the more powerful figure in any clash. And that more powerful figure was never the victim, who was often, instead, vilified. "I've got to be honest," Dr. Breakey said. "If I were a victim, I'm not sure I would come forward."

Although they both would bristle at the comparison, Meeker and Redburn were alike in one way. Both tried hard to do well but were out of the mainstream, socially and temperamentally out of step with their classmates that year. If you mention either of their names, their squad mates seem to step back, waiting to hear of the latest gaffe or blowup, as if they are beyond surprise.

For a three-degree like Redburn, ostracism translates into social distance and loss of respect. But as an upperclassman, he would not have ordinarily been second-guessed over his treatment of doolies. For an already powerless SMACK, however, ostracism multiplies his or her vulnerability. Watson, the popular flight commander for First Beast who was himself accused, and cleared, of singling out a basic cadet for humiliation, said that upperclassmen often see complaints of harassment or illness as a ruse to avoid training, a sign of social immaturity akin to "crying for Mommy and Daddy." Four-digs like Meeker, who was already tagged as a "problem child," carry even less credibility among the upperclassmen who run the squadrons.

As a woman, Meeker undoubtedly met extra skepticism. The 2006 Department of Defense report on sexual harassment and assault at the military service academies noted that sexual harassment and abuse were "highly correlated" with power and that women at the service academies were triply disadvantaged from the start: they were minorities, accounting for less than 20 percent of the population; they were barred from some combat specialties; and they had to meet lower training standards.

Meeker had her own record, with her early expletive-laced explosion on the assault course, working against her. "Once somebody is ostracized or disliked, then everything they do is going to be painted in the worst light," said Elizabeth Simpson, the squadron's representative to the honor board.

That is why MacKenzie and Winter's response, teaming Redburn up with another upperclassman for training, might have seemed a wise solution, but it did little to mitigate Meeker's misery. It is also why Redburn, despite the warnings, would have felt comfortable singling out Meeker again at Recognition, in full view of his squad mates.

As the year ended, Redburn told me that he would not be training incoming cadets at Jacks Valley that summer but would be on the airfield. At the time, he said nothing of the harassment accusation, and even within Squadron 13, most cadets were unaware of it. Rather, he said, he didn't enjoy yelling at kids frozen with fear for two weeks straight. "Some people really love it," he said. "It doesn't do anything for me at all."

35 | Taking Off

The morning of graduation offers perfect flying weather: chilly, with clear skies and a soft breeze. In Falcon Stadium, a human flag is taking shape in the stands as families from throughout the country fill the seats. Some families count three generations in uniform. There are immigrant families from the boroughs of New York a few seats away from autoworkers from Michigan and farmers from Iowa. There is a family of Native Americans, the men in cowboy boots and southwestern bolo ties and the women in woolen ponchos.

These are the parents and the grandparents, the siblings and the friends of the 980 cadets of the Class of 2007 who will be graduating as the air force's newest officers after four arduous, exhilarating, and at times maddening years.

As the marching band strikes up, the graduates file onto the field, snappy in their parade dress uniforms, which were designed by Cecil B. DeMille, the legendary Hollywood director. (DeMille staked his own claim in aviation history by starting Mercury Aviation, the first passenger airline to fly regularly scheduled flights, in 1919.) Cropped dark blue jackets with double rows of brass buttons top high-waisted white pants. The pants legs seem to stretch for miles, and, true to DeMille's penchant for the big picture, the thousand uniforms streaming onto the field make an arresting tableau. A bright gold sash catches the sunlight, and the cadets are wearing white gloves. Instead of wearing the usual graduation mortarboards, they wear white hats with dark blue visors. Though the morning is cold, the cadets' excitement seems to warm the stands.

Throughout their four years here, the cadets have forged closer bonds and more intense relationships than they probably would have at any civilian university: living, eating, sleeping, studying, and training with the same group of cadets for three years, imbibing a culture that aimed not just to teach them but also to transform them. They entered a few weeks out of high school, when their friends at civilian campuses were enjoying their first taste of freedom, and they surrendered themselves to a campaign that began by storming their defenses.

At its most excessive, the academy aimed to rebuild not just their bodies and minds but also their souls. At its best, it uncovered unimagined reserves of strength and will. For four years, they crossed milestones: basic training and boot camp, Acceptance Day, Combat Survival Training, Commitment, Hundred's Night. Each year they trooped out to watch another batch of firsties toss their hats to the sky. Just days ago, they joined in another academy ritual for the first time: they leapt into fountains to celebrate finishing their last final exams as cadets. Now it is their turn to graduate.

This is one of the first classes to have applied to the academy after the attacks of September 11, 2001, when the number of candidates for admission surged amid a wave of patriotic fervor. They began their cadet careers with the country at war on two distant fronts, Afghanistan and Iraq. Those conflicts await them still. About 60 percent of this year's graduating class is slated for pilot training.

The firsties receive their commissions as second lieutenants before graduation, at ceremonies scattered across the academy. Squadron 13 holds its ceremony at the Officer's Club in a room with floor-to-ceiling windows that look out on the woods. Each cadet comes forward upon hearing his or her name, raising a hand to take the oath, and standing as parents or designated others pin on shoulder boards marking the cadet's new rank: second lieutenant.

Some firsties, like Matt Adams and Jonathan Elliott, are commissioned by their fathers, who served before them. At the ceremony, the Class of 2007 gives gifts to its active-duty officers. Jonathan Elliott hands Master Sergeant Mark Winter a Cadet Plaque and Saber, the highest honor cadets can bestow. Major Robert MacKenzie receives a gift certificate to REI, a national chain of stores that specialize in outdoor sports gear. Technical Sergeant Jeannette Copeland receives a gift certificate to a local restaurant.

For Lance Watson, whose gift is a Rambo costume in tribute to his love of bodybuilding, leaving the academy is both exhilarating and sad. After taking sixty days of paid vacation, which he'll spend white-water rafting and tramping through Europe, he will head to Beale Air Force Base in northern California to handle aircraft maintenance for the Ninth Reconnaissance Wing—home of the country's fleet of U-2 spy planes and Global Hawks, forty-foot-long unmanned surveillance aircraft that can fly up to thirty-five hours.

Watson looks forward to joining the active-duty force, but he also expects it to be more lonely. The camaraderie borne of living in close quarters with people who are all going through similar experiences at the same time will vanish after today. "Got to keep up that social network," he says.

Matt Takanen, who was initially troubled by his assignment to a naval air station for pilot training, is instead bound for Misawa Air Base in Japan, home of the Thirty-fifth Fighter Wing. However, he will not be allowed to fly. A few weeks earlier, he was disqualified from pilot training because of a problem with depth perception that cannot be corrected through laser surgery. Thus, he will go into communications at Misawa, where he expects to serve three to four years.

Takanen leaves here as a Distinguished Graduate—the academy's equivalent of summa cum laude. As squadron commander, he produced results, lowering the number of cadets on probation for poor grades and having none on probation for alcohol violations. Squadron

13 finishes first in overall performance for its group of ten squadrons, which is a tribute to both Takanen and his first-semester predecessor, Adrian Peppers.

As he moves toward his first active-duty assignment, Takanen thinks that a less exalted position, such as element leader or flight commander, might have given him more useful experience. As squadron commander, he was the link between the upperclassmen who were training the four-digs and the active-duty officers who were overseeing the squadron. Takanen didn't get as much personal, direct experience training four-digs as he had hoped, however.

On good days, "it was really fulfilling," he says. "I learned a lot about communication: giving people deadlines that make sense; giving them time to act; allowing them to come up with the best solutions." Takanen realizes that he needs to improve his organizational skills. There is also something else he picked up, which is not very obvious when you're standing near the top of a strict hierarchy: "Never assume you know the right answers all the time. Always ask questions. Look for advice. Look for different perspectives." Before shipping off to Japan, Takanen will take time off in Greece and Hawaii.

Although the cadets grow attached to their closest friends, there can also be something claustrophobic about living alongside the same group of people for so long and putting up with the endless rules.

"I don't think anyone misses the academy on graduation day," says Nick Mercurio, a two-degree, as he watches the firsties graduate. "They're all ready to see it in the rearview mirror. But I will miss it." Mercurio expects to miss his friends, and the small ways they find "to make it fun" at the academy. "My four best friends are here—well, my five; one of them's my roommate," he adds, remembering Syed Saad Javaid. "The other four live on either side of me. So it's gonna be sad to split off and go our separate ways."

A few days before graduation, the two-digs have their own rite of passage in Ring Dance, the academy's answer to senior prom. Girlfriends and boyfriends of next year's firsties fly in from around the country for the formal dinner, at which the two-degrees receive their class rings.

As with everything else, receiving the ring is bound up in ritual: The two-degree takes his or her ring from its case and drops it into a glass of champagne or—for the under-twenty-one crowd—sparkling cider. The cadets drink the champagne until the rings rest in their mouths. With kisses, they pass the rings into the mouths of their dates, who slip the rings on the cadets' fingers. If the relationships are serious, the cadets and their dates typically spend the weekend together in the mountains with friends, renting homes, relaxing, and cooking. Cadets without dates skip the ceremony and just slip the rings on their fingers.

Mercurio, who is not accustomed to taking himself too seriously, has grown in unexpected ways in the last year. He feels surer of himself and speaks with fewer linguistic tics—fewer *um*s and *ah*s. He is handling his own expenses and not turning to his parents for financial help. As one of the top two students in his major, English, he is a serious contender for a coveted slot in graduate school. He has also fallen in love and is thinking of marriage. He met Abby the previous July, when he was briefly sent to Nellis Air Force Base outside Las Vegas. She lives in Iowa and works in marketing for a de-icing company that has contracts with the air force. They met away from the base at a chance encounter in Las Vegas.

"I never thought that I'd have a serious girlfriend or anything like that," Mercurio says, "but now I'm ready to live with her and, a couple years down the road, get married."

By graduation, Mercurio is already doing research at the John F. Kennedy Memorial Library in Boston. He flies back just for Ring Dance. The assignment is not far from his family's home in Rhode Island, and it gives him a chance to work on writing samples for his graduate school applications. He keeps a journal, jotting down observations and ideas that he might work into short stories. Mercurio admires Ernest Hemingway for "the masculinity of his prose; the way he evokes the same images that Virginia Woolf can, with a third of the words." He is considering the College of Charleston in South Carolina and the University of Iowa, which has a celebrated creative writing program. He might serve the air force as a speechwriter or come back to teach at the academy.

Although some graduates plan to relax during their sixty days off, others are plunging right into an even more lasting commitment: matrimony. Alan Rodriguez, a friendly, outgoing younger brother of an economics instructor then at the academy, will wed his high school sweetheart, Sarah, in two days. Rob Santos, who is heading to Eglin Air Force Base in Florida, is also planning to wed his fiancée, Laura, but he will wait a few months. "One major life change at a time," Santos says, with Laura on his arm.

This year's graduates choose as their Class Exemplar, or official hero, Lieutenant Colonel Virgil Ivan "Gus" Grissom, one of the original Mercury astronauts and the second American to go up in space. Grissom was favored to become the first man to walk on the moon, but he died in a prelaunch test for the Apollo I, which was plagued with serious design flaws. Whenever a speaker at graduation says, "Class of 2007," a thousand grads roar back, "Gus!"

Just before the graduating cadets receive their degrees, Defense Secretary Robert M. Gates speaks to them about duty and courage, urging them to strive for their best and to be mindful of the myriad eyes that will be watching their every move. At the time, Gates was consumed with prosecuting the wars and also with handling the fallout from Abu Ghraib.

"We live in an age where friends and enemies alike will seek out and focus on any and all mistakes made under great stress," Gates tells the graduates. "The slightest error in judgment or even the perception of an error can be magnified many times over on the Internet and TV and circulated around the globe in seconds."

Even though Gates does not bring up the troubles that have roiled the academy in the last four years, it occurs to me that this year's graduates—who have seen their academy pilloried and their training curtailed over allegations of sexual assault, religious intolerance, and cheating—have a visceral understanding of his point.

Forget the "liberal media," held in suspicion by conservatives as a matter of course. Newspapers and television were but two parts of a much larger phenomenon called openness, whose pillars were coming to include Web sites and Wikipedia, blogs and chat rooms, YouTube and, not long after graduation, Twitter. Although Gates is enmeshed in an avalanche of scathing reports in the *Washington Post* over conditions at Walter Reed Army Medical Center—reports that earn the paper a Pulitzer Prize the following year—he warns against giving in to bitterness and resentment at the oversight, calling Congress and the press "the surest guarantors of the liberty of the American people."

Gates casts the early days of the air force as a triumph over Luddites and skeptics, beginning with cavalry soldiers at the turn of the century, who lacked the foresight to grasp the potential of air power on the battlefield.

Robert Santos, in a moment of quiet triumph.

Lance Watson, elated upon receiving his degree.

Jeremy Putz.

Grace
Anderson.

"Airmen crashed the sound barrier many times over and extended the range, scope, and nature of air missions beyond what anyone could have imagined," Gates says. "It was upon this great tradition of technological innovation that the air force was formed." It was, undoubtedly, the daring of these figures—men like Chuck Yeager, Neil Armstrong, and Grissom—and their modern-day successors that attracted countless young people to join the academy.

As Gates speaks, however, the air force is undergoing a tectonic change, and this time, the fighter and bomber pilots, the heroes of the skies who inspired the graduates sitting before him, are the ones in history's sights. The air force is under growing pressure to shift its priorities. Critics are accusing it of being mired in a romantic past and of overspending on costly piloted jets, like the F-22 Raptor.

Every year, the Pentagon has been cutting back on manned aircraft in favor of remotely controlled drones that can keep constant watch over enemy territory—for longer periods, at a lower cost, and at no risk to American lives. The drones can drop bombs, fire missiles, and attack aircraft.

Within two years of Gates's speech, the air force would be training more officers to operate unmanned aircraft than to fly fighters and bombers combined. Many of today's graduates who are slated for pilot training will find their careers diverted toward a different kind of war, one that is played out in chat rooms and on computer screens. As Peter W. Singer describes in his study of robotics on the battlefield, *Wired for War: The Robotics Revolution and Conflict in the 21st Century*, the officers will go to battle in a cubicle in the afternoon and then go home in time for dinner.

This is not the stuff of spirited send-offs, however. Gates's graduation speech does not mention unmanned aircraft at all.

"We're engaged in a global ideological struggle with some of the most barbaric enemies we have ever faced," Gates says, adding that soon the graduates will finally get to use their skills as leaders. "The time for words has now passed."

Then it is time to deliver the diplomas. As each graduate's name is called, an elated cadet walks up to the dais, the picture of protocol: saluting the defense secretary and collecting his or her diploma. Then the joy explodes. The new officers exchange salutes and jump into the arms of the classmates who graduated just before them. As the cadets collect their diplomas, each squadron fills the aisle.

"We did it! We did it! We did it, man!" the cadets of Squadron 13 shout, jumping and hugging one another. Santos jogs toward the throng, punching the air in victory, and the cadets lift one another from the ground in their excitement, slapping shoulders, feeling giddy and euphoric. Their thrill is uncontainable, atomic, and spilling out of them. When the last graduate has collected a diploma, the cadets, back in their seats, raise their right hands. Brigadier General Susan Desjardins, the commandant of cadets, administers the oath of office.

"Class of 2007, you are dismissed," she says, releasing the throng before her from the academy. The second lieutenants hurl their hats high in the air, like a thousand white birds freed from their cages. At that exact instant, F-16s streak over the stadium in tribute. Inside the hats, which stay at the academy, the graduates have tucked an amount of money corresponding to their class year—twenty dollars and seven cents—for the children who will stream over the field and pick them up. (Some also contain self-addressed envelopes and a request for the money's return.)

Lance Watson springs from the row of chairs, his excitement like fireworks, lighting his face. The planes spin and twirl, tracing corkscrews that disappear vertically into infinity. The graduates light up cigars, congratulate one another, and crowd together, their faces shining, to pose for pictures. One graduate watches four fighter jets swoop across the sky in formation as he draws on a cigar. "That is so sweet," he says aloud, to no one in particular. Grace Anderson stands on a chair, looking for her family.

Gradually, the cadets who are scattered across the stadium drift toward the empty stands behind the dais. They climb the bleachers, as if drawn by invisible strings, to stand along the top row, the best spot for viewing the spectacular flights of the Thunderbirds. The fighter jets streak across the sky so fast that by the time their approach is heard, they are already halfway gone. They fly straight up in formation, then separate like streams of water from a fountain. They converge and shoot apart like starbursts. They form vertical loops and fly upside down.

Jeremy Thompson, a tall three-degree from Squadron 28, watches with his friends as if mesmerized. Thompson came here from Eielson Air Force Base; nearest town: North Pole, Alaska. "It's just beautiful," he says, not taking his eyes from the sky. "Two more years, and this'll be for me."

Epilogue

As this book was going to press, the four-digs I tracked, the Class of 2010, were in their final semester, heading toward graduation. Among them was Brad Bernard, who has surprised many, including himself: he had not only remained at the academy but thrived. He was on track to graduate in the top third of his class, and his horizon now stretched beyond anything he had imagined when he first came out from Georgia to play football.

Bernard had traveled to Las Vegas, New York, and Germany, flying on cargo planes from Peterson Air Force Base in Colorado Springs, along with four to five hundred other cadets, to support air force teams in athletic matches away from home. Bernard himself was no longer on the track team because he had torn a ligament in his elbow, which kept him from throwing a javelin. Now he was keeping up a 3.2 grade point average and had landed a pilot's slot.

"I'm actually really happy I stayed at the academy," Bernard said. "The stuff I've gotten to do—I didn't see all this in the beginning."

David Urban and Rhonda Meeker were also on track to graduate. As her doolie year neared its end, Meeker had spoken movingly of all that the academy meant to her. Its greatest gift, however, came a few months later, with the chance for a fresh start in a new squadron as a three-degree. With it, Meeker "adjusted beautifully" to life as a cadet, according to a friend. (She rebuffed my efforts to contact her directly.) The air force sent her abroad for the first time in her life, dispatching her for training in England and Kuwait.

Casey Jane Barrett, who'd left the academy, was studying aerospace engineering at the University of California at San Diego.

Of the 1,334 original members of the Class of 2010, 1,023 were still at the academy. If history is any guide, somewhere between 40 and 80 more students would not make it to graduation.

Jamal Harrison, the two-degree who had shepherded Meeker and Bernard through their first year, was in Afghanistan, working in communications. The day after he was scheduled to graduate, Harrison married Emily, his longtime sweetheart from back home in Texas.

Harrison's grades had slipped in his last semester—"senioritis, but a whole 'nother level," in the words of his best friend, Miles-Tyson Blocker—so Harrison did not graduate with the rest of his class in the spring of 2008. He had handed in his final paper in behavioral sciences a week late, losing so many points for lateness that he received an automatic F. In an almost painfully frank e-mail from Afghanistan, Harrison blamed himself for the mistake, saying he'd grown overconfident and lazy, accustomed to thinking that just passing was good enough.

"That was an expensive lesson to learn," he wrote, "having to tell Emily, my mom, Emily's parents that the day that everyone had been waiting for wouldn't happen, I wouldn't walk across the stage and shake the President's hand, I wouldn't be on the field when all my friends tossed their hats in the air.

"Knowing that I threw all of that away. It was sickening," he continued. "Once I told everyone, they were really supportive, especially Emily and Miles, but that may be what hurt the most, knowing that I let them down—not just them, but it felt like I let everyone down, everyone who along the way had believed in me, who had given me those second and third opportunities."

Harrison therefore stayed at the academy and did an independent research course, which involved keeping a journal to reflect on his mistake and reading Colin Powell's book, *My American Journey*. Harrison said, "I took that class to heart and tried to figure out who I am and who

I want to be." He ultimately graduated with seven other cadets on August 1, 2008, and Emily flew in from Fort Worth for the ceremony. Then the couple drove home. He was among the last to graduate in his class and the first to see combat.

Harrison spent half a year stationed in Germany with Emily, training at Spangdahlem Air Base to join the 606th Air Control Squadron for deployment in Afghanistan and Southwest Asia. The squadrons are new creations: mobile combat units that deliver real-time intelligence of events on the ground, using data from satellites, drones, and other sources.

One of their first jobs in the field was to install new radar and communications systems. As an officer, Harrison thought that his preparation at the academy had gone only so far. As flight commander during basic training, he had learned about the importance of taking care of the people he was training. Still, "there are a lot of things that can't be taught," he noted.

"As far as in the deployed environment, I think I felt prepared (as much as you can be)," Harrison wrote. "I knew (for the most part) what I was getting into, that there would probably be rocket attacks, that I would go to ramp ceremonies and see caskets with flags draped over them, and know that if I don't do my job, the radar doesn't spin or the radios don't work, and people don't get the close air support they need. That could lead to more caskets. That's pretty heavy, thinking that less than a year ago I was at the academy."

Harrison's classmate and buddy, Blocker, spent another month in Japan. His grandmother flew there from California to join him and to introduce him to the Japanese side of his family. Blocker met her older brother, his great-uncle, who was more than eighty years old.

Blocker was engaged to marry Rebecca Ross, a classmate from the academy. He was one of only three in the Class of 2008 to graduate to a career in airfield operations. He went for training at Keesler Air Force Base in Biloxi, Mississippi, and was stationed at the Air National Guard in St. Joseph, Missouri, thirty-five miles outside Kansas City. His experience at the academy was helpful, but he found that it was not much like the active-duty air force.

"The academy does a good job of aligning structure and groups, knowing what it feels like to be in a squadron," Blocker said, "but in terms of being like the active duty? It's a good stepping-stone, but it's not like it." The marching, the drills and the parades, the room, and the uniform inspections were no longer part of his life. "That's strictly an academy thing," he said. "It almost seems like a world away." He was not even living on base, but in an apartment on his own.

Graduation in 2008 had bordered on pitiless. The temperature was down to forty degrees, and it drizzled. Addressing the class was President George W. Bush, who had only a few months left in office. Fearing that the Thunderbirds would not fly through heavy clouds for them, the graduates cheered whenever the sun peeked through. For Nick Mercurio, it was "the happiest day of my life."

Mercurio and his pals had not made it to Europe after graduation. Instead they "took a detour" to San Antonio, where one of them, Mitchell Wills, got married. The graduates of the Class of 2008 had a reunion of sorts at the Air and Space Basic Course that many took at Maxwell Air Force Base in Alabama a few months later.

Mercurio landed at McConnell Air Force Base in Wichita, Kansas, after graduation. There he ran the Public Affairs Office, with fifteen people under him. "I was surprised when I showed up," he recalled. "I was expecting to be a deputy chief and to have another officer. But that wasn't the situation."

The academy gave him the confidence to take charge, but life gave him the maturity to understand the limits of his knowledge. Like many new officers, he realized he was in charge of people who knew more than he did about the specific operation he ran. That could come only with experience. At the academy, he'd learned to "find that senior enlisted person. Latch onto them. Ask questions," he said, adding, "They're the backbone of the air force."

Whereas Mercurio remained single, Elizabeth Simpson, who as a junior had planned never to marry, found love at the academy—specifically, down the hall in Squadron 13. She and Christopher Yarlett, Class of 2009, wed in Colorado a few weeks after his graduation.

They were stationed four hours apart: he trained at Little Rock Air Force Base in Arkansas to be a maintenance officer, and she began pilot training in Texas. Air force doctors never found the cause of Simpson's crippling headaches, which she had feared would disqualify her for pilot training. However, she found a massage therapist in Fort Collins who blamed the pain on tension in Simpson's neck, jaw, and back and managed to work it out of her. Simpson stayed on at the academy for a year after graduation, as an instructor and a squadron ethics officer, while she awaited pilot training.

From the Class of 2007, Jonathan Elliott also married after graduation. At that time his brother Stephen transferred into Squadron 13 as a legacy student. Elliott went from the academy to Hurlburt Air Field in Florida, where he was trained in special operations. He then went on to pilot training at Laughlin Air Force Base in Texas, where he began by flying single-engine T-6 turboprops. Out of the academy, Elliott found his schedule less cluttered. Pilot training, though demanding, was all that he was doing at the time. "It was a bit of a relief to not feel pulled in a million directions," he said.

Two weeks shy of finishing the initial phase of pilot training, however, Elliott ran into trouble mastering the proper responses to in-flight emergencies. He had to switch career fields and was working the night shift in the air terminal operations center at Dover Air Force Base in Delaware, awaiting his wife's arrival.

Matt Takanen, who'd been disqualified from pilot training because of a vision problem and sent to work in communications at Misawa Air Base in Japan, was enjoying his job. He hadn't yet decided on his future, but he thought he would most likely put in more than the mandatory five years.

Matt Adams also landed at Misawa, but from there he was deployed to Iraq as a civil engineer. He was working mostly on provincial reconstruction projects.

Grace Anderson, who had done her initial pilot training at Naval Air Station Whiting Field in Florida, was happy to dismiss the rumors of second-class status for air force officers. Her pilot's class had fifteen trainees: eight from the air force, three from the marines, and two each from the navy and the coast guard.

"You get teased a bit about being air force, but you get treated the same as any other student," she reported. "As far as getting leftovers, that was never the case. We were never separated in any way by service." Her training partner, in fact, was "a coastie." Nor did she find herself shunned upon returning to the air force for advanced pilot training at Vance Air Force Base in Oklahoma. On the contrary, she felt envied. The air force method of training involved more classroom instruction. The navy, in contrast, got students flying and immediately sent them on their way.

Anderson still did not know the specific aircraft she would be assigned, but since she was learning on T-1 trainers, she assumed that she would ultimately fly "something heavy," like tankers or transports, but it was by no means certain. She could still be diverted to operating an unmanned aerial vehicle—a drone—instead of a jet. Around her, officers training on T-38s—the fighter and bomber track—were being given C-17 and C-21 transport planes and KC-135 refueling tankers instead. Training on the fighters and bombers was already backed up, and that was before Secretary of Defense Robert M. Gates announced a major force reorganization that shifted the air force away from fighter jets and bombers in favor of unmanned aircraft. Anderson feared she might get elbowed out of any cockpit at all. The only sure jobs these days were flying helicopters.

Where was the challenge in a drone? The risk? The sacrifice? The definitions that Webster's dictionary offered, alongside "pilotless plane," all sounded like defeat: "a male bee . . . or ant which serves only in a reproductive capacity, has no sting, and does no work" or "an idle person who lives by the work of others; parasite; loafer."

Anderson and thousands of other graduates had trained in the mud, done thousands of push-ups, and run scores of miles. They'd swallowed bugs and dirt, bracing themselves for being shot down over a combat zone and evading an enemy. The academy aimed to make them warriors who aspired to heroism. What tied such stretching of their physical and psychic boundaries to sitting before a console, manipulating a plane thousands of miles away? Was this warfare?

"I would be one unhappy camper," Anderson said. "I would do it, but I'd be disappointed."

The overhaul that Gates announced in the summer of 2009 marked the end of an era in which jet fighters and bombers were prized as essential in dominating the battlefield. Even before the announcement, however, that era had been fading, eclipsed by changes in the kinds of wars facing U.S. forces. Battles were being won and lost on the ground, and unmanned drones were feeding intelligence to ground troops in close to real time.

In the debate over the air force's future, some questioned whether it should continue to exist as a separate branch of the service at all. Gates's plan called for retiring 254 fighter jets, mostly F-15s and F-16s, from bases around the world, and for diverting four thousand pilots and designated trainees for work in other fields, from running drones to special operations to maintenance. He capped purchases of the next-generation F-22 Raptors—a highly controversial jet fighter designed for air-to-air combat that would cost taxpayers a staggering $350 million each—at just four more than those already ordered. The new plan aimed to make the air force more responsive to the other branches of the service.

The air force's newest recruitment effort reflects this shift in its role. Its prior campaign promoted the air force "Above All," showing its most sophisticated aircraft, ending with the F-22 Raptor, tearing across the skies. The new commercials are more low-key. They feature the slogan "Air, Space, Cyberspace," with airmen discussing the importance of their work in each sphere. The new commercials play down the daring pilots, the celebration of the warrior spirit so vaunted at the academy, to celebrate the science fiction, "gee whiz" side of the service's mission.

Trent Redburn stayed on track for pilot training and spent part of his postgraduation vacation in Hawaii, giving private lessons in flying gliders. "I'm just thrilled to death to start flying for the real air force," he said. He did not nab one of the prized slots at Sheppard's Euro-Joint Jet Pilot Training Program, but that assignment no longer assured a future flying fighters or bombers. With technology changing the face of war so completely, there are few guarantees as Redburn and the hundreds of other aspiring pilots graduating the academy each year take their place in today's air force.

Index